Raymond Barr
1967.

# LECTURES

## ON THE

# HOLY
# SPIRIT

...

## GUS NICHOLS

$3.50

Order From
Nichols Bros. Publishing Co.
1107 Canyon
Plainview, Texas

# INTRODUCTION

Anything as basic as the GODHEAD deserves careful study by every child of God. Especially is this true of the neglected subject of the Holy Spirit. Moses E. Lard wrote: "An accurate scriptural view of Spiritual influence is something not hastily acquired. It requires not a little reading, much thought, and an unusual care to avoid falling into error. The most thorough investigation is not too sure to lead to the truth; while anything less is sure to miss it." It is thought by the publishers that this book will help sincere students in that "thorough investigation."

Perhaps no man in our brotherhood today is better acquainted with the BOOK than Gus Nichols. Five hours of daily study for fifty years has developed a naturally-gifted mind far beyond normal accomplishments. Many of his one hundred public discussions have dealt with errors about the Holy Spirit. By preparation and experience he stands with few peers in the ability to discuss this theme.

The Walnut Hill church in Dallas invited Gus Nichols to lecture for a week on THE NATURE AND WORK OF THE HOLY SPIRIT. The lectures were recorded, and then carefully edited by the author. This combined the fine qualities of a prepared manuscript and the fluency and appeal of an oral sermon. Thus, this volume is able to present a difficult subject in an "easy-to-read" and enlightening manner.

May the Lord bless the reader and his study of the Holy Spirit.

THE PUBLISHERS

# TABLE OF CONTENTS

# BIRTH OF THE SPIRIT

It is a great joy to study the subject of the Holy Spirit and his work. I'd like to think you will be honest of heart as we present what the Bible says on the subject. All we can know about the Holy Spirit and his work we must learn from the Bible. This is a timely subject. There is probably no other Bible subject concerning which there is more confusion than the subject of the Holy Spirit and his work. There is much superstition and error being taught to the disturbance of religious people throughout the world, and much of it centers around the Holy Spirit and his work.

## The Birth of the Spirit

At this time let us consider "The Birth of the Spirit." "There was a man of the Pharisees, named Nicodemus, a ruler of the Jews: The same came to Jesus by night, and said unto him, Rabbi, we know that thou art a teacher come from God: for no man can do these miracles that thou doest, except God be with him. Jesus answered and said unto him, Verily, verily, I say unto thee, Except a man be born again, he cannot see the kingdom of God. Nicodemus saith unto him, How can a man be born when he is old? can he enter the second time into his mother's womb, and be born? Jesus answered, Verily, verily, I say unto thee, Except a man be born of water and of the Spirit, he cannot enter into the kingdom of God. That which is born of the flesh is flesh; and that which is born of the Spirit is spirit. Marvel not that I said unto thee, Ye must be born again. The wind bloweth where it listeth, and thou hearest the sound thereof, but canst not tell whence it cometh, and whither it goeth: so is every one that is born of the Spirit." (John 3:1-8.) This quotation from Jesus' conversation with Nicodemus declares that there is such a thing as being "born of the Spirit." Of course, this means the "Holy Spirit."

### Human Spirit Born

From verse 6 we learn that it is the **human spirit** that is "born of the (Holy) Spirit." Man has a soul, or spirit, as well as a body. Jesus said, "Fear not them which kill the body, but are not able to kill the soul: but rather fear him which is able to destroy both soul and body in hell." (Matt. 10:28; Luke 12:4-5.) Man could so live and act as to "lose his soul." (Matt. 16:26.) Paul said, "Glorify God in your body, and in your spirit, which are God's." (1 Cor. 6:20.) The prophet Daniel said, "I Daniel was grieved in my spirit in the midst of my body." (Dan. 7:15.) The spirit is a part of man; it is the inward man, the knowing part of man. "For what man knoweth the things of a man, save the spirit of man which is in him? Even so the things of God knoweth no man, but the Spirit of God." (1 Cor. 2:11.) It is the spirit of man which needs to be saved. (1 Cor. 5:5.) It is the soul which can be lost, or saved. (James 1:21; Matt. 16:26.) The Bible says God is the "Father of spirits." (Heb. 12:9.) The spirit of man came from God, and at death it returns to God. (Eccl. 12:7; Acts 7:55, 59.)

By sin, man has become in spirit a child of the devil, and must have the new birth in order to enter the kingdom of God. The Bible uses the words "child of the devil" (Acts 13:10), "children of the devil" (1 John 3:10), and Jesus said, "Ye are of your father the devil, and the lusts of your father ye will do." (John 8:44.)

Nicodemus thought Jesus meant the **outward man** must be born again when he said, "Except a man be born again, he cannot see the kingdom of God." (John 3:3-4.) Then Jesus tried to show him that the new birth is not the old natural birth, but is a birth "of water and of the Spirit." (John 3:5.) Jesus said, "That which is born of the flesh is flesh: and that which is born of the Spirit is SPIRIT"— the human spirit. (John 3:6.) One's conduct, the way he lives, depends upon the kind of a spirit he has. (1 Peter 3:1-4; Psalm 51:10.) God has purposed to make man over by converting his spirit, and giving it a new birth. With a right spirit, or inward man, at the steering-wheel of one's life he will follow the Holy Spirit as he leads by his word (Rom. 8:14), and not follow the flesh. "For if ye live after the flesh, ye shall die; but if ye through the Spirit do mortify the deeds of the body, ye shall live. For as many as are led by the Spirit of God, they are the sons of God." (Rom. 8:13-14.)

## After Led By The Spirit

This does not mean that one is a child of God before he begins to be led by the Holy Spirit. While discussing with a denominational preacher the design of baptism, he asked me, "Were you led by the Holy Spirit to be baptized? Or, by the spirit of the devil?" He thought if I had been led by the Holy Spirit to be baptized, then I was a child of God before baptism, for "as many as are led by the Spirit of God, they are the sons of God." (Rom. 8:14.) I asked him if he were led by the Spirit of God to believe, repent, and pray for salvation (since he said these are conditions of salvation). He said he was led by the Spirit of God; to which I responded: "According to your logic, you were saved unconditionally, and before you believed, repented, and prayed for salvation."

## Our Spirit a Part of Man

This reminds me of a discussion which I had with a materialist, who contends that man has no soul or spirit, except the "breath." He said the spirit or soul is no part of man. I replied that if this were true, then that which is no part of man must be born again—and not the "man," as Jesus taught it. Jesus said, "Except a **man** be born again, he cannot see the kingdom of God." (John 3:3.) Again he said, "Except a **man** be born of water and of the Spirit, he cannot enter into the kingdom of God." (John 3:5.) Then he said, "That which is born of the flesh is flesh: and that which is born of the Spirit is **spirit**." (John 3:6.) It cannot be true that that which is no part of man experiences the new birth, for Jesus said, "**Ye** must be born again." (John 3:8.) Therefore, the soul or spirit is a part of man.

## Whole Man Baptized

Another man asked, "Do you baptize the body of a man,

or his spirit?" He argued that no bodily act can bring any blessing to the spirit, or soul, or inward man. I asked him if he preached so as to affect the inward man without reaching him through the outward man—through his physical ears, etc.? I asked him if he ever took the Lord's supper? If so, did he eat the supper to benefit the outward man, or the inward man? for the body, or for the spirit? He quickly declared that the blessings in the Lord's supper are for the spirit, or inward man. Only prejudice kept him from seeing that baptism is not for the benefit of the body, but is an act prompted by the Holy Spirit, by his word, and through the human spirit; and it is to bring blessings to the spirit of man. Baptism has to do with the salvation of the soul. (Mark 16:16; 1 Pet. 3:21.) The whole man—not just the body—is involved in scriptural baptism, just as is true of the Lord's supper. Speaking of baptism, Paul says, "Ye have obeyed from the heart that form of doctrine. . . Being then made free from sin, ye became servants of righteousness." (Rom. 6:17-18; cf. 6:3-4.) Since baptism must be "from the heart," or prompted by the conscience, it is not **merely** a **bodily** act. (1 Pet. 3:20-21.) To say a literal, physical, act could not affect the soul, is to say the blood of Christ was shed in vain—for that blood was physical, literal blood, just as much as mine or yours. And yet it was shed "for the remission of sins." (Matt. 26:28.) The physical act was unto our salvation. So is our obedience which is from the heart. (Heb. 5:8-9.)

### Our Spirit Born

We cannot overemphasize the fact that the new birth is for the inward man, and not just the outward, nor a matter of "formality." Those baptized without the inward and proper preparation of heart and spirit, need to be baptized over, as the twelve at Ephesus were. (Acts 18:24 to 19:7.)

### The "Wind" Illustration

It is the inward and invisible man which is born again, as Jesus taught. When Nicodemus thought and talked only about a natural, physical birth, Jesus used the "wind" illustration. He said, "The wind bloweth where it listeth, and thou hearest the sound thereof, but canst not tell whence it cometh, and whither it goeth; so is every one that is born of the Spirit." (John 3:8.) He did not say, "So does the Holy Spirit operate in the new birth." But he said, "So is every **one that is born** of the Spirit." They could not see the wind coming and going, like clouds; neither can one see the spirit of man being born of the Holy Spirit. As it comes out of satan's kingdom, it is invisible; and no man sees it as it is translated into the kingdom of Christ. (Col. 1:13; Rev. 1:9.)

### How Begotten?

Since becoming a Christian is similar to a birth, how is one begotten so as to be born again? Paul says, "I have begotten you through the gospel." (1 Cor. 4:15.) This is why he wrote, "I am not ashamed of the gospel of Christ, for it is the power of God unto salvation, to every one that believeth." (Rom. 1:16.)

But some one may be ready to ask, "Is the gospel the Spirit?" No; but the gospel was revealed and confirmed by the Spirit. It was preached "with the Holy Ghost sent down from heaven." (1 Pet. 1:12.) The Spirit guided the apostles "into all truth" as they preached the gospel. (John 16:13; 14:26.) They spoke "as the Spirit gave them utterance." (Acts 2:4; 1 Cor. 2:13.) The gospel was, and is, the very word and message of the Holy Spirit.

In order, then, for the sinner to be born again, he must be begotten by the gospel. (1 Cor. 4:15.) James says, "Of his own will begat he us with the word of truth." (Jas. 1:18.) This is why the gospel must be preached "to every creature" in "all the world," in order to salvation. (Mark 16:15-16.)

### Word of the Spirit

To be "born of the Spirit" is to be born by the word of the Spirit—to be begotten "through the gospel," and by "obeying the truth." Peter says, "Ye have purified your souls in obeying the truth. . . . being born again, not of corruptible seed, but of incorruptible, by the word of God, which liveth and abideth forever." (1 Pet. 1:22-23.)

This is the way the Spirit operates upon the heart (spirit) of man in the new birth. He does not miraculously make men children of God. If he operated in that way, he would make **all** men children of God, and salvation would be unconditional on man's part. Instead, men are begotten and born again by the word, or gospel—and not by a direct and miraculous work upon the sinner.

### "Born of the Spirit"

"So is every one that is born of the Spirit." (John 3:8.) What does it mean to be "born of the Spirit?" Well, it certainly means that the new birth is brought about through the leadership—through the agency and work of—the Holy Spirit; it means that the Holy Spirit makes people children of God. You just could not get less than that from this statement: "Except a man be born of water and of the Spirit, he cannot enter into the kingdom of God." (John 3:5.) "So is every one that is born **of the Spirit**" (v. 8) shows that the Holy Spirit has something to do in the new birth, to make us children of God. The apostle Paul said, "As many as are **led by the Spirit of God**, they are the sons of God." (Rom. 8:14.) To be "born of the Spirit" (John 3:8) one must be **led** by the Spirit. When a man has been "led" by the Spirit of God, he is a "son" of God, he is a child of God. The Holy Spirit's work in the process of the new birth is defined as "leading" us—which he does through the inspired word he revealed. Those who follow as the Spirit guides, have the new birth, or are "born of the Spirit." The Holy Spirit, then, makes us children of God. There is no controversy about that, I presume, among any of us.

We all admit the fact that the new birth is "of the Spirit." But the question is: HOW does the Holy Spirit make us children of God? Does he do it **directly**, or does he do it **indirectly**? Does he do it without medium, or does he operate through the medium of divine truth? Well, let me illustrate it. My right hand may represent the Holy Spirit, and my left hand may represent the heart of the sinner. All of us agree that the Holy Spirit must operate upon the heart of the sinner and bring about the new birth. The question is: HOW does he do it? Does he do it this way (author strikes his left hand directly with the right hand)? Does the Spirit operate directly upon the heart? —with no medium through which to work—a direct operation? That is the way the denominational people of the world think the Holy Spirit operates.

Or, does the Holy Spirit operate on the sinner's heart through the medium of divine truth, like this (with the Bible in his right hand, author strikes the Bible against his left palm)? Does the Holy Spirit use the truth to convert, leaving man to be a free moral agent, to accept or reject? —or is it miraculous, like this (again author strikes left hand directly with right)? Will all those be converted whom he wants converted, and nobody be converted whom the Spirit doesn't want converted? Does the Holy Spirit decide the whole proposition, leaving man to be nothing but a mere machine to be operated upon?

How is it brought about? Well, let us note the Scriptures on it: "Of his own will begat he us with the word of truth" (striking the left hand with the Bible being held in his right hand). (Jas. 1:18.) There is the begetting in the new birth: "Of his own will **begat** he us. . . ." How? Is it "without the word of truth," this way (striking the left hand directly with the right)? No! No! It is this way (striking left hand with the Bible held in the right hand). James says, God "begat . . . us **with the word** of truth."

Take Peter's statement: "Being born again, not of corruptible seed; but of incorruptible, by the"—direct operation of the Holy Spirit? No! No! That is not the way it is! Well, how is it, Peter? He said, "Being born again, not of corruptible seed, but of incorruptible, **by the word of God**" —(striking hand with the Bible)—"which liveth and abideth forever." (1 Pet. 1:23.)

### The Word By the Spirit

"Well," says one, "the word of God is not the Spirit." I know that; and this Bible here is not my right hand, either! But my right hand was "operating" on my left hand through the Bible—my right hand was doing it, but was doing it through the medium of the Bible. The Bible is actually the thing that contacted my left hand; and similarly, the Holy Spirit converts the sinner—but he does it through his word. So, Peter says "the gospel was preached . . . with the Holy Ghost sent down from heaven." (1 Pet. 1:12.) Hence, Paul says, "The gospel . . . is the power of God unto salvation." (Rom. 1:16.) The Bible says, "Receive with meekness the engrafted word, which is able to save your souls." (Jas. 1:21.) And speaking of the gospel, Paul said, "By which also ye are saved." (1 Cor. 15:2.)

So, the new birth is brought about by the Holy Spirit through the word that he revealed and confirmed through the apostles, and left on record in the revelation that we have, which is a revelation of the Holy Spirit, his very message—the gospel, the "good news" of salvation, through Christ. That's what it means to be "born of the Spirit."

After we have been born of the Spirit, the Holy Spirit dwells in us because we have been born of the Spirit. Paul said, "Because ye are sons"—because you have become children of God, because you have had the new birth—"Because ye are sons, God hath sent forth the Spirit of his Son into your hearts, crying, Abba, Father." (Gal. 4:6.) The Spirit doesn't come and dwell in our hearts until after he has converted us (through the medium of divine truth), and made the heart a fit place in which to dwell. But then he comes into a clean heart which he himself cleansed through the medium of divine truth, so that Jesus could say, "Ye are clean **through the word** which I have spoken unto you" (striking left hand with Bible held in right hand). (John 15:3.) The gospel is the  power.  (Rom. 1:16.)

### Spirit Uses the Word

The Spirit does not operate directly upon the sinner. But the Holy Spirit uses the gospel, or word of God, and the sinner is begotten by the word. He uses the  moral  and suasive power, the power of the gospel, to bring about the birth  of the Spirit.  Men are converted by the powerful facts, commands, threats, and promises of the gospel, which includes the whole story of Jesus and his love—the sweetest story ever told or heard!

## Power In The Word

There was power enough in the devil's word—the devil's lie—to lead man away from God, and make him a child of the devil. (Gen. 2:17-18; 3:1-6; 1 Tim. 2:11-14; 2 Cor. 11:1-3.) And there is power enough in the word of God, the gospel of Christ, to bring man back to God and make him a child of God. (Rom. 1:16; 1 Cor. 4:15; Jas. 1:18, 21; 1 Cor. 15:1-4.) The devil did not miraculously and directly operate on man, to get him into sin; neither does God, nor the Holy Spirit, operate directly and miraculously upon man to make him a child of God. The new birth (conversion) is a moral and spiritual change, and is brought about by moral and spiritual means—the gospel of Christ. O! There are so many people who need to know this!

## Born By Faith

Man is born again by faith, and not by the gospel while he rejects and disbelieves it. Only believers are given "power to become" the sons of God, or to be born again. (John 1:11-12.) Some believed on Jesus (John 8:30-32), but would not obey him, and Jesus called them the "children" of the devil later in the chapter. (v. 44.) Faith alone did not make them children of God. Repentance is "unto life" (Acts 11:18), which shows that one cannot be born again (have life) without it.

## Born of Water

The penitent believer must be "baptized into Christ" in order to be a child of God by faith. Unto members of the churches of Galatia, Paul wrote: "Ye are"—present tense —"all the children of God by faith in Christ Jesus. For as many of you as have been baptized"—past perfect tense— "into Christ have put on Christ." (Gal. 3:26-27.) Here the apostle called them children of God, but not until after they had been moved by faith to be baptized into Christ, where they were "all one in Christ Jesus." (v.28.) "If any man be in Christ, he is a new creature." (2 Cor. 5:17.) Therefore Paul said, "Know ye not, that so many of us as were baptized into Jesus Christ were baptized into his death?" (Rom. 6:3.)

## Water Baptism

But some one may be saying, "That would make water baptism a part of the new birth." Well, Jesus said, "Except a man be born **of water** and of the Spirit, he cannot enter into the kingdom of God." (John 3:5.) How could "born **of water**" mean "born **without water?**" If born **"of water"** means "born **without water,**" then "born **of the Spirit**" (v.6), must mean "born **without the Spirit!**" Of course, it does not in either case mean "without." One is "born of water" and "of the Spirit" (John 3:5) when he is taught and "led" (Rom. 8:14) by the Holy Spirit to believe in Christ, repent, confess Christ, and be baptized "for the remission of sins." (Acts 2:36-38; 8:35-39.)

## Raised From Burial

When Christ was raised from his burial and from his grave, he was said to be "the firstborn from the dead." (Col. 1:18.) His resurrection from the burial was a "birth" from the dead. Our resurrection in baptism is a "birth" of water, as taught and led by the Spirit. We are said to be "buried with him in baptism, wherein also ye are risen with with him." (Col. 2:12.) This resurrection in baptism is a birth of water. "We are buried with him by baptism into death; that like as Christ was raised up from the dead by the glory of the Father, even so we also should walk in newness of life." (Rom. 6:4.) Here we get the new life ("newness of life") after being "born of water and of the Spirit"—after coming forth from the water and from the burial in baptism.

## Very Important

This new birth is so very important, that I would like to persuade men, as Paul did. (2 Cor. 5:11.) Many now do not realize the need of it, even as Nicodemus did not. Christ said to Nicodemus, "Ye must be born again." (John 3:7.) He had not been born again.

**Nicodemus was a Pharisee, a member of the biggest "denomination" then in existence.** (John 3:1.) But he had not had the new birth! (John 3:3, 5, 7.) Many now in the denominations have never been "born of water and of the Spirit," and are not in the kingdom of God. They never will be, unless they obey the gospel. (John 3:5; 1 Pet. 4:17; 2 Thess. 1:6-9.)

**Nicodemus was a "ruler of the Jews"—an intelligent and educated man!** He held a good position, and was a religious leader of his people. (John 3:1.) But he had not had the new birth! (John 3:3, 5, 7.) Not many of the great men of earth, men of the elite class, have had the new birth. (1 Cor. 1:25-27.)

**Nicodemus believed in God, and said Christ was a teacher "come from God." (John 3:2.) He was no atheist, nor infidel.** But his "faith" alone did not make him a child of God, for he still needed the new birth. (John 3:3, 5, 7.) Faith must obey and include baptism, in order to save, or bring "remission of sins" and the new birth—the birth "of water" and "of the Spirit." (Acts 2:38; Mark 16:15-16; John 3:5; Acts 22:16.)

**Nicodemus was not only a religious man, a member of a big "church," a religious leader of his "denomination," an intelligent man, and a believer in God; but he was not a modernist nor a liberalist!** He did not quibble against miracles and signs done by Christ and his disciples. He said, "No man can do these miracles that thou doest, except God be with him." (John 3:2.) Believing that Christ wrought miracles, which established his claim to be the Son of God, Nicodemus believed in Christ. (John 20:30-31.) But he had not had the new birth! He did not "believe" obediently. He, like many today, did not believe Christ's teaching about the new birth. (John 3:11-12.) Many now claim to "believe" in Christ, while they reject what he says. (John 12:48; Mark 16:15-16.)

**Nicodemus believed that God was with Christ.** (John 3:2.) Yet Nicodemus would not stand with Christ! He was like many others who "believed" in Christ, but would not "confess him, lest they should be put out of the synagogue: for they loved the praise of men more than the praise of God." (John 12:42-43.) To be ashamed of Christ is to stay in sin, and remain a child of Satan. (Matt. 10:32-33; Mark 8:38; Rom. 1:14-16.)

**It seems that Nicodemus wanted to be some sort of "secret disciple"**—at that time. Three times the record says he came to Jesus "by night." (John 3:2; 7:50; 19:39.) He was, perhaps, like Joseph, who later was "a disciple of Jesus, but secretly for fear of the Jews." (John 19:38.) But we know that Nicodemus at first was not a child of God. (John 3:3, 5, 7.) A "secret" disciple is a false disciple. (John 8:30-32; Mark 8:37-38.)

**Finally, we may say Nicodemus was a "good" moral man, even a good religious man.** But his religion was vain, and his morality did not make him a child of God. He needed the new birth, without which no man can enter the kingdom of God. "Except a man be born of water and of the Spirit, he cannot enter into the kingdom of God." (John 3:5.)

### It's The Truth!

Jesus, in introducing the new birth, said, "Verily, verily . . . " This means, "Truly, truly," or "It's the truth, it's the truth. . ." Then he said a man "cannot see the kingdom of God" or "cannot enter into the kingdom of God" without the new birth. Friends, do you believe the Son of God? "He that obeyeth not the Son shall not see life." (John 3:36, A.S.V.)

# BORN OF GOD AND LED BY THE SPIRIT

We are to study one of the most difficult passages in the Bible—one that is so often misunderstood that some interpretations given it actually deny what it says. This is the text: "Whosoever is born of God doth not commit sin; for his seed remaineth in him: and he cannot sin, because he is born of God." (1 John 3:9.) John says in the next verse that "in this the children of God are manifest, and the children of the devil." Every man shows what he is by the life that he lives.

## Out of the Sinning Business

Jesus Christ came into this world to get us out of the sinning business. The apostle Peter said, "Repent ye therefore, and be converted, that your sins may be blotted out." (Acts 3:19.) Then, in verse 26, "God, having raised up his Son Jesus, sent him to bless you, in turning away every one of you from his iniquities." We must repent, which means: "A change of mind for the better, heartily to amend, with abhorrence of one's past sins." (Thayer.) Repentance is such a change of mind, and heart, and purpose as will get us away from sin, away not only from the love of sin and from the purpose to sin, but immediately get us away from the wilful practice of sin. It will eventually separate us from the power of sin, and the thralldom of it, and get us away from the powerful habit of sinning, and make us more and more like Jesus as we grow in the Christian graces. That is the purpose of Jesus' coming. Had it not been for this fact, God could have had universal salvation. If nothing is necessary in going to heaven other than just pardon or forgiveness of sins, we could have had that for all mankind, if no conversion were needed. But heaven would have been populated with unconverted people, with wilful sinners, people who love sin and revel in it; and heaven would have been no better than the devil's hell as far as the environment would have been concerned. Therefore, heaven would have been spoiled and ruined, just as man has spoiled and ruined this world by sin. Man would have spoiled heaven, too, because God could have raised the bodies of every lost and sinful and wicked man, woman, boy, and girl on earth and given them glorified bodies, if that is all that it takes to get people to heaven.

But man has a soul or a spirit as well as a body. Paul said, "Glorify God in your body, and in your spirit, which are God's." (1 Cor. 6:18-20.) The spirit is to become a new creature. Jesus said, "That which is born of the flesh is flesh; but that which is **born of the Spirit**"—meaning the Holy Spirit—"is spirit"—our spirit. He says it is the spirit of man that is born again. Materialists do not believe that a man has a soul or a spirit as a living thing. Jesus said, "Fear not them which kill the body, but are not able to kill the soul." (Matt. 10:28.) Here we learn that the soul has life just the same as the body. The body has life, and it can be killed; but the soul has life, and it cannot be killed. So man has within him a living soul, a living spirit that will not die when the body dies. Hence, Jesus said, "Fear him, which after he hath killed"—has killed the body— "hath power to cast into hell; Yea, I say unto you, fear him." (Luke 12:4, 5.) So man has a spirit; and this spirit must be converted. In its very purposes of heart, it must be turned away from the business of sinning, in order to be fitted for heaven and immortal glory.

### Soul Changed in Conversion

All the change that the soul, the spirit of man, will ever receive must be received in conversion, and as we live the Christian life. We must become Christ-like in life, not in the resurrection. It is plainly taught in the Bible that in the resurrection man will get a different body and that will be a miraculous change! Christ shall "change our vile body" and fashion it "like unto his glorious body." (Phil. 3:20, 21.) By His almighty power, God will see to that. "This corruptible must put on incorruption and this mortal must put on immortality," Paul says. "Behold, I show you a mystery. We shall not all sleep"—we as Christians will not all die, some will be alive when Jesus comes and they will escape death—"but we shall all be changed." There will be a change for the body. "This mortal must put on immortality," but there will be no change at that time for the soul. The soul must get its change in conversion, in growing in grace, in living the Christian life, and as we get ready for heaven by a continual process of conversion. So Paul says to Christians, "I beseech you therefore, brethren, by the mercies of God, that ye present your bodies a living sacrifice, holy, acceptable unto God, which is your reasonable service. And be not conformed to this world: but **be ye transformed by the renewing of your mind** ." (Rom. 12:1, 2.) We are not through with the process of transformation when we are initially converted.

When I was a young man we used to sing, "O, the best life to live is the life of a Christian, serving the Lord Most High. O, the best life to live is the life of a Christian, ready to live or die." That is a great Bible truth, and we have nothing but pity for people who prefer some other way of life. So, as we live the Christian life, we are being transformed and changed and better fitted and prepared for a heavenly society. Death and the resurrection of the body affect the body only; the spirit will not be affected at all. If you are expecting some great miraculous change to take place in your soul and make it fit for heaven when Jesus comes, you have been deceived. So, let us therefore emphasize (as God has emphasized it) the importance of a new birth, and of transformation. This takes place in meditation upon God's word and devout study thereof. In spiritual worship, our spirit—the whole inward man—is involved in singing, praying, and worshipping out of the overflow, not in a mechanical sort of a worship that becomes a curse instead of bestowing a blessing.

### Make Preparation Now

Jesus came to fit our souls, our spirits, for heaven. "Prepare to meet thy God." (Micah 4:12.) Prepare for the judgment; prepare for eternity; get ready. We are here just long enough to make preparation. We are deciding now—today, tonight—we are all deciding where we will be billions and billions of years from now. We therefore should not allow this world to detract, and decoy, and lead us astray, nor cause us to forget the most important thing that there is in life—that is, that we are to get ready to really live with God hereafter. If our souls are not ready, we just can't go to heaven, for God is not going to allow the wicked in heaven to spoil it, like they have spoiled this world and this environment down here. We read in Psalm 9:17, "The wicked shall be turned into hell, and all the nations that forget God."

This being the very purpose of the coming of Christ, the angel said, "Thou shalt call his name Jesus: for he shall save his people from their sins." (Matt. 1:21.) He came to get us out of the sinning business. He came to save us from sin, from the love of it, and away from the wilful practice of it. So it should be our determination and purpose to sin no more. Our purposes and our hearts are pure. "Blessed are the pure in heart: for they shall see God." (Matt. 5:8.) That is what Jesus came to do. He came to turn us away from the love and the wilful practice of sin. He came to get us out of the sinning business, just as a man may make up his mind to get out of one sort of business and get into another which he thinks would be better for him and more profitable. And so he gets out of one business to get into another business. He no longer is wilfully following the old practice, the old business. He is in a new work and a new sort of life, trying to find for himself a richer and better life.

### Vocation To Serve God

Man's business is to serve God. Paul said, "Walk worthy of the vocation wherewith ye are called." (Eph. 4:1, 2.) Being Christians is our vocation. Everything else is an avocation, a sideline, something we may do or may not do. If it is something clean and right within itself we may do it or may not. A physician's business, his vocation, is the practice of medicine. Day or night when he can administer to the welfare of mankind, he stands obligated. He has devoted his life to serve, so that he will minister to those who are in need of his services. And we stand pledged to God

Almighty that as Christians we will not commit any sin whatsoever. Our purposes are pure; our hearts are clean. We may not perfectly live up to it, but we will do the best we can and then God will do the rest. God wants us to do now that which will keep us out of sin later.

You know sin sometime grows in clusters, like grapes. And to commit one of them is to invite all the others to come in and cluster round about. Unbelief, for instance, is a root sin and out of that sin grows a great cluster of sins. Israel, at first, believed God. (Psalm 106:12.) But by the time you get to verse 24, it says, "They believed not his word." They had lost their faith and with the loss of faith, there came in all the sins that are the products of unbelief. God wants to get us away from those things which cause people to sin, such as **the love of sin**, and the **purpose to sin**. Covetousness is a root sin. It brings into our hearts and lives a great variety, or cluster of sins, because they perfectly fit into and grow in the hot-bed of covetousness. (1 Tim. 6:5-17.)

### Preventive Righteousness

We hear much about preventive medicine. The doctors are not just interested in curing diseases, but they are interested in preventing disease. But many members of the church are not enough interested in preventive righteousness. We believe in preventing diseases, and we therefore try to eat, exercise, and so live as to promote good health. We want to prevent sickness. We know that doctors can usually cure us if we are sick. But they can also prevent diseases. They have just about done away with smallpox as a result of vaccination—preventive treatment. And typhoid has largely been eradicated as a result of preventive medicine—preventive treatment. And so it should be in the religious life. If we are wise in the way of Christian living, much sin can be prevented. "The way of transgressors is hard." (Prov. 13:15.) DeWitt Talmadge visited Sing Sing prison, and looking back as he entered the big doors, he saw a big sign: **Proverbs 13:15.** "THE WAY OF TRANS-GRESSORS IS HARD." He said to his guide, "Man, in the name of God, why don't you put that on the outside to keep people from coming in here?" And the reply was given, "You look after those on the outside. We will try to look after those on the inside. We want those in here to know that the way of transgressors in here is hard—that if they do not submit to the rules regulating the prison itself, it will be hard on them. That is what we mean. You put it outside. You advertise it out there. We will emphasize it in here but it is true everywhere." "The way of transgressors is hard."

We are interested in prevention. We are interested in prevention concerning poverty. Henry Ford made the great statement that he had rather give people an opportunity to work so they could earn a livelihood, and prevent poverty, than to give millions to the poor. It seems that we are right on the border of inflation. Our citizens and statesmen are frightened. They don't want us to get into another depression, and we don't want the experience. Isn't it so much better and wiser for us to prevent a depression than to get out of it?

I had pneumonia in 1910. I got over it but I would have been so much better off if I had not had it. I have a scar on one of my lungs now nearly as big as a dollar that I did not know I had until less than ten years ago, when I had my lungs X-rayed. You can sin. You can get forgiveness provided you can obey—provided you can repent. Don't trifle with sin. Don't expose yourself and have pneumonia unnecessarily. We now have penicillin which will cure pneumonia in nearly all cases. We had no real cure at the time I had it. One out of every three who had pneumonia in 1910 died, and that is a narrow risk to run, isn't it? So it is much better not to have pneumonia, not to have a scar, than to have the disease and get over it. It is so much better not to sin than to sin and get forgiveness, even if you could be sure that you would be good enough of heart to repent and to obtain forgiveness.

## Can Fall Away

There are those who can't repent. People can go to the point where they can't get well of some disease. They can abuse the body where they can't live longer as a result of such abuse. They can go so far in sin that they can't turn back. You can go past the "point of no return." When Colonel Lindbergh was flying in his initial flight over the great Atlantic in his Lone Eagle plane, he felt somewhat safe and secure as long as he had gas enough that he could turn around and come back. Finally he passed what he called the "point of no return" and there his life was at stake. He knew that he must make it from there to the other shore on what gas he had. We can pass the point of no return. We can get to the point where we can't turn back and we need to know that.

In Hebrews 6:4-6: "For it is impossible for those who were once enlightened, and have tasted of the heavenly gift, and were made partakers of the Holy Ghost, and have tasted the good word of God, and the powers of the world to come, if they shall fall away," (the American Standard Version says, "and then fell away"—that it is impossible) "to renew them again unto repentance." If it is impossible to renew them, it is impossible for them to be renewed, and thus people can reach a point where they can't come back. They have fallen **away** and it is impossible to bring them back. Now, so long as one has not fallen "away"—has not given up faith,—he can come back. (Luke 8:13.) He can be renewed. He can be restored. Jesus said to the church at Ephesus that had left its first love but still held on to faith in Christ and to the divinity of the gospel and of the church and of their religion, "Remember therefore from whence thou art fallen, and repent, and do the first works." They had fallen —could return. But when they **"fall away"** that is different. If a man falls on the deck of a ship, he may get up. But if he falls overboard and **"falls away"**—the word **"away"** disconnects him from the ship—then he may not be rescued. And so when people simply fall—fall into sin, still believe in God, still believe in Christ, have their faith yet—they can come back and they can be renewed. But there is that danger that we may go beyond the point of no return, and therefore he pleads with people not to do that. We read of some who had gone beyond the point of return in their wilful practices of sin, "Having eyes full of adultery, and that cannot cease from sin." (2 Peter 2:14.) When people get to where they cannot quit the sinning business, they are gone! They are lost forever. There isn't any hope for them if they get where they can't cease from sin. So people can get so in love with sin that all sense of honor, and of the spiritual has been destroyed within them, with their hearts so hardened, and their consciences so seared the gospel won't reach them.

### Gospel Only Power God Uses

God has no other power that he uses in reaching men other than the gospel. God has miraculous, creative power. "In the beginning God created the heaven and the earth." (Gen. 1:1.) But he does not use that miraculous power in converting men. God has proposed to convert us through the persuasive power of the gospel. Paul said it is the power of God unto salvation. (Rom. 1:16.) God has other power but he doesn't use it in saving men. He deals with us as free moral agents, as creatures of responsibility and accountability and hence he appeals to us to be saved and he has stipulated that salvation must be upon certain conditions and these conditions are not for God's benefit. They are not meritorious. They do not earn salvation to any degree. It is entirely of grace in the sense that we don't pay for it. It is conditional on our part. And it is not all grace in the sense that it includes our obedience; but our obedience is itself also of grace in the sense that the gospel produces the obedience. God through his revelation has brought us to salvation, the gospel has brought us there, and hence faith is a part of grace in that sense; and repentance, confession, and baptism are all parts of grace—God's divine means that are graciously bestowed to bring us to Christ. Salvation is actually as much then a gift of God as if it had been unconditional. The reason that it is conditional is that the conditions are for our benefit, not to pay God for salvation. They fit us for heaven, and if it were not conditional on our part and God were to save us unconditionally, he would simply be pardoning and forgiving spiritual criminals and turning them loose on the society of heaven eventually to spoil heaven. This is the same conclusion we reached awhile ago from another reasoning viewpoint.

And so you can see why it is we have the gospel, why we have the church, why we have Christianity: it is to get us away from the sinning business and to get us fit for heaven. It is a prepared place, therefore, for a prepared people. If we don't prepare, we just can't go. He won't permit us to spoil it and ruin the place with sin. And we would be miserable there anyway if we had not been converted. People who don't love services like this, who do not love the praise of God in song and prayer, who do not love to worship God and serve him now, would not be changed one whit by being in heaven. They would still hate righteousness if they were in heaven. They would want the old gang, they would want the old sins, and the old lust satisfied, for the spirit would still be the same. It would not be changed.

The new birth, then, is to get us out of the sinning business, make us new, make us over, so that we won't wilfully sin. That is what John is teaching in our text. I have laid this background so that you can appreciate I John 3:9.

### Consider Context

May I suggest that all passages of scripture should be studied in the light of the entire revelation of God. We should study any given statement in the light of all that God has said from the first verse of the Bible to the last one. Our conception of its meaning and interpretation thereof should be in harmony with all that God has ever revealed and said concerning the matter under consideration. And then we should study a given statement, and especially one that is hard to be understood, in the light of the book in which it is found. For each book of the Bible had a general purpose—an overall sort of a purpose for its very existence. And then the statement should be considered in the light of its own immediate context as well. What is being said at the time the statement is made? What is he there talking about? To whom is he speaking? And who is speaking? And under what circumstances is he speaking? All of those things will help us to understand difficult passages of scripture. And we should study any word of the text that may be difficult to understand.

## A Difficult Text

I John 3:9: "Whosoever is born of God doth not commit sin." I think the hard word here, the key word to unlock the situation and give us understanding, is the word "commit." "Whosoever is born of God doth not **commit** sin." What did he mean by it? Well, the word commit is from a Greek tense that is in the present indicative. It means to "practice," as in the Living Oracles and other translations. "Whosoever is begotten of God doth not practice sin; for his seed remaineth in him and he cannot sin; because he is begotten of God." Well, what is the meaning? "He that believeth and is baptized shall be saved." (Mark 16:16.) When you trust in that promise, you are risking everything in this world and in the world to come on it. That is faith and that's what he is talking about. Now then, when a man has done that and has repented of all his sins, has faith enough to turn from sin, he will say, like Noah said to the old world, "Goodbye." (That's what he was saying by everything he did in building the ark. "Goodbye old world—I'm going to be done with you, I'm turning my back on you. I'm going to enter the ark and through the ark, I'm going to come into a new world. So, goodbye old world.") And until a man says that, he has never repented. He isn't fit to be baptized. Many people get nothing but a wetting when they are baptized. They go down into the water dry and come up wet. That is the only change they get. **They go right on living the same old life, telling the same lies over again and again, committing adultery and stealing and defrauding and being dishonest and hating, hating God and the Bible and showing their contempt by the very lives that they wilfully live and by continuing on in their wilful and purposeful practice of sin itself. They're in the sinning business and they're not born of God and John is telling us that when he says "whosoever is born of God doth**

**not practice sin."** If you say you are born of God and you are the same old sinner still, you are not born of God. That's what he is telling you.

He is trying to keep these brethren from being deceived and deluded into thinking they are children of God for some other reason than being born again—born of God. That is why children of God are new people. They have a new love, new affection. They have new ambitions and aspirations. They now have a new hope for they have a new life. Hence, inwardly, they are Christlike now. They hate sin and they love righteousness. They hate their own sins. They hate the sins of the wife or the husband. They hate the sins of the children. The children hate the sins of the parents. They're against the sinning business everywhere. All you have to do is identify a thing as sinful and a faithful child of God is against it.

### Be Against Sin

President Coolidge was a man of few words. One Sunday his wife was sick. He went to the denominational church of which he was a member. When he returned, the following conversation took place, "How were the services?" "Good." "How was the sermon?" "Good." "What did the preacher talk about?" "Sin." "What did he say about it?" "He was against it." That was the end of it. He was of so few words; but he said a mouthful, didn't he? He said the preacher was against sin. You can't say that about some church members, can you? They are not against the sinning business. They are against certain sins. They are against all sins except their pet sins. You know some people have pet sins. And they say, "You can preach all you want to—just stay off my pet sins. But when you get on my sins, then I don't like it." Well, what does he like? He likes his pet sin, and he is a wilful sinner.

Now I want to say this, and I'm not just a young preacher saying this because it came to mind. I've been saying it for nearly 50 years. A man who will **wilfully** practice one sin is going to hell if he does not repent of it—if he does not correct it and get away from that purpose—he is going to hell. You say not many people are going to heaven. I don't think you are right about that. I think there are literally millions of people who really are not **wilfully** practicing any sin. It is not my purpose to ever sin. David swore to it that he would not commit sin. And yet I can't get a lot of my brethren to even promise themselves, much less promise God, that they won't sin. There isn't a sin in the catalog that I am willing to ever practice or ever commit a single time. Now you say, "You claim perfection!" Oh, no. But all the defect has got to be in my **inability**, in my **weakness,** in my **ignorance, it has got to be somewhere other than in my heart.** I'm not going to be a **wilful sinner.** I don't know of a commandment in God's word that I am not doing my best to obey and I don't know of anything he has forbidden that I even want to practice.

A man said, "You need the second blessing." I said, "What do you mean by the second blessing?" He said, "You need to reach the point where the 'want-to-sin' is taken out of your heart." I said, "Conversion did that for me. I got that blessing when I got what you call the first blessing." That is what conversion does for a man. It turns him away from the desire to sin and from the purpose to sin and the will to sin and makes him pure and clean in his very heart. A heart that says, "Lord, I'll give up all my sins but my alcohol, I'm **not going to give that up,"** or "I'll give up all my sins **except adultery**," has not repented—he is not converted. He may have been baptized, but he just got wet. He is not saved. And if he goes on living like that, he is deluded if he thinks he is a child of God. God doesn't save men who have the purpose to commit any sin. If he could permit a man to purpose to commit one sin and be a child of God, he could permit another to commit two sins and another three and another a thousand and another all the sins in the catalog, and let them be children of God. No, God doesn't want us to come to the judgment with the love of sinning in our hearts. So people need to be converted. You can see what John means, "Whosoever is born of God doth not commit sin"—he doesn't **practice** sin.

The word "commit" here is from the Greek word used

in James 4:12-14, "Go to now, ye that say, Today or tomorrow we will go into such a city, and continue there a year,
and buy and sell, and get gain: whereas ye know not what
shall be on the morrow. For what is your life? It is even
a vapor, that appeareth for a little time, and then vanisheth
away." "I'll go to such a city and **continue** there a year and
buy and sell. . ." "Whoever is born of God doth not commit
sin"—doth not **"continue"** in sin. And that is the truth of
the passage, I John 3:9. That means then that if  we  are
Christians, if we are really children of  God—have  been
born again—that we're not **continuing** in sin. We gave it
up when we obeyed the gospel.

### Away From the Purpose To Sin

We died to the love and the practice of sin. We resolved
to turn from it and to get out from under it, as fast as God
could work through us and get us out. **That is our purpose.**
And so, in Romans 5, the closing verses, Paul said, "Where
sin abounded, grace did much more abound," meaning that
the more people were sinful, the more they needed the favor
and grace of God through Jesus Christ and the more they
needed a Saviour. He knew somebody would jump to the
conclusion that, if we want the abundance of God's grace,
we would have to be awful sinners to get it;  hence,  the
doctrine of the Bible would promote the sinning business.
So he says, "Shall we continue in sin,  that  grace  may
abound? God forbid." That is, God forbid that we jump to
such an unscriptural conclusion. "How shall we, that are
dead to sin, live any longer therein?" (Rom. 6:1, 2.)

Yes, Christ came to get us out of the sinning business—
away from it. And if we will worship and serve God as we
ought, if we will study the Bible and fill our hearts with
it, learn from one another, be encouraged by each other,
and if we make our fellowship sweet and complete, it will
help us to stay out of the sinning business. We get out of
more and more of it through experience, and practice, as
we grow in grace and in the knowledge of our Lord and
Saviour Jesus Christ, and as we are changed into the image
of Christ, from glory to glory, from one state of glory to a
higher state of glory. (2 Cor. 3:18; 2 Peter 3:18.) All of that

is involved in it. Getting out of the sinning business is the purpose of conversion, and the purpose of our worship. It is the purpose of prayer and the godly life—the whole of the Christian life is to help us get more and more away from sin, and into the work of the Lord. And that work itself also helps us to get out of the sinning business.

We are away from the purpose to sin. We want to do right. "If we walk in the light, as he is in the light, we have fellowship one with another, and the blood of Jesus Christ his Son cleanseth us from all sin." (1 John 1:7.) **Cleanseth** means God keeps us cleansed. "Cleanseth us from all sin."

### Away From Wilful Sin

Sometime ago, I was preaching in a gospel meeting and the brother who opened the services that day prayed that God would "forgive us of our many, many sins." I thought, "That is not the way Christians ought to pray, is it? If this group is guilty of 'many, many sins' since they prayed last night or this morning, they must be **wilful sinners**, and are involved in the sinning business." And I just didn't feel that I was a part of that sort of a group of people. I just did not believe that represented that group properly. Then the next brother who led a prayer had caught on to that same old expression and he prayed likewise that God would forgive us of our "many, many sins." I thought, "What have we done that is wrong, and so much of it, since we prayed a few minutes ago? Just what have we done? Did he pray in faith? Did the first man? Did the audience pray in faith when they asked Him to forgive their many sins? What are those many sins that they have committed in the last few minutes? And they are now in worship. If they sin in worship like that, and commit other 'many, many sins' out of worship, they must be **wilful sinners**." And I'm afraid the doctrine that people can be wilful sinners, and be Christians, is growing to be popular. And then the brother who prayed at the table, instead of giving thanks, prayed that we might be forgiven of our "many sins," so that we would be fit to partake of the Lord's Supper. I don't believe God is chalking up sin against me every day, much less every two or three ticks of the watch like that.

## God Will Keep Us Clean

I've heard denominational preachers say, "Churches of Christ teach the doctrine that you're saved this moment; but the next moment you will be lost, and you will be in need of pardon again." If you prayed a hundred times per day would you need to pray for God to forgive you of your "many, many sins" each time you pray? Jesus taught his disciples to pray, "Forgive us our debts," our "sins" (Matt. 6:12; Luke 11:4); but he had reference of course to all of the sins down through life as we are penitent and humble and prayerful—just keep us forgiven; keep us justified all the way to heaven. That is the Christian life. Thus, "if we walk in the light, as he is in the light, we have fellowship one with another, and the blood of Jesus Christ his Son cleanseth us from all sin." God will keep us cleansed because we are praying for him to **keep us cleansed,** to keep us forgiven, and that is a penitent, humble, pure, clean attitude toward God. And a person like that ought to go to heaven because he hates sin—his own sins. And he wants God to keep him justified and saved and on the way to heaven.

## Try To Be Perfect

There are extremes. One is that a child of God can't sin at all. Well, that is a false interpretation of John's statement. This same apostle said in the next verse, "If we say that we have no sin"—that is, that we never do anything wrong, why then—"we deceive ourselves and the truth" —God's truth, God's word—"is not in us." We are ignorant of the Bible if we say that. God says, "There is no man that sinneth not." (1 Kings 8:46.) And in Ecclesiastes 7:20, "There is not a just man upon earth, that doeth good, and sinneth not." In other words, there are no perfect people. There is no man who is entirely out of the sinning business, when it comes to the momentary acts of life. But a faithful Christian **wants** to be perfect. "Let us go on unto perfection." (Heb. 6:1.) Let us have maturity and perfection in mind.

A little child taking its first piano lesson would say, "I want to play perfectly," and will do its best. But the teacher says in her heart, "He made an awful mess of it," but gives him a good grade—100 or an "A" or whatever the method of grading the student—because he did his best. God is not going to say at the judgment, "Well done, thou good and **perfect** servant. Thou hast been **perfect** over a few things, I'll make thee ruler over many things. Enter thou into the joys of the Lord." If my Bible read like that, I'd want to cry forever! There would be no grace sufficient to save me and I don't think it would reach all of you either! But it is by the favor of God, his mercy and forgiving grace, that we are saved and kept saved and kept on the way to heaven. If lightning were to strike you and you had not had time to pray since this morning, what about it? You would go to heaven because if you hate sin and hate the sinning business you are not wilfully living in sin. I'm living in obedience to God. It is my all-consuming and rainbow purpose and plan in life never to commit a single sin. That makes me a Christian. What about the practice of sin? Like the little child, the practice is not up to the standard. Thus, we grow into maturity and the life may never reach that standard of perfection. "Whosoever is born of God doth not commit sin," that is, he does not practice sin or wilfully sin. He is a changed man. He is a new creature. But that does not mean that he is sinlessly perfect. It only means that he hates sin, his own sins; and is trying to get away from sin, and that he is no longer in rebellion against God.

### To Whom God Will Not Impute Sin

Little children do wrong. They violate the word of God just the same as adults. A little child, when he lies, does wrong. God would be displeased if you parents were to tell your children that it is right for them to lie, just because they are not accountable and responsible before God. What is the difference? God does not chalk their sins up against them. He does not chalk lying up against a child for it is not accountable and responsible. It is not able to do any better than it is doing. God does not chalk up stealing against a little child. But the very day that a youth becomes accountable before God, and responsible, God starts chalking up sin against him and then he is lost, and is a sinner before God. He will be eternally lost, just as anyone else, if he dies without obeying the gospel and without becoming a Christian. But God does not chalk up sin against the faithful child of God. He keeps us justified. He keeps us pardoned and forgiven of our sins. That is what Paul meant when he said in Romans 4:8, "Blessed is the man to whom God will not impute sin." The American Standard Version says, "to whom God will not **reckon   sin.**" What does **reckon** mean? It means to count it, to chalk it up, to put it on the record against one. "Blessed is the man to whom God will not impute sin." The Bible says, "If we say that we have no sin, we deceive ourselves, and the truth is not in us." (1 John 1:8.) Everyone has sins, but he does not have to be a **wilful sinner**. He will have enough of them if he is sinning only through weakness and when doing the best he can to overcome sin and to obey God in all matters. He will still have some sins, but if he is penitent and pure and clean in heart, in purpose of life, and is doing his best to be like Jesus, then **God will keep him cleansed** and that is the man to whom God will **not impute, not reckon,** not chalk up sin.

It is encouraging to the Christian to know that he can live the Christian life in spite of his weaknesses, and mistakes. If he is pure in heart, hates his sins and wants to live right, God will see him through. So I do not hesitate to tell the alcoholic that he can be a Christian. I do not hesitate to tell the thief and the robber that he can become a Christian. I tell everybody that if he will obey the gospel, God will forgive him and save him, and will keep him cleansed so long as he is not **wilfully sinning**, so long as he is pure in heart, he will see God. And God will not chalk up his sins against him, because he is praying for continued forgiveness every time he prays. Not, I've sinned so many sins here in the last few moments, or in the last few days; but, I want forgiveness for whatever sins I may commit while not in the sinning business. That is what John means. (1 John 1:7, 8.)

This is a field that is not being cultivated as it should be. Many become discouraged. But some fellow may say, "Why you preachers are hypocrites. You preach that if we will obey the gospel we will be saved. What good will that do us when the very first sin we commit we will fall from grace, and Paul said you can't be renewed unto repentance." And he says again, "If we sin wilfully, that there remaineth no more sacrifice for sin." They interpret this to mean there is no more forgiveness. I had a debate with one who affirmed this proposition: **"The scriptures teach that a child of God must succeed in living a perfect and sinless life, in order to see God in peace, and go to heaven when he dies."** Now you just think of a proposition like that! The scriptures teach that a child of God must **succeed** in living **a perfect and sinless life** in order to see God in peace and to go to heaven when he dies. My first argument in reply was that if that were so, every sin that a child of God may commit, even through weakness, off-guard, or under the stress and strain of some great temptation, in a moment of great weakness—the weakest link in his character maybe—and that if he yields, it would be an unpardonable sin and that every sin that a child of God commits **would be an unpardonable sin.** Thus, there would be no hope for anybody, and we might as well cry forever. That is exactly what the doctrine is. He quoted 1 John 3:9 to prove that doctrine. That passage does not teach it. It simply teaches that we, as Christians, are out of the sinning business.

Then there is another extreme, that one can **wilfully** sin and die in murder, or in adultery, as a man did in Numbers 25, and still go on to heaven—die robbing a bank and go to heaven—die drunk and go to heaven. This is the impossibility of apostasy, and is another extreme.

### Three Kinds of People
Now we close with this suggestion. There are three different characters, in God's sight, as far as responsible beings are concerned. There is the wilful sinner, the man who has become accountable, responsible, and has not been saved, never obeyed the gospel. He may have gotten drunk one

time, just once, and he may have said, "I will never get drunk any more." And he may have prayed for God to forgive him, but he did not forgive him. He may even be penitent. But God does not save a man piecemeal-fashion, like that. God never forgives a man of drunkenness to leave him guilty of all his other sins. That is not God's plan of salvation. It is a perverted doctrine. **He won't forgive you of any sin, until you repent of all sins,** and resolve to obey God in **all matters,** to the best of your ability. Your heart is not even pure until you reach that decision. God chalks up all sins against the alien sinner, and leaves them chalked up against him until he **obeys the gospel.** If he never obeys the gospel they will all remain chalked up against him, and be imputed at the judgment bar of God, and will damn his soul forever. They will remain piled up  mountain-high against him, millions of them—every impure thought, every sin he ever did, even his sins of weakness, will be counted against him for he had no forgiveness in his impenitence and his life of wilful sin. So he is lost.

Then there is the backslider. God also chalks all of his sins up against him, from the moment that he backslid, from the moment he made up his mind to wilfully sin, and go into sin, God started chalking them up against him. "If we sin wilfully after that we have received the knowledge of the truth, there remaineth no more sacrifice for sins." (Heb. 10:26.) Christ has made the only sacrifice that will ever be made, and if you do not obey the terms of  the Lord, the second law of pardon, which involves repentance, turning from sin, and prayer, that sacrifice Christ has made will avail you nothing as a child of God. You will be as lost as if he never had died for you if you backslide and wilfully or impenitently sin, and go back into sin. The Scripture says nothing remains "but a certain fearful looking for of judgment and fiery indignation, which shall devour the adversaries." (Heb. 10:27.) There is no hope for the backslider if he dies in his sins. He is a wilful sinner. He is impenitent. He sins wilfully and he stays in sin, if he does not confess his wrongs. He can come back if he hasn't gone beyond the point of no return. Hence, we are warned not to harden our heart, nor to sear the conscience.

Then there is the third person, the faithful Christian, who himself is imperfect. If, at the close of the construction of a great skyscraper, the impartial judge should put his hand upon the head of an old father who had had fifty years of experience in constructing great skyscrapers, and his other hand on the head of the son who had little experience in such work, and is just an apprentice, the judge might be able to say to both of them, "Well done, ye good and faithful servants." The son can be just as faithful as the father. But if he were to put his hand upon the one who is most nearly perfect, it would likely have to be on that old father's head. A new member of the church can be faithful. He can stay with God and stay with the Christian life, and do his best, just like anybody else, and he will be lost eternally if he does not do it. There are some in the church more nearly perfect than others, some more mature, of course.

We're going to sing a hymn of encouragement. You can be a Christian. Don't you see you can? Will you come tonight while we stand and sing the hymn of invitation?

# HOLY SPIRIT AND THE SPIRIT
# WORLD

Your presence is duly appreciated. My subject is one concerning which there is more misunderstanding and around which there has been thrown more mysticism, than any other Bible subject. I feel very humble in approaching this study, especially when I remember that we are studying about the Holy Spirit. We can only know what is revealed about the Holy Spirit. I may not even know all of that. The Bible does not tell us all about God, all about Christ, and the Holy Spirit. God has revealed whatever is necessary for us to know about the Holy Spirit, about God, and about Christ, and perhaps all we can comprehend. In Deuteronomy 29:29 we read, "The secret things belong unto the Lord our God: but those things which are revealed belong unto us and to our children." We want to confine our study to the things revealed and be satisfied with that.

## Mysteries In Religion

There are great mysteries connected with our religion, but they are over on the divine side. There is no mystery about what to do to be saved, how to worship and serve God, and to live the Christian life, and finally be able to go home to God in heaven. The mystery is on the divine side, and God will look after the mysteries. In 1 Timothy 3:16 he tells us, "Without controversy"—meaning without any argument, without any debate about it, there is nobody to deny it, it is admitted by all who know anything about religion—"without controversy great is the mystery of godliness." And he mentions some of those mysteries: "God was manifest in the flesh"—which certainly has reference to the virgin birth, a subject that we cannot fully comprehend; and then how that God—"was justified in the Spirit, seen of angels, preached unto the Gentiles, believed on

(39)

in the world, received up into glory"—great mysteries. We
can believe what is said about these mysteries, but we
cannot fully comprehend them.

## A World of Invisible Things

In the very first place, there is an invisible world. We're
so prone to look at everything through material glasses
and are so secular and so materialistic that it is difficult
for us to conceive of a spirit world—an invisible world. But
even in our world there are things which are invisible. We
know about the atom and remember that the Hebrew writer said, "Through faith we understand that the worlds were
framed by the word of God, so that things which are seen
were not made of things which do appear." (Heb. 11:3.) The
things which are seen were made out of things which do
not appear—of invisible things—and this includes the
atoms, of course. Now nobody has ever seen an atom. We've
been able to make bombs out of the atom. We won the last
World War by using the atomic bomb, but we still have
never seen an atom. Though everything is made out of
atoms, we haven't seen a single atom. And yet, all of us
know that they exist.

The same is true of other things that are invisible. I remember a man came from Thailand to the University of
Alabama to take some post graduate work. He was a graduate of some university somewhere near Thailand, and
being a Buddhist, he was an atheist, and was brought by
a doctor's wife, who was a friend of mine, for me to talk
to him. She thought I might be able to convert him. He said
he could not believe in God because he could not believe
in anything that he could not see. I asked him if he believed that there is such a thing as an atom, and he said
that he did. I said, "Did you ever see one?" He said, "No."
"Well, do you have any evidence that anybody ever saw
one?" He said, "No." I said, "Then, there are invisible
things!" Take the subject of gravity. No one has ever seen
gravity. It is an invisible thing. Yet it is connected with
our world. So right here in our world there are invisible
things. Also, we cannot see the wind. In John 3:8 we have
a clear statement concerning the wind that the "wind

bloweth where it listeth, and thou hearest the sound thereof, but canst not tell whence it cometh, and whither it goeth." They could not tell from which direction the wind was coming and which way it would go because of the fact that it is invisible. Had it been visible like clouds, an airplane, or something like that, you could tell which way it was coming and which way it would go. Wind is invisible. Our very homes and lungs are filled with invisible air. There are things invisible.

Electricity is an invisible thing. You may say you see lights produced by electricity. Yes, **produced by** it. But we do not see electricity. We only see its product. Electricity is invisible, and it is a great and mysterious thing, traveling about 186,000 miles per second, surrounding this earth at the equator about seven times in one second. There are mysteries connected with a thing that can travel that fast. But there are mysteries everywhere.

Some people refuse to believe in God because they can't see him, and reject the truth about the Holy Spirit because he is invisible, and reject the Lord Jesus Christ because he is now glorified, and has become an invisible being, as far as we are concerned. We cannot look upon his glorious presence with our human eyes and not be blinded as was Saul of Tarsus (Acts 26), and as was John when he beheld him in his glory when he appeared unto him (Rev. 1). There are invisible beings and things.

Gravity itself is suggested in Job 26:7 when the Lord stretched "out the north over the empty place, and hangeth the earth upon nothing." It is now hanging up in space. Here we are, millions of miles above stars and beneath stars, stars all around us millions of miles away. We are up here in orbit, going around the sun once a year, traveling at tremendous speed—held up by what is commonly called gravity, but the Bible calls it the power of God. "Upholding all things by the word of his power." (Heb. 1:3.) There are invisible things connected with this world.

Even our very minds are invisible. Nobody has ever seen the human mind but that does not mean we are idiots

—that we don't know anything. Nobody has ever seen a thought or an idea. But such things exist. We can see the brain, but we can't see the mind.

Right here in Dallas, once lived a preacher of the gospel and defender thereof by the name of Joe Warlick. He was about to catch a train out of the city to some point and a little boy came into the depot with a Bible under his arm. An atheist was sitting by who said, "What is that you have under your arm?" The boy said, "My Bible." "Well," he said, "you don't believe in God, do you?" "O, yes," he said, "I believe in God." "You go to Sunday School?" "Yes." "Did you ever see God?" "No." "Did you ever contact him with any of your five senses?" And he enumerated them. "No." "Well, how do you know there is a God, then?" Well, the little fellow was very much embarrassed and Warlick then took his part and said to the atheist, "Do you have a mind or are you an idiot?" He said, "That is an insulting question. Of course I have a mind." "How do you know you have a mind? Did you ever see it? Did you ever smell it? Did you ever feel it? Did you ever taste it?" and so forth. He said, "No." "Well, you are an idiot then. You can't believe in God because you have never seen him, and yet you claim to believe that you have a mind when the facts are that you have never seen it either. According to your logic and reasoning you would have to be an idiot, to be consistent." So there are those who claim they can't believe in God because of the fact they've not seen God.

There are invisible things and there is an invisible world that we cannot see. We could not see those beings with our naked eyes unless they assume some human shape or form. Scientists now tell us that there are trillions of little things in this world that we cannot see, even with our most powerful microscopes. But there is a great world of living beings which we cannot see. But we believe in them because we have proof of their existence, as we have of the atom, without ever seeing one of them. So there is an invisible world of beings, and things not visible, some in this world where we live.

### God Is Spirit

Therefore, it is not inconsistent for us to believe in the Holy Spirit, an invisible being, and to believe in God and to believe in angels and spirits. Traveling in Egypt we had a guide who, immediately after we had started on our journey from Cairo to the airport, said, "I presume you are teachers." I said, "Yes, and No." "What do you mean by 'yes' and 'no'?" I said, "We are religious teachers. Three of us are preachers." (With my wife and me were our son Flavil and Brother W. Gaddys Roy.) I said, "Three of us are gospel preachers; so we're teachers in that sense." "Yes," he said, "and what church are you members of— what religion have you embraced? Are you Mohammedans? Catholics?" I said, "We're not Jews nor Catholics, neither are we Mohammedans. We are trying to be Christians only, with no denominational affiliation, just following Christ as Christians ought." And he said, "I'm glad to meet you, indeed. I have been a Christian for some time." But we had not gone very far until he said, "However, concerning the matter of religion, I fear that the time is at hand when no one in all the world will any longer believe in God. We are just about to create life and if we succeed in doing so, then the idea of God will be given up by all intelligent people." I said, "I don't see how you can reach that conclusion from the premises. It takes so much intelligence to create life that we have never been equal to the task, as of now. We have never created life as of yet. We have never had enough sense to do it. It takes so much intelligence that we've never been able to create the tiniest form of life. And if we were to succeed in creating life, it would not shake my faith in the Bible one whit. It would, in fact, confirm me in the belief that all life originates in background intelligence—and that no life comes by accident and chance. We've never known any life to come by accident or chance. Spontaneous generation is a mere theory. It has never been established. It is not a science. We know nothing of such, it is nothing but an unproved theory." After he had attended to our business at the airport for us he said he would go his way. But he came back in a few minutes and said, "I want to apologize for the statement I made concerning the creation of life. I have been thinking about it and I have decided, too, that if they succeed in creating life it will only prove that the first life came from a great intelligence and therefore, of God." Mr. Edwin Conklin who is a great scientist and a biologist of Princeton, made a statement that the idea that life originated from non-living matter by accident and chance, by the blind forces of nature, guided by no intelligence, is equal to the idea of the unabridged dictionary originating from an explosion in a print shop. So we can see that there is just no reason to think life came by accident and chance. There is life. There is a world, an earth, a universe, and it had to have a maker. It has every mark of divine causation and of having been designed and fashioned and made. As Paul said, **"Every house is builded by some man; but he that built all things is God."** (Heb. 3:4.) If a house like this **proclaims its builder**, whether you have ever seen him or not, **proclaims that it was designed**, fashioned and made, then the world and universe proclaim their Builder. Then, of course, the existence of the world, of the universe and man and all things would proclaim a great, divine Builder equal to the task of creating all things. So there is a God.

The very first of these invisible beings introduced to us in the Bible is God. Genesis 1:1: "In the beginning, God created the heaven and the earth." And of course God is a spirit being and is an invisible being. John 4:24: "God is a Spirit; and they that worship him must worship him in spirit and in truth." And Jesus said, "Handle me, and see; for a spirit hath not flesh and bones, as ye see me have." (Luke 24:39.) God has always been. If there ever had been a time when there was no God, there never could have been anything. If you could think of a time when there was nothing, you would be logically driven to the conclusion that nothing ever could have existed for something never comes from nothing. Something always comes from something—all the way back to the eternally existent something—God. Hence, God always has existed. Psalms 90:1,2: "Lord, thou has been our dwelling place in all generations. Before the mountains were brought forth, or ever thou hadst formed the earth and the world, even from everlasting to everlasting, thou art God." So God is just as everlasting back the way we've come as he is the way we're going. Hence, in Romans 16:26 he is called "everlasting God."

Of course we cannot fully comprehend a being so great as God, any more than a little spider down by the railroad tracks could comprehend a great railroad system with the trains moving so rapidly where there are a hundred cars and traveling at tremendous speed. Of course a little spider wouldn't understand all that because it's far beyond his ability to comprehend. But that is not as far beyond the spider's ability as God, and the comprehension of God, is beyond our ability. So we therefore do not reject the existence of God on the ground that we cannot understand him. A flea on an elephant couldn't understand the elephant. It would be so much larger and such a great animal in comparison with himself, so far beyond anything that he knew about other than just to merely see him to know he existed, but he couldn't comprehend him. But that wouldn't prove there's no elephant, even if the flea were to reach such a conclusion. So it is with man and God. We are nothing but fleas in comparison with God Almighty. We are nothing but dust worms of the earth, and are not worthy to be compared with our Maker.

## Christ Is A Spirit Being Now

Christ is himself also a glorified being, an immortal being. You will recall that the Bible says that Christ, our Lord, is a spirit being now. "The Lord is that Spirit," (2 Cor. 3:17) and he is no longer in flesh and blood as he once was. In 2 Cor. 5:16, "We have known Christ after the flesh, yet now henceforth know we him no more." So we don't know Jesus after the flesh any more. He is now glorified. Paul's statement in Philippians 3:21 says, "He shall change our vile body, that it may be fashioned like unto his glorious body, according to the working whereby is able even to subdue all things unto himself." And so Jesus Christ is no longer a physical, material, fleshly being; but he is a great spiritual being.

Before this world ever was, Jesus was, and existed as an invisible Being. We could not have seen him with our eyes. We read in John 1:1-3, "In the beginning was the Word, and the Word was with God, and the Word was God. The same was in the beginning with God. All things were made by him." Christ was back there before the creation. "All things were made by him; and without him was not anything made that was made." And in verse 14, "The Word was made flesh"—virgin birth—"and dwelt among us, (and we beheld his glory, the glory as of the only begotten of the Father,) full of grace and truth." So he was an invisible being, and yet conscious, and of course, infinitely intelligent, back there before the world ever was. In John 17:5, in his prayer to the Father, he said, "Glorify thou me with thine own self with the glory which I had with thee before the world was." And in verse 24, "Thou lovedst me before the foundation of the world." So Jesus existed back there—not in flesh and blood. But finally, God prepared for him a body and he came down from heaven to live and dwell in a little virgin born body. "A body hast thou prepared me." (Heb. 10:5.) And thus Jesus took upon himself flesh to dwell among us. He came from a spirit world. In John 6:38 he says, "I came down from heaven." In verse 62 he said, "What and if ye shall see the Son of man ascend up where he was before?" He was up there before he was down here. We read in John 3:17, "God sent not his Son into the world to condemn the world; but that the world through him might be saved." So Jesus came into the world from a spirit world, from where God dwells, where the Holy Spirit dwells. And he said in John 16:7, "It is expedient for you that I go away; for if I go not away, the **Comforter** will not come unto you; but if I depart, I will send him unto you. And when he is come, he will reprove the world of sin" . . . and thus he goes on to describe the work of the Holy Spirit. He would send the Holy Spirit, but he himself should first ascend unto heaven. We know he safely arrived there because he fulfilled his promise and on Pentecost in Acts 2 he sent the Holy Spirit. Now, Jesus has been glorified so the Spirit could come. In Acts 2:4 we read, "They were all filled with the Holy Spirit, and began to speak with other tongues, as the Spirit gave them utterance."

## Human Spirits Invisible

Also, our own spirits are invisible. Our own souls are invisible beings. (Matt. 10:28.) Hardly a man could be found who would deny that he has a soul or a spirit, yet he has never seen it. He has never contacted it with his five senses. He believes it solely and only upon the statement of God's word, such as Daniel 7:15: "I Daniel was grieved in my spirit in the midst of my body." And he believes it 'because of Ecclesiastes 12:7: "Then shall the dust return to the earth as it was: and the spirit shall return unto God who gave it." Acts 17:28, 29: "We are the offspring of God," and it is our spirits which are his offspring. "We have had fathers of our flesh which corrected us, and we gave them reverence: shall we not much rather be in subjection unto the Father of spirits and live?" It is the spirit of man that is the offspring of God and causes God to love man. He is interested in man because we are thus his offspring—just like grandparents love their grandchildren, for instance. They are their offspring, and they especially love them for that reason. Remember that the spirit of man is a part of man. Some think that the soul, the spirit, is just the breath —that it is no part of man. Well, if the spirit is no part of man, then Jesus said that which is no part of man will have to have the new birth. He said, "Except a man be born again, he cannot see the kingdom of God." (John 3:3.) "Except a man be born of water and of the Spirit, he cannot enter into the kingdom of God." (John 3:5.) Then, in verse 6, he said, "That which is born of the flesh is flesh; and that which is born of the Spirit is spirit." It is the spirit that is born again. But if the spirit is no part of man, then that which is no part of man is born again instead of man. And the man himself would not be born again, and could not enter the Kingdom of God. (John 3:6.) That is the uncertainty to which it leads when people begin to deny what the Bible says about the spirit.

## Angels Are Spirit Beings

The angels of God are spirits and are invisible beings.

Of course, they sometimes assumed the shape or form of man in order to talk and converse with man. "Who maketh his angels spirits," (Heb. 1:7) and so there are such beings as spirit beings. Remember that in Acts 23:6-8, Paul said that he was a Pharisee and the record says that Pharisees **believed in angels and spirits** whereas the Sadducees did not believe in either. There are people who are materialists now, like the Sadducees, and they do not believe in anything invisible except when they begin to make exceptions. Also, the demons are spirits. In Mark 5:13 they are called "unclean spirits" and also Luke 7:21. And then the angels have appeared here upon earth and have been seen. When Lazarus died the angels came and carried Lazarus to Abraham's bosom. (Luke 16:22.)

Balaam's eyes were opened so that he could see an angel that he had not been seeing. And a great warrior was permitted to open his eyes, by the power of God, to look on a great host of angels, and soldiers, and chariots and horses out yonder and things that he hadn't seen. And God only knows what all we could see if we had the right kind of eyes to see. (2 Kings 6:17.)

### Holy Spirit Invisible

The Holy Spirit, likewise now, is one of these invisible beings and we, therefore, believe in such. In Cruden's Concordance he says, "In the scripture the word **spirit** is taken for the Holy Ghost, the third person in the **Trinity."** And in the next place that the word spirit refers to the "spirit of man." The word **"Trinity"** of course means **three.** In Matthew 28:19 the Lord in giving the Great Commission said, "Teach all nations, baptizing them in the name of the Father, and of the Son, and of **the Holy Ghost."** And we read of the Father, Son, and Holy Ghost; the three of the Trinity, in many scriptures, though not in that order all the time. In 2 Cor. 13:14: "The grace of the Lord Jesus Christ, and the love of God, and the communion of the Holy Ghost, be with you." In Ephesians 4 we read, "There . . . is one Spirit," (verse 4) and there is "one Lord," (verse 5) and "one God" (verse 6). Well, that would be three ones together and the Trinity, the **"one spirit," "one Lord,"** and "one God." Three "ones" make three, and thus the Trinity of the Godhead. These are united. Jesus said in his prayer for the unity of his disciples that he wanted them to be one as he and his Father are one. (John 17:21, 22.) In 1 John 5:3-7 we read that the "three" bear record. There were the Father, and the Son, and the Holy Spirit, making the three thus mentioned, again. The Godhead is mentioned three times in the scriptures and I believe the Greek word is used in another passage where the Apostle Peter says, "According as his divine power hath given us all things that pertain unto life and godliness." (2 Peter 1:3.) The three passages using the word Godhead are Romans 1:20; Acts 17:29; and Col. 2:9. Hence, the Godhead is composed of the three persons, the three intelligent divine beings that make up the Godhead. Of course, the Father is God. The word God means Deity. Sometimes it refers to all three of the Godhead. "In the beginning God created the heaven and the earth." (Genesis 1:1.) Sometimes as you'll find in that chapter, the Hebrew word for God is plural. In verses 26 and 27: "Let us make man in our image, after our likeness." And thus, God, Christ, and the Holy Spirit were involved in the creation. Christ is Deity as I showed awhile ago. He was back there at the creation. "All things are made by him; and without him was not anything made that was made." (John 1:3.) Hence, he existed before the world was. (John 17:5.) And the Holy Spirit is God, or Deity, and a real personality, or divine being, and not a mere thing like wind or electricity, or something of that sort that has no intelligence. The Holy Spirit is infinitely intelligent, as God and Christ, and as a member of the Godhead. In Genesis 1:1, we read, "In the beginning God created the heaven and the earth." But in John 1:1-3 we learn that he did it through Christ. (Heb. 1:1, 2; Col. 1:13.) The Holy Spirit created. "And the Spirit of God moved upon the face of the waters." (Gen. 1:2.) I read from Job 26:13, "By his Spirit, he hath garnished the heavens; his hand hath formed the crooked serpent." So God garnished the heavens by his Spirit. The Holy Spirit gave laws to regulate all things. He was in the creation of man and of the earth and of all things. We read also where Elihu made the statement, "The Spirit of God hath made me, and the breath of the Almighty hath given me life." (Job 33:4.) And when it is said in Genesis 2:7 that God "formed man of the dust of the ground and breathed into his nostrils the breath of life; and man became a living soul," the Holy Spirit had a part in that creation of man. But I read again in Psalm 104:30, "Thou sendest forth thy Spirit; they are created: and thou renewest the face of the earth." There the Holy Spirit is in creation, back there in the beginning.

## The Holy Spirit Works Through Law

But the Spirit gave laws, when he garnished the heavens and when God created everything through Christ, the Holy Spirit then gave laws to the creatures of the world to reproduce their kind, and gave laws to Adam and Eve to "multiply and replenish the earth." (Genesis 1:28.) He gave the seed in the vegetable world and the seed has in it the power to reproduce its kind. About nine times in the first two chapters of Genesis it is said that everything will bring forth after its kind.

The power to convert the world and to make Christians is wrapped up in the seed, the word of God. The Holy Spirit has put the power there. Jesus used the parable, "The seed is the word of God." (Luke 8:11.) "The sower soweth the word." (Mark 4:14.) There's not an idea in religion today, which is true, that is not wrapped up in the seed, the word of God. There are no direct ideas. You had just as well expect to produce a crop out here by going out to the farm and praying to God to send down direct power and operate upon the soil and produce a crop and a harvest as to expect a direct revelation of God's will to man now. He has finished his revelation. We sing the old song, "How firm a foundation, ye saints of the Lord, is laid for your faith in his excellent word. What more can He say than to you He hath said? Ye who unto Jesus for refuge have fled." So we should stay with the seed, the word of God. We should depend upon it to produce the harvest. "They that sow in tears shall reap in joy. He that goeth forth and weepeth, bearing precious seed, shall doubtless come again with rejoicing, bringing his sheaves with him."

(Psalms 126:5, 6.) So there is not a true religious idea in the world not from the Bible. No man has such an idea except as he receives it from the seed, the word of God. It just narrows down to that. Everything else is false and extraneous.

Now people sometimes have imagined that the Holy Spirit was inspiring them, revealing something to them, when it was not true. I remember that I was in a discussion with Mr. Busbee of a denominational church over in Mississippi many years ago. He spoke very rapidly and in his haste he couldn't quote certain scriptures. He would get them backward and all tangled up in his haste and finally he would stop and he would say, "Help me, Holy Ghost!" And about that time, he would pick up the passage and here he would go with it and he would quote it; then say, "Thank you, Holy Ghost." He was taking the audience away with that trick. That's exactly what it was, a trick of the devil. People usually can be exposed when they get off on something like that, and I kept looking for a place to expose his trickery. Finally, he misquoted one and said, "Help me, Holy Ghost," and he imagined that the Holy Spirit had helped him and he said, "Thank you, Holy Ghost." But he had perverted it, did not quote it correctly. I turned then and read the passage and pointed out the fact that he and his Holy Ghost (?) had made a blunder and that his Holy Ghost was not the Holy Ghost. That the ghost he was depending on was another, a wicked spirit, and quoted several passages such as 1 Tim. 4:1, "The Spirit" —that is God's Spirit—"speaketh expressly, that in the latter times some shall depart from the faith, giving heed to **seducing spirits**, and **doctrines of devils**." I said, "There it is, a 'seducing spirit.' You are under the influence of the spirit of the devil." He didn't like it, but I could not help it. I had to expose him because he had no right to resort to such trickery in the first place, to try to delude the people into thinking that he was inspired. He had claimed it and then went down. Well, he never did say, "Thank you, Holy Ghost," any more during the rest of the discussion of the three nights. The Holy Spirit is **a person—a real being.**

And we will take that up tomorrow evening. We hope that you will be with us. Bring your neighbors and your friends and we will study these things.

Don't forget there is a spirit world and we are deciding now where we will be millions of years from now. So to-night, will you follow the teaching of the Holy Spirit? If you already know what to do to be saved, will you do it tonight? If you don't know, come and we will be glad to help you and instruct you, from the Bible itself. We will let you read it for yourself, what to do to be saved. You can obey the gospel and go on your way tonight, saved, your name written in heaven and be under the leadership of the Holy Spirit rather than following the flesh, and go to heaven rather than perdition when you leave this world. We are going to stand and sing the hymn of invitation at this time.

## QUESTIONS AND ANSWERS

**Question:** Had the word been translated Spirit rather than Ghost, would that not have prevented some of the confusion about the Holy Spirit?

**Answer:** The American Standard Version and modern translations leave out the word Ghost and put the word Spirit there. The facts are that the same original Greek word "pneuma" is translated Spirit in the King James Version in many places where it is occasionally translated Ghost. Hence, it is the same identical original word. The word used by Christ and the apostles is the same word **PNEUMA**—a form of the word is pneumatic. You talk about a pneumatic tire because the word pneuma primarily had reference to air and wind. But it has no such meaning in the Bible in passages refering to God, the Holy Spirit, Deity. For instance, when it says, "God is a Spirit" (John 4:24), it does not mean that God is a wind or that God is just hot air. It doesn't mean that. He is a being of intelligence, Almighty power, infinite wisdom, and the like. So the correction in the translation did go a long way in getting people to thinking aright.

At the time, however, the King James translation was made, the word Ghost carried with it the idea, largely, of guest; a visitor; one who had come to make his abode with us, and thus guest. At that time, when they would read about the Holy Ghost, it just meant a being who had come to live with man, dwell in man. So they didn't get the wrong idea back there in 1611 when the King James Version was made. A Holy Guest. But finally the word ghost came to connote in our changing, growing, language something it didn't mean then. It came to mean a sort of a goblin or something like that—something that is mysterious in the sense that they didn't know what it was—didn't know anything about it at all. Hence, false doctrines began to develop and people began to teach accordingly. Now that we have the corrected translation, we ought to use the word Spirit as often as possible and we are not misquoting the Bible because the Lord did not write in English. But the New Testament was written largely in Greek and the Greek word, pneuma, is the word that is translated both spirit and ghost.

**Question:** What evidence do we have of demons at work today?

**Answer:** I don't know much about demons, either. All I know about them is what God says about them and may not know all of that. But remember that in Deuteronomy 29:29, God's great declaration is: "The secret things belong to the Lord our God: but those things which are revealed belong unto us and to our children." We don't have to understand demons and know all about them, tell of their origin and all of that in order to believe what God said. He says that there were demons and I do not know all of their functions, all of their activities. But there are times you read of devils instead of demons. For instance, when James says, "The devils also believe, and tremble" (James 2:19), it is translated "demons" in the American Standard Version. I gave some Scriptures tonight where the Lord spoke of these demons as "spirits." We don't know all about them. It may be, as I thought of it this night, when God sent his Son into the world that he allowed people to be demon possessed so that the Lord might have an opportunity to counteract demoniac power and to show his superiority over the demons. That's exactly what he did whether demons possessed people for that reason or not. You remember when God called Moses, he offered some excuses and God said, "What's in your hand?" "A rod." He threw it down and God turned it into a serpent before his eyes and he fled from before it. God said, "Take it by the tail." And he did. Then following those signs of which this is the first mentioned, the magicians threw their rods down and they turned to serpents. That is, it seems that they did. It may be that they even had power, that God had somehow allowed them power or they had demoniac power to turn their rods to serpents. God may have permitted such in the first century so that Christ would come and conquer the demons and old satan—overpower them. In Mark 3:22 beginning and Matthew 12:22 beginning you will find that they accused Jesus of casting out demons by Beelzebub, the prince of the demons or devils. And Jesus, in defending himself against this very dangerous doctrine, made the statement that he cast them out by the power of the Holy Spirit. "And if I by Beelzebub cast out devils, by whom do your children cast them out?" (Matt. 12:27.) Their children claimed to cast them out, also. If just the casting out of demons proves one is in league with the devil, in league with Beelzebub, in partnership with him, then your children would be in partnership with him for they claim to cast them out. With withering logic he attacked their pretense and repudiation of the miracles of the Son of God and of the gospel. And then Jesus said, "No man can enter into a strong man's house, and spoil his goods, except he will first bind the strong man; and then he will spoil his house." (Mark 3:27.) If you leave him untied, unharmed, while you're trying to take his furniture and spoil his goods, he would perhaps be striking you upon the head with a chair or something, and you will not get by with it. So you have to first bind him before you can spoil his goods. As much as to say in this little parable, "I have bound Satan and that's why I can spoil his goods. That's the reason I can cast him out." He had cast Satan out of the man born blind and unable to speak. They couldn't deny that it was a real, actual miracle and so they just impugned his motive and his power as best they could by saying that he got his power from Beelzebub, the prince of the devils. And incidentally, he could say that was blasphemy against the Holy Spirit. In Mark 3:28, 29 he said, "He that shall blaspheme against the Holy Ghost has never forgiveness, but is in danger of eternal damnation," and in verse 30 he says, "Because they said, He hath an unclean spirit." So, to accuse Jesus of casting out demons by the power of Beelzebub was to call the Holy Spirit Beelzebub, was to call the Holy Spirit an unclean spirit, and that is what blasphemy is. It is to speak against that which is sacred and holy. And so they had blasphemed the Holy Spirit. He said they were guilty of an eternal sin and would never have forgiveness in view of that fact. He, also, in this connection showed his power, of course, over the devil. Satan cannot harm us if we will follow Christ. He came to destroy the works of the devil (I John 3:7). If we will follow him we will win, we will be victorious, and we will conquer over all the works and power of Satan. So it may be that God permitted people to be devil possessed. So Christ cast these demons out of people to show his superiority over the power of wicked spirits.

Sometimes people raise the question, "Where did Satan come from? Where did Satan originate?" First of all, it seems from the teaching of the Bible that Satan was in heaven. In Luke 10:18-20 Jesus said, "I beheld Satan as lightning fall from heaven." He was cast out. It seems that he was cast out up there because of his rebellion against God, that he was a great angel at one time, a good angel at first. We read in 1 Timothy 3:6 about an elder of the church, "Not a novice," he said (which is a young, or recent convert) "lest being lifted up with pride he fall into the condemnation of the devil." That does not mean that he would fall into the condemnation which the devil would

heap upon him. For the devil would not condemn a man
for being proud and haughty. He would approve of that.
That passage is nearly always misunderstood, mistaught.
It means, lest being lifted up with pride he would fall into
the condemnation that the devil fell into when  he  was
lifted up with pride and became haughty, conceited, arro-
gant, and violated the law of God in heaven. Hence, "fall
into the condemnation of the devil," means the condemnation into which the devil fell through his pride. Pride
and a haughty spirit go before a fall. We should look out
if we are haughty and "stuck-up" and proud. Be humble
and remember that God gives grace to the humble. But he
resists the proud and hates a proud heart. (Proverbs 6:16-
19.)

Further illustrating the matter—since this is  the  last
question, I will add these points here before we close—
that in John the ninth chapter connected with the healing
of a blind man, they asked Jesus, "Who did sin, this man,
or his parents, that he was born blind?" They thought it
had to be one or the other—that he sinned before he was
born so as to be born blind or else his parents had sinned
so that he might be born blind. Jesus said, "Neither hath
this man sinned, nor his parents," that he was born blind.
He is not here saying that no parents have ever sinned in
such a way so as to cause their children to be born blind,
for many are born blind because of sins of parents, sins
that brought on disease which caused  blindness.  They
were born blind because of the parents' sins. He says that
was not the case here. In this instance, God had a purpose
and this man was born blind that the purpose of God might
be manifested, "that the works of God should be manifest
in him"—that he might be an occasion, an  example  so
Jesus could demonstrate his great and mighty power in
giving him his sight—so he could establish his claim as
the Messiah, the Christ, the Son of God, the Saviour and
hope of the world. Hence, God is in the background here,
in his rich provisions—providence—provide-ance, if you
please. God is the one who provides. God, himself, had
purposed and planned this birth to be as it was—had a

child born blind that the power of God might be demonstrated in him. He did a great deal of good, maybe more
good than a thousand normal people of his day, in being
(what we might be pardoned for saying) the guinea pig
of the occasion for Jesus to demonstrate his power as the
Son of God. Christ opened the eyes of the blind. Behold
the signs, said John, truly done by Jesus—besides this
one. "Many other signs truly did Jesus in the presence of
his disciples, which are not written in this book: but these
are written, that you might believe that Jesus is the Christ,
the Son of God; and that believing ye might  have  life
through his name." (John 20:30, 31.) I think this is as far
as we will go on this occasion. May God richly bless the
study of his word! May we go away with reverence and
a greater desire and determination to be led and guided
by the Holy Spirit and to know more about how he deals
with us down here in the world.

# HOLY SPIRIT AND REVELATION

I could not feel that I had done justice to myself, nor been courteous to you, without joining in the words of welcome and expressions of appreciation in the introduction.

Our overall subject is: THE PERSON AND WORK OF THE HOLY SPIRIT.

All we know about the Holy Spirit is what is revealed in the Bible concerning the subject. We know nothing "directly" about the Holy Spirit. We have never seen the Holy Spirit. We are not inspired, and we have wrought no miracles by the power of the Holy Spirit. There are deceptions around about, everywhere, concerning the work of the Holy Spirit, and even concerning the very nature of the Holy Spirit.

### Spirit a Person

Yesterday evening we tried to learn something of the personality of the Holy Spirit. Remember that the Spirit is not a mere 'essence' of some sort, like water, air, or electricity, or something of that kind. Although figurative expressions are used in the Bible (such as, "I will pour out my Spirit" and "the Holy Ghost fell on them," Joel 2:28; Acts 11:15), the Bible does not teach that the Holy Spirit is a liquid, like water. These are figurative expressions.

The Holy Spirit is actually a person, a divine Being, as is God our Father, and the Lord Jesus Christ. The Holy Spirit is "eternal" (Heb. 9:14), just as God (Rom. 1:20) and Christ (1 Tim. 1:17) are eternal. He is one of the Godhead, is of the 'Trinity,' as in Matt. 28:19, and many other such kindred passages.

### Spirit in the Old Testament

I would like first to point out something about the Holy Spirit, and his teaching concerning himself, in the **Old**

**Testament.** We read of the Holy Spirit, beginning with the second verse in the Old Testament: "The Spirit of God moved upon the face of the waters." (Gen. 1:2.) Hence, the Spirit was "brooding" (as some translations put it) upon the face of the waters back there in the first chapter of Genesis.

The Holy Spirit could move men to speak and to write Scripture. "Knowing this first, that no prophecy of the scripture is of any private interpretation. For the prophecy came not in old time by the will of man: but holy men of God spake as they were moved by the Holy Ghost." (2 Pet. 1:20-21.) Peter's statement that "no prophecy of the scripture is of any private interpretation," should be obvious: it simply means that the prophecy of the scripture did not come by the will of man, as he goes on to say. Some 'Drew Pearson' back there did not take into consideration the facts concerning the trend of the times, and then interpret these to mean that in the future certain things were going to happen. The prophecies did **not** come "by the will of man" in such fashion. It was not some prediction based upon even a good knowledge of the facts concerning the 'trend' of things at that time. In the next verse Peter affirms: "Holy men of God spake as they were moved by the Holy Ghost." (2 Pet. 1:21.) Thus the Holy Spirit moved men to speak and to write the Old Testament scriptures, even prophetic scriptures.

### "Spirit of Christ"

We also read that "the Spirit of Christ" was in those prophets back there. (1 Pet. 1:10.) The "Spirit of Christ" was the Holy Ghost. He was sometimes called "the Spirit of Christ" (Rom. 8:9-11), and sometimes "the Spirit of God," as well as "the Holy Spirit."

The Holy Spirit spoke **through men** in Old Testament times. David said, "The Spirit of the Lord spake by me, and his word was in my tongue." (2 Sam. 23:2.) Peter said, "Men and brethren, this scripture must needs have been fulfilled, which the Holy Ghost by the mouth of David spake . . ." (Acts 1:16.) And so, the Holy Spirit spoke the scriptures of the Old Testament, and the Spirit was in the inspired men who spoke and wrote.

### Spirit Interested

God said, "My spirit shall not always strive with man." (Gen. 6:3.) This indicates that the Spirit is interested in man. However, the flood would come in "one hundred and twenty years," which would be early in life for many, and they would not live out their usually-allotted time of eight or nine hundred years. So, the Spirit was striving—but would not always strive—with man. David prayed in the great "Confession" Psalm, "And take not thy Holy Spirit from me." (Ps. 51:11.)

### Spirit Strives With Man

From Gen. 6:3 we learn that the Holy Spirit "strives" with, and is interested in, man and his welfare. He strives with man to get him to do right. He does not just leave man alone, and leave him to be lost, without making an effort to reach him, and without trying to influence him for good and for God. So, he is striving with men. He strove with people then through the preaching of God's word. Of Noah we read that he was "a preacher of righteousness." (2 Pet. 2:5.) Hence, Noah, as one of God's "holy men," "spake as" he was "moved by the Holy Ghost." (2 Pet. 1:21.) It was the Holy Spirit, then, who moved such "holy men of God" as Noah, to speak to the people, and warn them, and plead with them to turn and live. Hence, the Holy Spirit was "striving" with man.

### Noah Preached By The Spirit

This may help us to understand and appreciate the statement that Christ was raised from the dead by the same Spirit by which he had "preached unto the spirits in prison; which sometime were disobedient, when once the long-suffering of God waited in the days of Noah, while the ark was a preparing, wherein few, that is, eight souls were saved by water. The like figure whereunto even baptism doth also now save us (not the putting away of the filth of the flesh, but the answer of a good conscience toward God) by the resurrection of Jesus Christ: who is gone into heaven, and is on the right hand of God; angels and authorities and powers being made subject unto him." (1 Pet. 3:18-22.) Christ did not go in person; he went by the Spirit in the person of Noah, for it was the "Spirit of Christ" who was in those prophets back there. (1 Pet. 1:10.) Since "Spirit of Christ" is just another name for the Holy Spirit, Christ by the Holy Spirit (in Noah) preached (2 Pet. 2:5) unto the spirits in prison. Christ preached by the Holy Spirit.

He preached to them "while the ark was a preparing." (1 Pet. 3:19-20.) That is when they "were disobedient." They are called "spirits in prison," first of all, because they were "shut up" under a destruction that was to come in 120 years: "yet his days shall be an hundred and twenty years." (Gen. 6:3.) And they were "in prison" in the sense that they were involved in sin, and were in the "prison" of sin. We read (Luke 4:18) that Jesus was to "preach deliverance to the captives, . . . and to set at liberty them that are bruised." This evidently has a direct reference to the "prison" of sin. So, Christ's preaching by the Spirit through Noah was done to those who were in "prison." And it was done to those only who lived in the days of Noah: "which sometime were disobedient when once the longsuffering of God waited in the days of Noah, while the ark was a preparing." Hence, the preaching was done through Noah, done by the Holy Spirit, done unto the people before the flood came; and in that manner the Holy Spirit was "striving" with them.

### Words Of The Spirit

The Spirit put his words in the mouth of Isaiah the prophet (Isa. 59:21); and Ezekiel said, "The spirit entered into me when he spake unto me." (Ezek. 2:1-5.) This was also true of the other prophets. We read (Mic. 2:7) that the words of the Spirit were for the good of God's people. The Holy Spirit spoke always in behalf of the best interest of the people. (cf. Deut. 6:24.)

But the Spirit did not then work miraculously upon people to make them better. God has always dealt with sinners with regard and respect for their free moral agency.

Man is not a mere "machine," to be operated upon by God Almighty himself, nor by the Holy Spirit, for the purpose of making him better. God works through moral means to bring about a moral change which would fit man to dwell in a perfectly moral society in heaven.

### Spirit In Prophets

The Spirit was in the prophets, and God through that means taught the masses of the people. He did not send the Spirit directly to all the people to teach them. But he sent the Spirit to his inspired men, that through them he could teach the people. In Nehemiah's prayer to God, he said: "Thou gavest also thy good Spirit to instruct them." (Neh. 9:20.) The Spirit never did come to "confuse" people, but to teach and instruct. Now, from this verse alone, I will admit that you could not know whether he gave his Spirit directly to each individual, or whether he gave the Spirit to inspired men to (through them) instruct the people. But just ten verses later Nehemiah says God "testifiedst against them by thy spirit **in thy prophets**." (Neh. 9:30.) So the Spirit was in the prophets, and through them testified against God's people, who at that time were wicked and sinful, in rebellion against God.

With this in mind, we read again of "the words which the Lord of hosts hath sent in his spirit by the former prophets." (Zech. 7:12.) Hence the Spirit was God's spokesman through inspired men to the masses of the people. So the Holy Spirit back in Old Testament times called upon his prophets, one of whom was Ezekiel, and said, "Speak," and then guided them in their speaking. (Ezek. 11:5.)

We have in Joel 2:28-30 a prophecy fulfilled beginning on Pentecost. Quoting this prophecy, Peter said, "These are not drunken, as ye suppose, seeing it is but the third hour of the day. But this is that which was spoken by the prophet Joel; And it shall come to pass in the last days, saith God, I will pour out of my Spirit upon all flesh: and your sons and your daughters shall prophesy, and your young men shall see visions, and your old men shall dream dreams: And on my servants and on my handmaidens I will pour out in those days of my Spirit; and they shall prophesy: And I will shew wonders in heaven above, and signs in the earth beneath; blood, and fire, and vapour of smoke: The sun shall be turned into darkness, and the moon into blood, before that great and notable day of the Lord come: And it shall come to pass, that whosoever shall call on the name of the Lord shall be saved." (Acts 2:15-21.)

### "This Is That"

Peter said, **"This is that."** You can be certain you are right when you find where some New Testament writer quoted an Old Testament prophecy and said, "This is that which was spoken by the prophet." "This is that." Peter did not say, "Something that will happen way down yonder in the twentieth century, somewhere, will be that which was spoken by Joel," but he said "This that is happening here on Pentecost, A.D. 33, in the city of Jerusalem, is it." Nearly nineteen hundred years ago Peter said, "This is that" which was spoken by the prophet Joel. And Joel said, "It shall come to pass **in the last days** . . ." So Pentecost (Acts 2) was in **"the last days,"** according to Peter. "Last days" has no reference to the end of the world, nor necessarily to the twentieth century. But it has reference to the **last dispensation** of God's mercy to man, the **Christian age** of the world. So, God said, "In the last days" I will pour out the Spirit; but he poured it out on Pentecost; therefore Pentecost was in the "last days." Concerning the outpouring of the Spirit, God said, "I will pour out my spirit unto you, I will make known my words unto you." (Prov. 1:23.)

### Nature Of Spirit

But now study with me some of the characteristics of the Holy Spirit, and see that the Holy Spirit is a divine person or being, an intelligent being, and not some unintelligent something, nor a mere essence, like water, or wind, or electricity, or such like. We read that the Spirit could be blasphemed: "But he that shall blaspheme against the Holy Ghost hath never forgiveness, but is in danger of eternal damnation." (Mark 3:29.) Thus one could blaspheme the Holy Spirit. One could not blaspheme electricity, nor water, nor wind, nor some mere essence, nor a stone, nor a stump; he could not blaspheme anything less than a person or that which is connected with a divine person—like the word of God, which is connected with God himself. Hence, the Holy Spirit is a divine being, the same as Christ is. "Whosoever speaketh a word against the Son of man, it shall be forgiven him." That is, this is a "pardonable" sin; upon proper conditions, man can obtain pardon for it. "But whosoever speaketh against the Holy Ghost" (that would be "blasphemy" against the Holy Ghost, v. 31) "it shall not be forgiven him, neither in this world, neither in the world to come." (Matt. 12:32.) "Because they said, He hath an unclean spirit." (Mark 3:30.)

Again: people can lie to the Holy Spirit: Peter asked, "Ananias, why hath Satan filled thine heart to lie to the Holy Ghost?" (Acts 5:3.) Man could not lie to electricity, water, wind, or something of that sort; but man can "lie" to the Holy Spirit; hence the Holy Spirit is a divine Being, as God—to whom also Ananias "lied." (v. 4.)

### Spirit Knows

The Spirit is intelligent, or knows: "What man knoweth the things of a man, save the spirit of man which is in him? Even so the things of God knoweth no man, but the Spirit of God." (1 Cor. 2:11.) The Spirit of God, then, knows the things of God, as the spirit of man knows the things of man. And if the spirit of man is intelligent, then the Spirit of God is intelligent. If the one is a person because it can know, then so is the other.

### Spirit Grieves

And then, the Spirit could be grieved: "And grieve not the Holy Spirit of God, whereby ye are sealed unto the day of redemption." (Eph. 4:30.) Thus people can grieve the Holy Spirit, just as children by their waywardness and sins can grieve their parents, and as a husband by his sins can grieve his wife, or the wife can grieve her husband. Just so, people can "grieve the Holy Spirit." (This proves the Holy Spirit is not a mere essence, like wind, electricity, etc., for man cannot "grieve" them.) The Holy Spirit is in-

terested in us, and in our welfare. He grieves over our sins
more than our parents, because they don't always know
all about their children, but the Holy Spirit does know.

### Spirit Can Be Vexed

But then again: the Holy Spirit can be vexed, or aggra-
vated, or fretted, and that by men's sins, just as God can
be angered by sin. Isaiah (63:10) said, "They rebelled, and
vexed his holy Spirit." "Vex" means to harass, annoy, or
trouble grievously. Only a person could be "vexed;" therefore the Holy Spirit is an intelligent person of the godhead,
which consists of the Father, Son, and Holy Spirit. (Matt.
28:19.)

### Spirit A "Comforter"

The Holy Spirit could "comfort," for Jesus said, "He shall
give you another Comforter . . . even the Spirit of truth."
(John 14:16-17.) Christ was the first Comforter considered
there; he had been comforting them in that very chapter.
(John 14:1-3.) He was their present Comforter; but he spoke
of "The Comforter, which is the Holy Ghost, whom the
Father will send in my name." (v. 26.) He again called the
Spirit "the Comforter" in John 15:26 and 16:7. Of course,
he could not be a "Comforter" unless he were an intelligent
Being.

Of course, the Holy Spirit "comforts" by his word, which
he spoke through the apostles, which would comfort them
as they were taught. He would show them how to live as
teachers, and through them would show to others the way
of life and salvation. Hence we read: "Whatsoever things
were written aforetime were written for our learning, that
we through patience and **comfort of the Scriptures** might
have hope." (Rom. 15:4.) Again Paul said, "Comfort one
another with these words." (1 Thess. 4:18.) So the words
of the Holy Spirit comfort man. When the Holy Spirit
dwells in men, he does not comfort them **directly**, in any
miraculous way; but he comforts now just like he always
has comforted—like he did the apostles and other people
in apostolic days—through his word which he spoke
through inspired men. He guided them "into all truth."

(John 16:13.) And as the Spirit spake by David, and his word was in David's tongue (2 Sam. 23:2), it was to comfort people then, and encourage them, or to reprove them. As we have seen, God "testifiedst against them by thy Spirit in thy prophets." (Neh. 9:30.)

### Spirit Masculine In Gender

The Holy Spirit is referred to in the masculine gender, and is presented to us as "He." (John 16:13.) I know the King James Version often reads "it" (as in Rom. 8:16, 26); but the Holy Spirit is never called "it" in the better translations—but is referred to as "He."

In discussing the new birth at Huntsville, Alabama, I pointed out the fact that Jesus said we are "born of water and of the Spirit." (John 3:5.) My opponent ridiculed the idea that men are born "of water," and said that made "water" our **mother**! So he said I have a "Water Mother." Of course I did not say "water" is our mother, for Paul said, "Jerusalem which is above is free, which is the mother of us all." (Gal. 4:26.) I simply quoted what Jesus said, that "Except a man be born of water and of the Spirit, he cannot enter into the kingdom of God." (John 3:5.) Jesus was "born" from the dead (Col. 1:18); does that make the grave his mother? Of course not! Figures of speech cannot be made to creep on "all-fours," as logicians would say.

But I asked my respondent who—according to **his** doctrine—is the "mother?" "Who is the 'mother' in the new birth?" He said, "The Holy Spirit." To this I replied, "Then you have a 'HE' mother in the new birth, for Jesus said, "Howbeit when **he**, the Spirit of truth, is come, **he** will guide you into all truth: for **he** shall not speak of **him**self; but whatsoever **he** shall hear, that shall **he** speak: and **he** will show you things to come." (John 16:13.) The Spirit is called "he" six times in this verse, and twice in v. 14;—so my friend would have a "he" mother.

### Spirit Begets

But the Holy Spirit is the "begetting" agency, rather than the "mother." In James 1:18 we read, "Of his own will begat he us with the word of truth." But remember, "the word of truth" or gospel is preached "by the Holy Ghost sent down from heaven." (1 Pet. 1:12.) And so, the Holy Spirit uses the word by which to beget people. Paul said, "I have begotten you through the gospel" (1 Cor. 4:15), but that gospel is the message of the Holy Spirit. The Spirit begat people through the preaching of the gospel, and by that means.

### Guided By Spirit

Then again, the Holy Spirit could "guide," as I have just quoted from John 16:13: "He shall guide you into all truth." As the driver guides the automobile, so the Holy Spirit guided the inspired man. He did not take away all the man's personality, and destroy that; he did not reduce the inspired man to nothing more than a "microphone," but he **guided** him nevertheless. I think it was Bro. J. W. McGarvey who illustrated it by a man driving down the street a horse hitched to a buggy. So long as the horse was going exactly like he wanted him to go, the driver did not pull either the right rein nor the left. But if, before the driver wanted to go home, the horse started to turn homeward, his master would pull the rein, guiding the horse and causing him to go exactly where the driver desired. After this fashion the Holy Spirit did the guiding (John 16:13), but left the inspired man free to use his own vocabulary in speaking or writing. When the inspired man might be about to go wrong, or use the wrong word, the Holy Spirit would then guide and direct him. This gave us the verbally inspired Bible. (1 Cor. 2:13.)

### Spirit Bears Witness

Again, I call attention to the fact that the Holy Spirit could bear witness. We read of the Holy Spirit, that "he shall testify of me." (John 15:26-27.) That is, he would come, take possession of the apostles, and through them he would preach the gospel, thus testifying of Jesus—that he died for our sins, God raised him up, and he is alive and at the right hand of God to make intercession for us. Hence, the Holy Spirit testified through inspired men. Jesus said, "Ye also shall bear witness, because you have been with me from the beginning." (John 15:26-27.) These apostles had been with him during his personal ministry, even from the beginning, and they would bear witness of Jesus.

Again we read: "The Spirit itself (ASV: himself) beareth witness with our spirit, that we are the children of God." (Rom. 8:16.) Through inspired men, the Holy Spirit has laid down the plan of salvation. The conditions of pardon, revealed and confirmed by the Holy Spirit, are: faith in Christ, repentance of sin, confession of Christ, and baptism. (Acts 2:4, 36-38; 8:35-39.) And then our spirits testify as to whether or not we have met these terms. (1 Cor. 2:11.) If we have complied with them, then there are two witnesses to the fact that we are saved: our human spirits testify that we are in the group who have done what the Holy Spirit testifies must be done. Thus, the Holy Spirit does not bear witness "to"—but "with"—our spirits. Hence, it is a matter of faith, and Paul speaks of drawing nigh "with a true heart, in full assurance of faith." (Heb. 10:22.)

It is not a matter of physical knowledge that we know we are saved, like a man knows he has a dollar in his hand. It is not that kind of knowledge, but is a matter of "faith" —"full assurance of faith."

### Spirit a Teacher

The Holy Spirit could **teach**. Jesus said, "He shall teach you all things, and bring to your remembrance all things whatsoever I have said unto you." (John 14:26.) He could "instruct," for "Thou gavest also thy good Spirit to instruct them." (Neh. 9:20.) This was done "by thy Spirit in thy prophets." (v. 30.) So, the Holy Spirit can instruct or teach.

### Spirit Could Hear

The Holy Spirit could speak, and he could **hear**. "Howbeit, when he, the Spirit of truth, is come, he shall guide you into all truth, for he shall not speak of himself; but whatsoever he shall hear, that shall he speak: and he will show you things to come." (John 16:13.) So he came and took possession of the apostles, and through them he spoke the word of God which he himself had heard from the Father and the Son. In his prayer to the Father, Jesus said,

"I have given them"—the apostles—"the word which thou gavest me" and "I have given them thy word." (John 17:8, 14.)

## Spirit Could Speak

Then again we read, "He that hath an ear, let him hear what the Spirit saith unto the churches." (Rev. 2:7.) And you will find this admonition in each of the letters to the seven churches of Asia: "Hear what the Spirit saith unto the churches." What the Spirit had to say to the churches, he did not say directly to each individual member of the church in some mysterious way; he did not inspire the members, but through John the apostle the Spirit delivered his message, saying it in the letter that was to be read to the churches. When they heard that, they were hearing "what the **Spirit saith** unto the churches." The Spirit spoke through inspired men, and could thus be heard by the people.

"The Spirit speaketh expressly" (1 Tim. 4:1-3)—so he did not stammer and stutter around when he spoke, like many do. He could speak plainly; he is supposed to be understood, hence it says, "The Spirit speaketh expressly." And we know what he had to say, because it is recorded in scripture: "The Spirit speaketh expressly, that in the latter times some shall depart from the faith, giving heed to seducing spirits, and doctrines of devils;" and so on. (1 Tim. 4:1-3.)

Paul said, "Which things also we speak, not in the words which man's wisdom teacheth, but which the Holy Ghost teacheth." (1 Cor. 2:13.)

## Spoke By Men

We learn (1 Cor. 2:13) that the Holy Spirit taught the apostles the words to speak; he did not give them just the idea, and let them use their own judgment in the selection of words—and allow errors to thus creep into **revelation**. But they were verbally inspired. The Spirit selected the very words. So when the Holy Spirit came upon the apostles, "They began to speak in other tongues, as the Spirit gave them utterance." (Acts 2:4.) The Spirit gave them the utterance to say those things in other languages which the apostles previously knew nothing about. They spoke in the languages of the people, to teach them in their own tongues. The people understood that the apostles were talking about "the wonderful works of God" in raising Jesus from the dead, seating him at his own right hand as Lord and Christ. They understood. It was not "jabbering" such as modern deceivers and deceived people try to palm off on us.

### Spirit Could Witness

Paul said, "The Holy Ghost witnesseth in every city, saying that bonds and afflictions abide me." (Acts 20:23.) The Holy Ghost **witnessed** by saying this—not by a still small **voice** that was no voice at all—was nothing but **imagination**! The Holy Spirit is an intelligent being, and always acted in an intelligent manner.

### Spoke the Scriptures

The Holy Spirit spoke the scriptures. We read that "the Holy Ghost saith" (Heb. 3:7-11) what was recorded in Ps. 95:7-11. Paul said, "Well spake the Holy Ghost by Esaias (Isaiah) the prophet unto our fathers, saying . . ."—and then he quotes from Isa. 6:9-10 and Isa. 44:18. So the Holy Ghost "said" what was recorded by Isaiah. These scriptures are quoted as the words of the Holy Spirit. This is what the Holy Ghost had to say on the subject.

Jeremiah 31:33-34 is quoted in Hebrews 10:14-18, and in connection therewith the author says, "The Holy Ghost also is a **witness** to us"—that is, a witness that under the new covenant, sins would not be remembered again, as they were under the old. But the Spirit's "testimony" is contained in the scripture: "For after that he had said . . ." and then follows the quotation from Jeremiah; but it is attributed to the "Holy Ghost." Therefore the Spirit spoke the scriptures.

### Could Be Resisted

The Holy Spirit could testify in words that can be understood. God "testifiedst against them by thy Spirit in thy prophets." (Neh. 9:30.) And if they wanted the testimony

of the Spirit, they had to listen to the prophets. That is
why Stephen says, "Ye stiffnecked and uncircumcised in
heart and ears, ye do always resist the Holy Ghost." (Acts
7:51.) Like the Old Testament prophets, Stephen spoke by
inspiration of the Holy Ghost (Acts 6:3, 5); but he said,
"As your fathers did, so do ye." (Acts 7:51.) How did their
fathers "resist" the Spirit? Well, when God " testifiedst
against them by thy Spirit in thy prophets: yet would they
**not give ear**." (Neh. 9:30.) Therefore in rejecting the prophets' word, they were rejecting and resisting the Spirit's
word—because the Spirit was speaking through the prophets who testified against them. And Stephen said, "You
are doing the same thing your fathers did."

The Spirit could strive with men (as we pointed out in
Gen. 6:3), and they resisted the Holy Ghost back there
by resisting what the Holy Spirit had to say to them
through inspired men. People today resist the Holy Spirit
in the same way that it has always been done—when they
resist the words of the Holy Spirit revealed through inspired men. (Neh. 9:20, 30; 2 Sam. 23:2; Acts 1:16.)

The Holy Spirit did not speak directly to the masses of
the people, but spoke to the fathers by the prophets, and
to us through the apostles and other inspired writers of
the New Testament. And we can understand what he has
to say. Paul says, "**By revelation** he made known unto me
the mystery; (as I wrote afore in few words, whereby
**when ye read, ye may understand** my knowledge in the
mystery of Christ) which in other ages was not made
known unto the sons of men, as it **is now revealed unto his
holy apostles and prophets by the Spirit**; That the Gentiles
should be fellow-heirs, and of the same body, and partakers of his promise in Christ by the gospel." (Eph. 3:3-6.) So,
when we read we can understand what the Holy Spirit
wrote (through inspired men), and spoke, when he through
them spoke the scriptures. (Acts 1:16.) When the word of
the Spirit is rejected and resisted, the Holy Spirit is rejected and resisted.

### His Word Perfect
We must not add to the words of the Holy Spirit. His

word is perfect, for we read, "The law of the Lord is perfect, converting the soul." (Ps. 19:7.) So the law of the Lord
is able to do a perfect job of converting men.    It is able
to save: "Receive with    meekness    the    engrafted    word,
which is able to save your souls." (Jas. 1:21.) "The law of
the Spirit of life in Christ Jesus has made me free." (Rom.
8:2.) The Spirit is able to convert and save—but that does
not mean he does the pardoning. By his "law" (Rom. 8:2)
he influences us to turn from sin and become—and be—
Christians, and to live faithfully the Christian life. The
Holy Spirit is able to do that job; but he will not miraculously do it. He works through the gospel.

### Preached Gospel

Paul says the "gospel" is "the power of God unto salvation, unto every one that believeth." (Rom. 1:16.) And Peter
says this "gospel" was preached "with the Holy Ghost sent
down from heaven" (1 Pet. 1:12)—not directly by the Spirit,
but through the inspired apostles. To them Jesus said, "Go
ye into all the world, and preach the gospel to every creature." (Mark 16:15.) People were led by the Holy Spirit,
then, when they were led by the words of the Holy Spirit,
as spoken and written by these inspired men. And so, we
read: "As many as are led by the Spirit of God, they are
the sons of God." (Rom. 8:14.)    The Holy Spirit seeks to
"lead" all people aright. "God is no respector of persons."
(Acts 10:34.) He does not "will" that "any should perish,
but that all should come to repentance." (2 Pet. 3:9.)

### Revelation Complete

Therefore, we can be sure that we do not need any additional revelation from the Holy Spirit. He has said all that
is necessary. In closing the New Testament scriptures, he
warned: "If any man shall add unto these things, God shall
add unto him the plagues"—and one of them is hell fire!—
"that are written in this book: And if any man shall take
away from the words of the book of this prophecy, God
shall take away his part out of the book of life, and out
of the holy city, and from the things which are written in
this book." (Rev. 22:18-19.) So we are not allowed to add

to, to take from, nor to substitute anything else for, the word of God. It is complete.

### His Word In Bible
Hence, James says, "Receive with meekness the engrafted word" (ASV: "the implanted word") "which is able to save your souls." (Jas. 1:21.) The same writer then goes on, "Whoso looketh into the perfect law of liberty" (Jas. 1:21-25)—and called the word the "perfect" law.

Therefore the Holy Spirit has given us a "perfect" revelation. There is not a true religious idea on earth today which is not found in the seed, the word of God. If you want that idea perpetuated, just preach the word—and you will do all that God ever intended for you to do in reaching a world of lost people with the word of the Holy Spirit. The Holy Spirit does not reveal ideas and thoughts to people directly, nor guide them directly in some mysterious way, leaving them to wonder whether it is the spirit of the devil, or the Spirit of God that is doing the suggesting, and the leading, and such like. The Holy Spirit has no suggestions to make, no instruction to give, **other than what he has given in the Bible.**

### Deception Explained
It is possible for someone with only a meager knowledge of the Bible, to sum up in his mind certain great facts and truths, which he cannot express in Bible words; and he may imagine that the Holy Spirit is telling him, whispering to him, or making him to feel in a certain way, that a certain thing is true. He may imagine that this is a direct operation of the Spirit—when perhaps it was nothing more than a summing up of what he already knows as revealed in the Bible! There are **no new ideas** in the religious world which are true, which are from heaven. We have nothing that is true except what is revealed in the Bible. Paul said, "All scripture is given by inspiration of God, and is profitable for doctrine, for reproof, for correction, for instruction in righteousness; that the man of God may be perfect, thoroughly furnished unto all good works." (2 Tim. 3:16-17.) The Spirit does not have to detour around the scrip-

tures to aid and assist us in any good work. Every good work has been authorized and has been directed by the Holy Spirit in the scriptures, his word.

### Strives With Man

Tonight, the Spirit is striving with you to become a Christian, if you are not such. He is striving with all of us to be consecrated, dedicated Christians. He is striving with us through his word. (Gen. 6:3; 2 Pet. 2:5.) He has in that word offered incentives and motives, which are as vast as all eternity, and in which he has wrapped up the mighty, moral, persuasive power of Almighty God to save a lost world.

If God **could have put** into the gospel any more power than he did put into it, he **would have done** so. His great interest in us and in our salvation, his great love for us, his great throbbing heart of love, would not have permitted him to rest a moment without putting that extra power into the gospel—if he could have put it there and leave man a free moral agent. Hence, God has gone "all-out" in his efforts to save a lost world. He has put into his truth the power to make us free. Jesus said, "Ye shall know the truth, and the truth shall make you free." (John 8:32.) The Spirit guided the apostles "into all truth." (John 16:13.) So, by the time the last apostle died we had "all truth." Therefore Jude says, "Earnestly contend for the faith which was once" (ASV: "for all") "delivered to the saints." (Jude 3.)

### Revelation Complete

We do not need a new revelation of God's truth. We have that very truth—"all truth"—in the old revelation. This old truth needs no new "revelation;" and it needs no new "confirmation" by miracles today. (That will come up in a subsequent lecture, which we are very eager for you to study with us.)

I appreciate the good attention you have given. Let us now stand, and sing the hymn of invitation, with the hope and prayer that some lost soul will respond to the Lord's invitation.

## QUESTIONS AND ANSWERS

**Question:** Please explain the 'Blasphemy against the Holy Ghost'.

**Answer:** Although I would like to speak forty-five minutes about the blasphemy against the Holy Spirit, I will have to be brief. (Nearly a dozen questions have already been turned in for tonight.)

The word "blaspheme" means "to speak against." Jesus said, "All manner of sin and blasphemy shall be forgiven unto men: but the blasphemy against the Holy Ghost shall not be forgiven unto men. And whosoever speaketh a word against the Son of man, it shall be forgiven him: but whosoever speaketh against the Holy Ghost, it shall not be forgiven him, neither in this world, neither in the world to come." (Matt. 12:31-32.)

When Jesus said, "All manner of sin . . . shall be forgiven him," he meant those sins are pardonable. But he warned the blasphemy of (or speaking against) the Holy Spirit "shall not be forgiven him, neither in this world" (and the word "world" is from the Greek **aion**, which means "age"); it would not be forgiven him in "this world or age"—the Jewish dispensation, during the personal ministry of Christ—"neither in the world to come,"—during the Christian dispensation. It would not be forgiven in either of these dispensations.

To "blaspheme" the Holy Spirit is to "speak against" the Holy Spirit. In the context they had done that very thing. "By the Spirit of God" Christ had cast out devils. (v. 28.) But they said he cast out devils "by Beelzebub, the prince of the devils." (v. 24.) Mark (3:30) explains that they said, "He hath an unclean spirit," whereas Jesus claimed he had the "Holy Spirit." So to "blaspheme" the Holy Spirit was to **speak against** the Spirit, as they did. They denied that the Holy Spirit wrought the miracles that Jesus did, but attributed them to the devil, and gave the credit, glory, and honor unto the devil for that which the Holy Spirit instead did.

That will be all the time we have for that question.

**Question:** If the Holy Spirit is not the same as God, how could Christ be called the Son of God, when the Holy Spirit made Mary conceive? (Luke 1:34-35.)

**Answer:** An illustration helps clarify this matter: God sent the Holy Spirit through the apostles, to **convert us.** We are converted by the Holy Spirit; we are "begotten" by the **Holy Spirit** through his word. (1 Cor. 4:15; Jas. 1:21); and yet we are "children of **God.**" "Behold, what manner of love the Father hath bestowed upon us, that we should be called the children of God." (1 John 3:1-4.) Now, if **we** can be sons of "God" because we are begotten by the **Holy Spirit** through his word, then why could not  Christ  be called "the Son of God" when he was **directly** begotten by the Holy Spirit? The angel Gabriel told Mary, "The Holy Ghost shall come upon thee, and the power of the Highest shall overshadow thee: therefore also that holy thing which shall be born of thee shall be called the Son of God." (Luke 1:35.) Hence, I see no real problem, whatsoever, there.

**Question:** What is it that is being revealed through unrighteous men? (Rom. 1:18; et al.) Is it only what we read in the New Testament? Do these men get it from the New Testament?

**Answer:** Unrighteous men reveal many things, of course; but they reveal only human information. We can learn from unrighteous people many things concerning unrighteous people—because they reveal, make known, things of themselves.

But where is the scripture that says unrighteous people are revealing the will of God today? I deny that there is any such passage.

Voice: "Isaiah 64:6."

Gus Nichols: Someone has given me a passage of Scripture which says, "But we are all as an unclean thing, and all our righteousnesses are as filthy rags." (Isa. 64.6.) They did not have any righteousness at all! Their 'righteousness' was actually unrighteousness, and was as "filthy rags." Now, true "righteousness" is not as "filthy rags." "All thy commandments are righteousness." (Ps. 119:172.) "Everyone that doeth righteousness is righteous, even as he is righteous." (1 John 3:7.) "He that . . . worketh righteousness, is acceptable to him." (Acts 10:34, ASV.) Such obedience "from the heart" (Rom. 6:17-18) is not filthy and unclean in God's sight. But God's people Israel were wicked at the time Isaiah was prophesying concerning them and said, "All our righteousnesses are as filthy rags."

But note: it was Isaiah (who was an inspired prophet) who is saying this to the people. Hence this was not some revelation made to Isaiah by the people themselves.

**Question:** Is the 'angel of his presence' (mentioned in Isa. 63:9) the same as 'his Holy Spirit' (in v. 10)?

**Answer:** I think the "angel of his presence" was something different. Of course, the "angel of his presence" means a messenger from God's presence. God sometimes spoke by angels. Angels came and talked with Abraham, and with Lot, who entertained them. "Be not forgetful to entertain strangers: for thereby some have entertained angels unawares." (Heb. 13:2.)

The Bible does not say the Holy Spirit is the same as an "angel." We need to get away from that idea.

**Question:** Did Christ himself speak to Saul in Acts 9:5, or in the sense of through the Holy Spirit, as you discussed in 1 Pet. 3:18?

**Answer:** Christ spoke to the apostles through the Holy Spirit. So far as we know, all his speaking was done through the Holy Spirit. John says, "He whom God hath sent, speaketh the words of God: for God giveth not the Spirit by measure unto him." (John 3:34.) The context shows he is speaking of Christ. So Christ spoke the words of God, because God had not given unto him (that is, Christ) the Spirit by measure. Hence, when Christ spoke, it was by the Spirit which he had without measure.

Then we read, "The former treatise have I made, O Theophilus, of all that Jesus began both to do and teach,

until the day in which he was taken up, after that he"—
that is, Christ—"**through the Holy Ghost** had given commandments unto the apostles whom he had chosen." (Acts
1:1-2.) So Christ did his teaching, and did his   speaking,
"through the Holy Ghost." Not only so, but he wrought
his miracles through the power of the Holy Spirit: "I by
the Spirit of God cast out devils . . ." (Matt. 12:28.)

**Question:**  Did you understand that this question deals
with the conversion of Saul? In Acts 9, did Christ himself
speak with Saul? or did he speak to him through the Holy
Spirit?—at the time of his conversion.

**Answer:** Of course **Christ** spoke to him, for he said, "I
am Jesus." (Acts 9:5.) But the Holy Spirit was, through
Christ, giving the message. (John 3:34.) I do not see any
problem there.

**Question:**  How would you define (simply) the role of
the Holy Spirit in the Trinity?

**Answer:** The role of the Holy Spirit is to work with God
and Christ, the other members of the  Godhead  or  the
Trinity. (Trinity means three: they are the Father, Son,
and Holy Spirit.)

The Father planned and purposed our redemption. "God
. . . hath saved us, and called us with an holy calling, not
according to our works, but according to his own purpose
and grace, which was given us in Christ Jesus." (2 Tim. 1:8-
9.) The church (Eph. 3:10) and the preaching of the gospel
(v. 8) were in "the eternal purpose of God" (v. 11) before
the world was. Hence, God "purposed" our redemption, our
salvation. The church was not an "afterthought" with God,
nor an "emergency" measure that just came up when he
did not know what else to provide—and this was the best
thing he could plan in an emergency! But the church was
in the "purpose" of God from eternity, and our salvation
likewise. So God drew up the great "blueprint" of Christianity, we might say; and then he sent the Son.

So we read: "God sent not his Son into the world to condemn the world; but that the world through him might be

saved." (John 3:17.) Jesus said, "I came down from heaven, not to do mine own will, but the will of him that sent me." (John 6:38.) There it is: God sent the Son to do the Son's work. The Son was to die for our sins, and do all else that was necessary to be our mediator between us and God. (1 Tim. 2:5.) In the shadow of the cross he said, "I have finished the work which thou gavest me to do." (John 17:4.) Jesus went back to heaven, and sent the Holy Spirit, for he promised, "If I depart, I will send him unto you." (John 16:7.)

The Holy Spirit then came to do his work, which was to reveal and to confirm what God had purposed, and what Christ had wrought out in our behalf. The Holy Spirit was to make known (to reveal), and to confirm for all time to come, the glorious gospel of Christ. The Spirit thus guided in the establishment of Christianity in the earth when this gospel was preached by men, as God put it into the hands of "earthen vessels." (2 Cor. 4:7.) When that gospel is preached, and when people believe and obey it to become Christians and to live according to the words and teaching of the Holy Spirit, they are "led by the Spirit" (Rom. 8:14), and are comforted by the Spirit. They are encouraged by the Spirit. They have the Spirit's incentives and motives and inducements—vast as all eternity—to be Christians. And if the Spirit were to do his work over, he could not do any better! He did his best—he did a perfect job.

God is not going to do his part over, and get up another religion. Christ is not going to come back and be born (again) of a virgin, and do his work over. Neither does the Spirit need to do his work over. It is now time for **us** to work—and we ought to be at it.

**Question:** Should an answer of 'Yes' or 'No' be given to the question, 'Is the Holy Spirit God'?

**Answer:** Well, some questions cannot be answered with a 'yes' or 'no.' Brother F. B. Srygley was in a discussion with a Seventh Day Adventist who asked him a question, and demanded a "yes-or-no" answer. Brother Srygley from his seat responded, "Some questions cannot be answered in that fashion." His opponent said, "Well, I will answer any question you ask me with a 'yes' or 'no'." Whereupon Bro. Srygley asked, "Sir, **have you quit whipping your wife?**" (If he said,"Yes," that would imply that he had been whipping her; but if he said, "No," then he still whips her!) So, some questions cannot be answered with a "yes" or "no."

But this one can: "Yes." The Holy Spirit is "God." "God" is not narrowed down to the Father. In some passages "God" includes the whole GOD-HEAD. The word "God" means "Deity," or "Divinity," as in the definition of the word "God-head," the state of being God, or divine. So, the Holy Spirit is divine; the Holy Spirit is "God."

Christ is "God." Listen to John: "In the beginning was the Word, and the Word was with God," —now listen to the next statement—"and the Word was God." The Spirit is not the "Father" God, but he is "God" or "Deity." He is one of the "Godhead." That is why the "Father" (one of the Godhead or Deity) said, "Let **us** make man in **our** image, after our likeness." (Gen. 1:26-27.) The plural pronouns no doubt refer to the Holy Spirit, and to Christ—who were back there. Christ said he had glory with the Father "before the world was." (John 17:5.) He was not the "Father," but he was "with" the Father "before the world was." He said, "Thou lovedst me before the foundation of the world." (v. 24.) We also read that "God" (the Father) created all things "by" his "Son." (Heb. 1:2; Col. 1:13-18.)

**Question:** Here is another question: "If the Holy Spirit is a **person,** why can we not see him?"

**Answer:** Well, you cannot see any spiritual "beings" or **persons.** Last night I took the time to show that there is a spirit world, an invisible (to us) world. We cannot see God; we cannot see Jesus Christ now; we cannot see the angels up in heaven; neither can we see the "Holy Spirit." (But there are things down here on earth we cannot see. We cannot see atoms, gravity, electricity, the wind, love, instinct, nor thoughts.) So, there is a spirit world. The "Trinity" are spirit beings—and that is why I took the time and trouble last night to establish that fact.

**Question:** Why would anybody 'lie' to the Holy Spirit?

**Answer:** That is what I'd like to know! Ananias did it, and I suppose he did it through ignorance, or in a thoughtless manner. But today, why will brethren 'lie' about their contributions? "Uncle Sam" says that if Churches of Christ are receiving all the money their members are reporting as contributions on their income tax deductions, he does not understand how in the world we are going to spend all that money! So, not all of the 'liars' are yet dead!

In Ananias' day some could "discern" spirits. One of the nine gifts of the Spirit (1 Cor. 12:8-10) was "discerning of spirits." Peter must have been a discerner of spirits. He, by the Holy Spirit, seemed able to discern a man's spirit and know when he was lying to God and the Holy Spirit. Ananias probably did not know he could do that. Perhaps presumptiously, he thought that the Holy Spirit would not be able to detect the error. Hence he told and acted a lie —and God killed him. (Acts 5.) That is the reason Peter told Simon, "Repent therefore of this thy wickedness, and pray God, if perhaps the thought of thine heart"—that he could buy the gift of God with money—"may be forgiven thee." (Acts 8:22.)

There are people today so foolish as to think that they can sway God Almighty with numbers, or by counting noses, or by taking a vote, or with money.

**Question:** How do you know that the Spirit of Christ, and the Spirit of God, are the same as the Holy Spirit? Does not the Holy Spirit have his own spirit?

**Answer:** First of all, we do not read in the Bible where the Holy Spirit has his own 'spirit'. But the Bible speaks of "the Spirit **of Christ** which was in" the Old Testament prophets. (1 Pet. 1:10.) But Nehemiah said God "gavest also **thy** good Spirit to instruct them"—but this was done "by **thy Spirit** in thy prophets." (Neh. 9:20, 30.) However, other scriptures (such as Acts 1:16 and 28:25) show that it was the **"Holy Ghost"** or **"Holy Spirit"** who spoke through the prophets. Hence we must conclude that the "Spirit of Christ," the "Spirit of God," and the "Holy Spirit" are identical. The "Spirit of God" and the "Spirit of Christ" are used interchangeably in Romans 8:9-11. A "Thus saith the Lord" ought to be the end of all controversy. There is no reason to argue against the Scriptures which say that the Holy Spirit in the prophets was called the "Spirit of Christ."

**Question:** Does the Holy Spirit speak through men today in a direct way? Does he motivate them to speak by 'influence' on their behavior?

**Answer:** The Holy Spirit now through the Bible influences us to speak; but there is now no direct 'independent-of-the-word' operation, or revelation, for us. Such ideas "make the word of God of none effect." (Mark 7:13.) Such 'traditions' will make God's word of none effect today because people will 'turn up their noses' at the word, and look forward to, or expect, imaginary direct revelation. This is absolutely a 'decoy' to get people away from the word of God. The whole thing is a work of Satan, who wants to belittle the "word" of God and render it ineffective.

**Question:** Are angels agents of the Holy Spirit, or do they act independently?

**Answer:** They are agents of God, the Father. God sends angels—or did send them. He dispatched (Luke 1:26) them for his work. You will often read of the "angel of God" (as in Acts 10:3), but I do not know where the Holy Spirit sent angels. No such scripture comes to my mind.

**Question:** Is there any Biblical proof that the miracles stopped with the last person on whom the apostles laid hands and gave them power?

**Answer:** Of course there is! That will come up in about two more nights, and I prefer not to enter into it now. Time tonight forbids a mature study of it. And any other question that arises, if I am planning to discuss it thoroughly later, I will defer it likewise. In the meantime, study 1 Corinthians 13:8-13.

**Question:** 'Does the Holy Spirit guide men today other than through the word?

**Answer:** Tonight I have been saying over and over that he does **not**! The Holy Spirit's guidance in the written word of God, and by it he does a thorough job of guiding us. "Thou shalt guide me with thy counsel." (Ps. 73:24.) He does not guide us with 'imaginations.' But concerning such Paul wrote, "Casting down **imaginations** . . ." (2 Cor. 10:4, 5.) He did not say, "Exalt your imaginations, and follow them instead of the written word of God."

**Question:** Will you comment a little on the passage in Romans that says, 'The Spirit maketh intercession for us.' Is this the Holy Spirit as a person?

**Answer:** Yes, I think that is the Holy Spirit making the intercession; but his intercessions are his prayers for us. They are made to God. He is working with God for us, in our behalf. But he is not working directly upon us. There is a world of difference! He is not operating on us, and inspiring us, when he is praying for us! When I pray for you, I am not operating and working directly upon you in any miraculous way. Abraham interceded for Sodom (Gen. 18:16-33)—but he was not operating on Sodom in any mysterious manner. There are many illogical conclusions being reached by some.

**Question:** Please give some reasons why you believe such expressions as "the Spirit of Christ," "the Spirit of God," and "the Holy Spirit" all refer to the same one.

**Answer:** I did not say they refer to the same one: they refer to the same Godhead, the same Trinity. (Rom. 8:9-11.) But God, and Christ, and the Holy Spirit are not the same person. If that is what you mean, then I did not say that, nor do I believe that. Many times in debate have I defended the fact that there are three persons in the Godhead.

**Voice:** "The question concerns the "spirit of God," "Spirit of Christ," and the "Holy Spirit" being the same."

**Answer:** It depends on what verse is under consideration. The context shows whether it refers to the Spirit of Christ

**himself**—his own spirit. For instance, he said, "Father, into thy hands I commend my spirit." (Luke 23:46.) Well, that did not refer to the Holy Spirit, but to his own personal spirit. So the context must be considered.

**Question:** Romans 8:13 says, "If ye through the Spirit do mortify the deeds of the body, ye shall live." Does this teach that we have personal, daily, help in living the Christian life? If so, would this not be a great encouragement to him who says, 'I would become a Christian, but I am afraid I could not live it'?

**Answer:** Oh, yes! the Spirit encourages us very much to live the Christian life; but he does it through his word. When we study that, and follow his word, we are encouraged by it, strengthened by it, and by it mortify the deeds of the body. But when you imagine that the Spirit in some direct way encourages you, how would he do it? What sort of thought would he present? How much more could he say than has been said? The grand old song, How Firm A Foundation, stresses this:

"How firm a foundation, ye saints of the Lord,
Is laid for your faith in his excellent word!
What more can He say than to you He has said,
You who unto Jesus for refuge have fled?"

**Question:** I have heard so much about the unpardonable sin, which is supposed to be the sin against the Holy Spirit. What is the sin? Do you intend to discuss this more fully later?

**Answer:** Later; and I have already said enough about it tonight in answering another question. It was to say the Holy Spirit in Christ was an "unclean" or wicked spirit. (Matt. 12:22-33; Mark 3:22-30.)

**Question:** Was the baptism of the Holy Spirit necessary to perform miracles? Our brethren also believe in water baptism. In view of 'one baptism' (Eph. 4:5), would this now answer our few brethren who believe in 'speaking in tongues?' Please give your views.

**Answer:** That will come up tomorrow night. I am deferring this one until that time, hoping you will come back. That will be the main subject tomorrow night.

**Question:** If the Holy Spirit does not still guide us, and perform for us, what good are some of our prayers for a heart to be moved toward God and Christ?

**Answer:** Because the Holy Spirit does not have to operate **directly** upon a heart to move it. There are many things God providentially does—not miraculously—in answering our prayers. There is a difference between providence and miracles. Providence is the word "provide" plus "-ance" (with a slight change in pronunciation). God provides without miracles (necessarily) in many cases, and always has done so.

For instance, when Elijah prayed for rain, his servant saw a cloud about as big as a man's hand, coming from over the Mediterranean Sea; and it rained out of that cloud. (1 Kings 18:41-46.) There was no miracle about that: it was providence, and it was in answer to Elijah's prayer. But if it had rained out of a clear sky, or if the cloud had come up from the desert, and brought rain—that would have been miraculous! (When I was travelling over there in 1962 our guide told us that if the cloud had come from the wrong direction, it would have been a miracle!) But the cloud arose over the sea, and it rained out of the cloud! That was providential.

A mother bird, taking care of the young in her nest, can go out in search of food for which her babies have been begging ('praying' if you please!); she can go out and "answer" their plea for food—without working a miracle! Yet some folk cannot believe (it seems) that God can use the laws of nature and bless us! Some think every such blessing would have to be a 'miracle!'

I would just like to say, in closing, that I very much appreciate your questions. I want you to feel free to ask questions. If I cannot answer them, I will just say that I do not know. I have, over the last fifty years, had to say many times, "I do not know," because I do not believe God has revealed all matters, or I have not yet learned the answer. I am not here to be a 'smart-aleck,' if you please. I am very happy to think that these questions may be helpful, even to those who did not ask them. May all find it interesting to think upon them. God bless you.

# BAPTISM OF THE HOLY SPIRIT

This evening we are to study "The Baptism Of The Holy Spirit." Of course, our general over-all theme for the week is, "The Holy Spirit and His Work." Certainly, we do not know too much about any vital Bible subject. If we knew all that God has revealed about any given subject, we would not know too much. We can learn more and more about God, Christ, and the Holy Spirit by prayerful study of what he has revealed. One text we have used in the background study says, "The secret things belong unto the Lord our God: but those things which are revealed belong unto us and to our children." (Deut. 29:29.) We are interested in the things which are revealed, not in some speculative theories, nor in some imaginary system which someone has worked up and thought out for the rest of us.

## Was A Promise

First of all, the baptism of the Holy Spirit was a promise made unto the apostles of our Lord. John the Baptizer made the statement: "I indeed baptize you with water unto repentance: but he that cometh after me is mightier than I, whose shoes I am not worthy to bear: he shall baptize you with the Holy Ghost, and with fire: whose fan is in his hand, and he will thoroughly purge his floor, and gather his wheat into the garner; but he will burn up the chaff with unquenchable fire." (Matt. 3:11-12.) Beside water baptism, two other baptisms are mentioned in this context. "I indeed baptize you with water" assuredly refers to water baptism, with which the people who heard John were familiar. It is stated in this same chapter that the people "were baptized of him in Jordan, confessing their sins." (Matt. 3:5-6.)

## Baptism An Immersion

**Baptism** is an immersion. The English word BAPTISM is from the Greek BAPTIZO, which means to dip, immerse, overwhelm, submerge, and such like kindred ideas. It never meant to sprinkle or pour. It has reference to the burial, as mentioned in connection with baptism. The apostle Paul says, "Therefore we are buried with him by baptism into death: that like as Christ was raised up from the dead by the glory of the Father, even so we also should walk in newness of life. For if we have been planted together in the likeness of his death, we shall be also in the likeness of his resurrection." (Rom. 6:4-5.) Hence baptism is a burial. Paul also used the word "planted" here in describing the act. So, regardless of what the element might be in which one is baptized, the **baptism** itself is always an immersion, submersion, or overwhelming of some sort. Baptism never meant a sprinkling. It never meant just a bit of the element referred to. This is true of the baptism of the Holy Spirit the same as it is true of baptism in water.

### Baptism Of Suffering

Jesus said, "Are ye able to be baptized with the baptism that I am baptized with." (Matt. 20:22.) He was talking about his suffering. Who would be so blasphemous as to say that Jesus endured only a little "sprinkling" of suffering?— that when he called his a "baptism" of suffering, he meant that there was just a small bit of suffering connected with his death? No! The Bible teaches us that he suffered terribly in death for us—that he suffered indescribably for us that he might bring us unto God. (1 Pet. 3:18.) His suffering was beyond what any human tongue can describe. That suffering was a "baptism" of suffering! It was an **overwhelming** of suffering, and a **submersion**, as it were, in what is figuratively referred to as the "element" of suffering. Hence, the word "baptism" connected with anything, any element—literally or figuratively—describes an overwhelming. This word necessitates a large measure of the element, rather than just a small amount of it.

### Greek Literature

In classical Greek literature we find the word "baptism" connected with such experiences, for instance, as a man being "drowned" with questions. He was said to be "baptized" with questions. That didn't mean only a few questions, but had reference to a great quantity of questions. If a man were overcome with debt—so deeply in debt that he could not pay—he was said to be "baptized" in debt. This is the use of the word "baptize" in the language of the people whom Jesus addressed in the New Testament. The Holy Spirit, through the apostles and other inspired writers of the New Testament, addressed the people in their own—the Greek—language. They understood that language, and received the word of the Lord in the new covenant in that language. To them the word BAPTIZO (baptize) meant to overwhelm, submerge, and the like. When water is the element, "baptize" has reference to a burial, and a resurrection. (Rom. 6:4-5.) It refers to a "planting" in the likeness of his death—thus a covering up—for when we plant our seeds we cover them up. Not only so, but Paul says we are "buried with him in baptism, wherein also ye are risen with him." (Col. 2:12.)

So, baptism has reference to the act of submersion. It has reference to an act which differs from receiving just a bit of the element considered. Of John the immerser we read that the people "were baptized of him in Jordan." (Matt. 3:6.) One man quibbled, "Well, it didn't say River Jordan." True, that text doesn't; but Mark 1:5 does: "They were baptized of him in the river of Jordan." Later we read, when the Ethiopian eunuch was baptized, that "both Philip and the eunuch" first "went down into the water" preparatory to the performance of the act of baptism. (Acts 8:35-39.) Then the Bible says, "And he baptized him." After the baptism we read: "They were come up out of the water . . ."—that is, they came back up on the land.

Now, the word "baptize" connected with the Holy Spirit carries with it the idea (although figuratively expressed) of the **amount of the Holy Spirit** given and received in the case. Our Lord's baptism of suffering implies the great amount of suffering he endured. The one baptized in debt was overwhelmed in the enormous amount of his debts. One baptized with questions was submerged or "drowned" in the multitude of inquiries. So likewise we refer to a certain large, voluminous measure (we might say) of the Holy

Spirit when we talk about the **baptism** of the Holy Spirit. It is no ordinary gift of the Holy Spirit under consideration.

## Christ To Administer Holy Spirit Baptism

John said Christ, whom he referred to as coming "after me," "shall **baptize you** with the Holy Ghost" or "Holy Spirit." (Matt. 3:11.) Christ was to administer Holy Spirit baptism. When you find the Holy Spirit administered by some man, as by the laying on of some apostle's hands, such is not the "baptism" of the Holy Spirit—because only Christ was the administrator of that. The baptism of the Spirit was not given through the imposition of apostolic hands. (Tomorrow evening we will consider **that** measure, which in the Bible is never called the baptism of the Holy Spirit. We will see that it was bestowed by the laying on of the apostles' hands.)

God had given John a sign that, when he baptized Jesus, he would see the Spirit descending in the form of a dove. (John 1:33-34.) He said, "This is he"—the Messiah, the Savior and hope of the world—". . . the same is he which baptizeth with the Holy Ghost." So, Jesus alone, is said to baptize with the Holy Ghost.

## Baptism Of The Great Commission Not Holy Spirit Baptism

We know by this that the baptism of the Great Commission is not the baptism of the 'Holy Spirit. Jesus said to his disciples, "Go ye therefore, and teach all nations, baptizing them . . ." (Matt. 28:19.) Who were to do the going? The disciples. Who were to do the teaching? The disciples. Who were to perform the baptizing? The disciples. Hear Jesus again: "Go ye"—you disciples—"and teach all nations, baptizing them." That was **water** baptism; for only Jesus could administer **Spirit** baptism, as we have seen.

Another reason for saying the baptism of the Great Commission is water baptism is that it is to be performed "in the name of the Father, and of the Son, and of the Holy Ghost." (Matt. 28:19.) Certainly, Holy Spirit baptism would not be "in the name of . . . the Holy Ghost"—by the authority of the Spirit himself. Great Commission baptism

is in the name of the Father, Son, and Holy Spirit. Therefore **water** baptism is the "baptism" of the Great Commission. Except the Society of Friends (Quakers), every religious body or denomination in my knowledge baptizes (?)
some way or other, according to their ideas of baptism.
And they never administer what they call "water baptism"
without doing it in some "name."

## Some of the Differences

Let us note some of the differences between water baptism and Holy Spirit baptism.

1. Water baptism is for "all nations," and is required of
"every creature" who is a gospel subject. (Matt. 28:19; Mark
16:15-16.) Holy Spirit baptism was not for all men, for in
speaking of "the Spirit of truth" Jesus said, "whom the
world cannot receive." (John 14:17.)

2. Water baptism is a command of God. (Matt. 28:19; Acts
10:48; 2:38; 22:16.) Holy Spirit baptism was a promise of
God unto a very few. (Acts 1:2-5.)

3. Water baptism is an act of obedience, an act of man.
(Acts 2:38; 22:16; 10:48.) Spirit baptism was an act of the
Lord, not an act of man. (Acts 1:5.)

4. Water baptism is administered by men, by those doing
the teaching. (Matt. 28:19; 1 Cor. 1:14.) Spirit baptism was
administered by the Lord himself. (Matt. 3:11; John 1:33.)

5. Water baptism is a condition of salvation to a lost
world. (Mark 16:15-16; 1 Pet. 3:20-21.) Spirit baptism had
to do with either revealing the gospel, or confirming it.
(John 16:13; Heb. 2:4.)

6. Water baptism is "in the name" (or by the authority)
of Christ, and "into the name of the Father, and of the Son,
and of the Holy Spirit." (Matt. 28:19, ASV; Acts 2:38; 8:14-
16; 22:16.) Holy Spirit baptism was in no name at all—was
not performed by man. (Matt. 3:11.)

7. Water baptism is an act of faith. (Gal. 3:26-27; Mark
16:15-16; Col. 2:12.) Spirit baptism was not an act of man,

hence it could not have been an act of faith. (Luke 24:48-49.)

8. Water baptism has in the action both a burial, and a resurrection—as Christ was buried and raised. (Rom. 6:4; Col. 2:12.) Spirit baptism had no resurrection, and no visible burial. (Acts 1:5; 2:4.)

9. Water baptism is a baptism "of repentance" (Mark 1:4; Luke 3:3; Acts 19:4; 2:38)—that is, it belongs to, and grows out of, repentance. But Holy Spirit baptism came three-and-one-half years after the apostles repented and were baptized in water. (Mark 1:4; Luke 7:29-30; Acts 1:5; 2:1-4.)

10. Water baptism is a condition of cleansing one from the guilt of sin. (Acts 22:16; Eph. 5:25-26.) Spirit baptism came long after the apostles were already "clean" (John 15:3) through the word.

11. Water baptism puts one "into Christ." (Rom. 6:3-4; Gal. 3:26-27.) Spirit baptism of the apostles came after they already were "in" Christ, and had been urged to "abide in" Christ. (John 15:1-6; Acts 2:1-4.)

12. Water baptism is in order to "receive" the ordinary "gift of the Holy Ghost." (Acts 2:38; 5:32.) Spirit baptism itself was a reception of the miraculous "gift of the Holy Spirit" administered by Christ. (Acts 1:5; Matt. 3:11.)

13. Water baptism is to continue in God's program "always, even unto the end of the world." (Matt. 28:19-20.) There is no promise of Holy Spirit baptism this side of A.D. 64, when Paul wrote Ephesians 4:5.

14. You can obey the Lord's command to be baptized in water. (Acts 2:38; 10:48; 22:16.) But there is not now a thing you can scripturally do to obtain Spirit baptism—for there is only "one baptism" now. (Eph. 4:5.)

It is just like old Satan to get people to refuse to obey God, and instead, spend their time trying to "get" something which God has not promised us today, and which is not for us at all.

## Holy Spirit Baptism Promised

John promised that the disciples of Jesus would be baptized with the Holy Spirit: "I indeed baptize you with water . . . but . . . he shall baptize you with the Holy Ghost" or "Holy Spirit." (Matt. 3:11.) Baptism in water—even in the case of the apostles—would not take the place of, be a substitute for, Holy Spirit baptism. Neither would Holy Spirit baptism alone be sufficient. As apostles, they first had to be baptized with water. (Matt. 3:11; Luke 7:29-30.) But cases are not always uniform: we find a vast difference between the baptism of the **apostles** in the Holy Spirit, and the Holy Spirit baptism of the Gentiles at the house of Cornelius. (Acts 2 with Acts 10 & 11.)

## Promised To Apostles

We notice next that Jesus (in addition to John) promised to the apostles the baptism of the Holy Spirit. Let us read from Acts the first chapter. I want you to get the noun and the pronouns that follow clearly in mind. (You may not have read it carefully!) Luke says, "The former treatise have I made, O Theophilus, of all that Jesus began both to do and teach, until the day in which he was taken up, after that he through the Holy Ghost had given commandments unto the **apostles** . . ."—there is our plural noun, apostles; now watch the pronouns which follow all the way down for the next twelve verses—". . . he had given commandments unto the apostles **whom** . . ."— the very next word after 'apostles' is a plural pronoun, referring to the noun 'apostles'—". . . unto the apostles whom he had chosen. To **whom**"—the same pronoun—"also he showed himself alive after his passion by many infallible proofs, being seen of **them**"—that's another plural pronoun, referring to the apostles—". . . being seen of **them** forty days, and speaking of the things pertaining to the kingdom of God: and being assembled together with **them**"—the apostles—"commanded **them**"—that's the apostles again—"that **they**"—another pronoun referring to the apostles—"should not depart from Jerusalem, but wait for the promise of the Father, which, saith he, **ye**"—another plural pronoun referring back to the noun 'apostles'—"ye have heard of me.

For John truly baptized with water;"—as we quoted from
Matt. 3:11—"but **ye**"—a plural pronoun again, meaning the
'apostles'—"shall be baptized with the Holy Ghost not
many days hence." (Acts 1:1-5.) Pentecost follows in the
next chapter, and it was "not many days hence"—usually
considered to be about ten days after the ascension.

But let us read the sixth verse, going right on without
skipping a verse: "When **they**"—the apostles—"therefore
were come together, **they**"—the apostles—"asked of him,
saying, Lord, wilt thou at this time restore again the kingdom to Israel? And he said unto **them**"—the apostles—,"It is
not for **you**"—the apostles—"to know the times or the sea-
sons, which the Father hath put in his own power. But **ye**"
—the apostles—"shall receive power, after that the Holy
Ghost is come upon **you**"—the apostles—"and **ye**"—that, too,
is the apostles—"shall be witnesses unto me both in Jerusalem, and in all Judea, and in Samaria, and unto the uttermost part of the earth."

### At The Ascension

Luke continues: "And when he had spoken these things,
while **they**"—the apostles—"beheld, he was taken up; and
a cloud received him out of **their**"—still talking about the
apostles—"sight. And while **they**"—that's the apostles—
"looked steadfastly toward heaven as he went up, behold,
two men stood by **them**"—by the apostles—"in white apparel; which also said, **Ye**"—apostles—"men of Galilee,"—
these apostles were men of Galilee,—"why stand **ye**"—you
apostles—"gazing up into heaven? This same Jesus, which
is taken up from **you**"—all these pronouns refer to the
noun 'apostles' back in the second verse. But we continue
in verse 11: "This same Jesus which is taken up from **you**
into heaven, shall so come in like manner as **ye**"—you
apostles — "have seen him go into heaven. Then returned **they**"—the apostles—"unto Jerusalem from the
mount called Olivet, which is from Jerusalem a sabbath
day's journey." We have considered this meeting until it
broke up. The apostles went out and saw the Lord ascend;
now they have come back into the city for some things
that occurred during the interval between the ascension

and Pentecost, which is usually regarded as a ten-day period.

### Apostles Needed Holy Spirit Baptism

Now, I wish to call attention to the fact that these apostles were just fallible men. They were not qualified as yet to go out and preach the gospel under the Great Commission. (Matt. 28:18-20; Mark 16:15-16.) In a "former treatise" (Acts 1:1) by this same author, we have another record: "Thus it is written, and thus it behooved Christ to suffer, and to rise from the dead the third day: and that repentance and remission of sins should be preached in his name among all nations, beginning at Jerusalem. And ye are witnesses of these things. And, behold, I send the promise" —here's the promise about which we have been talking (Matt. 3:11); the baptism of the Holy Spirit was to take place later, on Pentecost day. (Acts 2.) "And, behold, I send the promise of my Father upon you"—Jesus was talking to his apostles, and was here giving them the Great Commission—"but tarry ye"—that's the apostles—"in the city of Jerusalem, until ye be endued with power from on high." (Luke 24:46-49.) So the promise is made unto the apostles; and the noun "apostles" (Acts 1:2) is the antecedent of the pronouns which we have followed all the way down until our Lord ascended to his throne in heaven. Those "apostles" turned back unto the city. (Luke 24:50-53; Acts 1:12.)

### Apostles Received Holy Spirit Baptism

There was no promise of the Holy Spirit to be poured out in a baptismal measure upon all mankind, nor on the multitude of people, nor on the "hundred and twenty." We have seen that this promise was to the apostles. Of them we read further in Acts 1. The last word in the closing verse of Acts 1 is the noun "apostles." Remember that God did not divide the Bible into chapters and verses. (This was done by men for convenience.)

Let us read the last verse of Acts 1, with the first four verses following it, ignoring the division into chapters: "And they gave forth their lots; and the lot fell upon Matthias; and he was numbered with the eleven **apostles**." There is the noun 'apostles;' it is the last word in the first chapter. We read right on: "And when the day of Pentecost was fully come, **they** . . ."—'they' who? The **apostles!** The pronoun 'they' refers back to the preceeding noun 'apostles.' "And when the day of Pentecost was fully come, they"—the apostles—"were all with one accord in one place. And suddenly there came a sound from heaven as of a rushing mighty wind, and it filled all the house where **they**"—there's the same pronoun again, referring to the apostles—"were sitting." (Note that Luke does not say, 'where they were wallowing or rolling in the sawdust, or down in the dirt,' but they were 'sitting'—in an orderly fashion, 1 Cor. 14:40, of course.) "And there appeared unto **them**"—that again is the apostles—"cloven"—or forked— "tongues like as of fire . . ." (These "tongues" were "cloven" or forked, like flames of fire leaping up, forking out this way and that.)

## No Fire Baptism On Pentecost

"And there appeared unto **them** cloven tongues like as of fire . . ." There was no "fire" **baptism** on Pentecost. Good people were not promised "fire" baptism. Fire baptism is **hell fire**! We read that the wicked "shall have their part in the lake which burneth with fire and brimstone." (Rev. 21:8.) Hell is here spoken of as a "lake" of liquid brimstone (sulphur) on fire. Now, John said Jesus would baptize with two baptisms: (1) one would be the baptism of the Holy Spirit, and (2) the other would be the baptism of fire. In this context John mentions this "fire" on both sides of verse eleven. (Matt. 3.) He says, "And now also the axe is laid unto the root of the trees; therefore every tree which bringeth not forth good fruit"—that is not **good** people—"is hewn down, and cast into the fire." (v. 10.) Now, that fire is not something to be prayed for, and sought after; it's for the bad and fruitless trees. John also said Jesus "will gather his wheat"—those are the good people—"into the garner; but he will burn up the chaff with unquenchable fire." (v. 12.) Don't you see that is **hell** fire? "Unquenchable fire" is never said in the New Testament anywhere to be for the righteous, for good people; but it is for the wicked, and has reference to eternal punishment in torment. Later, when Jesus repeated this promise to his faithful apostles only, Jesus omitted any reference to the fire baptism. (Acts 1:5.) Hence, when John said Jesus would "baptize you with the Holy Ghost, and with fire" (Matt. 3:11), we know the apostles were in one group, apart from those for whom fire baptism is intended—for they received the Spirit baptism, as we are tracing the account in Acts 1:26 to 2:4. In Acts 1:5 Jesus renewed the promise to the apostles that they would be baptized in the Holy Spirit "not many days hence." And they did soon receive Him. (Acts 2:1-4.)

### Both Visible And Audible

Thus we learn that the "fire" mentioned on Pentecost (Acts 2:3) was not real, literal, fire. Luke simply said the tongues were cloven or forked "like as of fire." He did not say they were actually tongues of fire. So down goes the theory that the apostles would be, and were baptized with the Holy Ghost **and with fire** on Pentecost! There isn't a word of truth in that idea; it is false doctrine! Your Bible says, "There appeared unto them cloven tongues like as of fire, and it sat upon each of them"—there on each of these apostles was a visible appearance. The multitude, when they assembled (v. 6) could all see that forked or cloven tongues sat upon the apostles. That was not something which depended upon the apostles' testimony. One apostle did not get up and claim, "I've got it!" and then another eventually arise, saying, "Well, I've got it, too! It's come upon me, too!" The audience that "came together" (v. 6) did not have just the apostles' word for their baptism in the Holy Spirit. The multitude could see this demonstration of Holy Spirit baptism upon the apostles. That is why Peter says Christ "hath shed forth this, which **ye now see** and hear." (v. 33.) And the people could hear the apostles speaking in their language, which is another mighty miracle connected with the baptism of the apostles in the Holy Spirit. (Acts 2:1-4.)

We read right on in Acts 2: "And **they**"—that is still talking about the apostles—"were all filled with the Holy Ghost, and began to speak with other tongues"—that is, other languages —"as the Spirit gave **them**"—the apostles —"utterance." (Acts 2:4.) Now the apostles have been baptized with the Holy Spirit by the time we finish this verse.

### Apostles Only On Pentecost

It was the **apostles** who received Spirit baptism on Pentecost, not the "hundred and twenty," not the multitude, nor everybody in the city round about. But let us read further: "And there were dwelling at Jerusalem Jews, devout men, out of every nation under heaven. Now when this"—the Spirit's coming upon the apostles—"was noised abroad"—when people of the city heard that the apostles had been baptized with the Holy Ghost, or heard the 'sound . . . as of a rushing mighty wind'—"the multitude came together." (v. 5-6.) The multitude was not present when this great miracle occurred. "The multitude came together, and were confounded . . ."—the multitude, not the apostles, were confused—"because that every man"—every one of the multitude—"heard **them**" —the apostles—"speak in his own language." The apostles were enabled to speak in the languages of the people of the multitude, even though they had never studied those languages a day in their lives! "And they were all amazed, and marvelled, saying one to another, Behold, are not all **these**"—these apostles—"which speak Galileans?" Remember, we read (Acts 1:9-11) where two men (angels) in bright apparel at the ascension called the apostles "men of Galilee." The apostles were "Galileans," whereas the multitude were from all over the civilized world. "And how hear we every man in our own tongue, wherein we were born?" They could hear the gospel as it was preached to them in their own language which they could understand. No miracle was performed on the multitude. It did not take a miracle for a man to **hear** the gospel preached in his own tongue when by the power of the Holy Ghost a man preached it in that tongue. This miracle was still upon the **apostles**, not upon those who heard.

The apostles were not 'jabbering' or 'muttering' something that nobody could understand! The multitude inquired, "How hear we every man in our own tongue"—or language—"wherein we were born?" The audience spoke different languages in the communities where they were reared; but the apostles were enabled, by the baptism of the Holy Spirit, to "speak with other tongues, as the Spirit gave them utterance." (v. 4.)

Then Luke lists fifteen countries from which the multitude had come. He says there were "Parthians, and Medes, and Elamites, and the dwellers in Mesopotamia, and in Judaea, and Cappadocia, in Pontus, and Asia, Phrygia, and Pamphylia, in Egypt, and in the parts of Libya about Cyrene, and strangers of Rome,"—then he explains that all of them worshiped according to the Old Testament, for they were all "Jews and proselytes," which are not places;—"Cretes and Arabians, **we**"—the multitude—"do hear **them**"—the apostles—"speak in our tongues . . ." (Now, were the apostles really 'speaking,' or were they just 'jabbering' something? Let's read that again.) "We do hear **them** speak in our tongues the **wonderful works of God**." They knew what the apostles were talking about! They were telling about God's wonderful works in raising Jesus, and exalted him!

## How Audience Reacted

"And they"—the audience—"were all amazed, and were in doubt, saying one to another, What meaneth this?" (There are many people who do not yet know the meaning of it!) "Others mocking said, These **men**"—there were no **women** in the group baptized by the Holy Spirit on Pentecost! The people were right there looking at the group that had been baptized by the Holy Spirit; they could see the "cloven tongues like as of fire" sitting upon them, and they could hear them in their own language as they told the multitude the "good news" (gospel) of the great works of God in raising Christ, and exalting him. They knew who received Holy Spirit baptism that day! Some who stood by said mockingly, "These **men** are full of new wine." They did not say any ladies as well as men were filled with the Holy Spirit **on this occasion.**

Sometimes some fellow will say, "Well, God said, 'On my servants and on my handmaidens will I pour out in those days of my Spirit.' (Joel 2:28-30.) Thus there had to be some 'maidens' there—unless one of the apostles was a 'daughter' or a 'maiden'." The truth of the matter is, Joel's prophecy only **began** to be fulfilled on Pentecost. Later, at the house of Cornelius, the Spirit was poured out upon the whole household, and it involved **ladies** as well as **men.** You remember that Cornelius had invited his friends and his kinsmen. (Acts 10:26-27.) Hence men and women, his friends in general, were present; and all of them were baptized with the Holy Spirit. (Acts 10 & 11.) Then, and not before then, was Joel's prophecy completely fulfilled so as to include the pouring out of the Spirit on the hand-maidens, as well as upon "all flesh." (Cf. Luke 3:6.)

Returning to Acts 2, we continue our reading: "But Peter, standing up with the eleven"—Peter was not standing up with the hundred and twenty, nor standing up with the three thousand, nor standing up with a lot of men and women; but he was 'standing up with the eleven,' the other **apostles!**—"lifted up his voice and said unto them, Ye men of Judaea, and all ye that dwell at Jerusalem, be this known unto you, and hearken to my words." Now the multitude must be converted by words that they must quietly hear, consider, and understand, believe, and obey, in order to be saved.

### Apostles Not Drunk

"For **these**"—here is a plural pronoun again; 'these' who? Well, 'these **men**.' Some had said, "These men are full of new wine," and Peter said, "These"—meaning these men—"are not drunken, as ye suppose, seeing it is but the third hour of the day. But this is that which was spoken by the prophet Joel . . ." Then follows Joel's prophecy, and Peter's sermon reaches this conclusion: "Therefore being by the right hand of God exalted,"—that's Christ's exhaltation—"and having received of the Father the promise of the Holy Ghost . . ."—this does not mean Christ received, after he got to heaven, the Holy Ghost which God had promised to give him. No; but he received from God

the "promise of" (or made by)"the Holy Ghost"—the promise upon which Peter at that moment was commenting.
What was that "promise?" That Jesus would be **raised to
sit upon David's throne**. The Holy Spirit promised that
to David. (2 Sam. 7:12-13.) And now Christ has been raised,
and has ascended into heaven, and has received David's
throne, which was the thing promised by the Holy Ghost.

"And having received of the Father the promise of the
Holy Ghost, he"—Christ—"hath shed forth this"—the baptism of the apostles in the Holy Spirit—"which ye now
see and hear." Peter did not say some **apostle** shed it forth
by laying hands on somebody, but **Christ** has "shed forth
this"—for only Jesus could administer Holy Spirit baptism. (John 1:33; Matt. 3:11.) Peter proceeded to preach
further to them: "Let all the house of Israel know assuredly"—believe most confidently—"that God hath made that
same Jesus, whom ye have crucified, both Lord and
Christ." (v. 36.)

### What The Multitude Needed

Note the result of this sermon: "Now when they **heard
this**, they were pricked in their heart"—the hearers were
pricked in their heart by the gospel which they heard,
which is 'sharper than any two-edged sword' (Heb. 4:12)
—"and said unto Peter and to the rest of the **apostles . . .** "
They didn't inquire of Peter and the "rest of the hundred
and twenty." Neither did they ask Peter and the "rest of
the three thousand," nor ask Peter and the "rest of the
multitude." But—"they said unto Peter and to the **rest of
the apostles**, Men and brethren . . ."—and sisters? No! Just,
'Men and brethren.' "Men and brethren, what shall we
do?" This question was propounded to nobody but the
apostles; they were the only ones who were qualified to
answer it. That the apostles were the proper ones to ask,
was demonstrated in the presence of the multitude by the
"cloven tongues like as of fire" sitting upon the apostles,
and by the fact that the apostles miraculously preached
the gospel in the languages of the people present. (v. 37.)

Remember that the Holy Spirit is speaking through the

apostles, for "they began to speak in other tongues as the Spirit gave them utterance." (Acts 2:4.) The Spirit, speaking through the apostles, is now directing the multitude, and telling them what to do to be saved: "Then Peter said unto them, Repent, and be baptized every one of you in the name of Jesus Christ for the remission of sins, and ye shall receive the gift of the Holy Ghost." (Acts 2:38.) "For the promise is unto you,"—you Jews—"and to your children,"—they will be Jews, too—"and to all that are afar off,"—that is us, Gentiles—"even as many as the Lord our God shall call. And with many other words did he testify and exhort, saying, Save yourselves from this untoward generation." (v. 39-40.)

Notice that the multitude did not receive any direct revelation of the Spirit to them; but of the audience we read: "Then that that gladly received **his word** were baptized: and the same day there were added unto them about three thousand souls." (Acts 2:41.)

## Why Were The Apostles Baptized With the Holy Spirit?

We have found that the Holy Spirit fell upon the apostles (Acts 1:26-2:4), and it came upon them as sent by Jesus, and was thus administered by Christ—that **Christ** did baptize them in the Holy Spirit. (Matt. 3:11; John 1:33.) Now, **why** were the apostles baptized with the Holy Spirit?

1. In the first place, these apostles were baptized with the Holy Spirit in order that they might be enthroned. Jesus said they would "sit upon twelve thrones, judging the twelve tribes of Israel." (Matt. 19:28; Luke 22:28-30.) They were enthroned, in power, and made to sit upon these twelve (figuratively called) "thrones" when they were thus given power. Jesus promised, "But ye shall receive power, after that the Holy Ghost is come upon you . . ."(Acts 1:8.)

2. That they might be empowered to function as apostles. We read: "Ye shall receive power, after that" (A.S.V. 'when') "the Holy Ghost is come upon you: and ye shall be witnesses unto me . . ." (Acts 1:8.) Again: "But tarry ye in the city of Jerusalem, until ye be endued with power from on high." (Luke 24:49.) Holy Spirit baptism was to give

them supernatural power, to reveal and confirm the gospel, the New Testament, for all time to come.

3. It was to make them able ministers of the New Testament. Paul wrote that Christ "hath made us able ministers of the New Testament; not of the letter, but of the spirit; for the letter killeth, but the spirit giveth life." (2 Cor. 3:6.) Hence, this was to make them "able ministers" of the New Testament, by enabling them to reveal the gospel, and to confirm the New Testament, for all generations to come, so long as the world stands.

4. The baptism of the Spirit was to enable the apostles to fulfill this promise of Jesus: "Greater works than these shall ye do; because I go unto my Father." (John 14:12.) After his ascension they would do greater **works** (not greater miracles). Holy Spirit baptism was to enable them to perform these greater works, which would involve bringing people into the kingdom of God. Remember that Christ ascended before the kingdom was established. (Mark 9:1; Acts 1:8; 2:4.)

5. It was to confirm through the apostles the word or gospel, which "was confirmed unto us by them that heard him; God also bearing them witness, both with signs and wonders, and with divers miracles, and gifts of the Holy Ghost, according to his own will." (Heb. 2:3-4.)

6. The Spirit was to be their Comforter. While with them, Jesus comforted them: "Let not your heart be troubled..." (John 14:1.) But now he says, "I will pray the Father, and he shall give you another Comforter." (v. 16.) Of course, the Holy Spirit now **comforts** by his promises, by teaching and encouraging us, through the apostles. They would, through the revelation of the Holy Spirit, be comforted. Hence we read of the "comfort of the Scriptures." (Rom. 15:4.) Paul said, "Comfort one another with these words" —words just revealed and written by the inspiration of the Holy Spirit. (1 Thess. 4:18.) The Spirit used words; the words of inspired men are written by the Spirit for our comfort. Therefore, we do not have any direct comfort of the Spirit. Some erroneously imagine that we must have

the Comforter come and do his work "in addition to, and independent of, the written word of God."

7. Jesus said the Spirit would teach the apostles all things. "Thou gavest also thy good Spirit to instruct them," and "testifiedst against them by thy Spirit in thy prophets." (Neh. 9:20, 30.) Jesus said, "He shall teach you"—the apostles—"all things, and bring all things to your remembrance, whatsoever I have said unto you." (John 14:26.) They could not remember everything Jesus had personally taught them; but the Holy Spirit would enable them to accurately recall what Jesus had taught, and bring it to the apostles' remembrance when needed. This prevented their leaving out something that ought to have been in the gospel, or in the new covenant.

8. Then, "He will guide you into all truth." (John 16:13.) They didn't have a line of the New Testament in writing. They had to give the world the New Testament, orally at first, then put it in writing. Without any guide, depending on fickle human judgment and memory in giving us a testament, they may have mixed and scrambled truth with error—like vegetable soup! But the Spirit guided them to give us a book of truth, without error.

9. The Holy Spirit was to show the apostles "things to come." (John 16:13.) He foretold of the apostasy (2 Thess. 2:4), and predicted that false teachers would come. (Acts 20:29-30; 1 Tim. 4:1-3.)

10. He was to enable these apostles to lay hands on others, to confer the miraculous power of the Holy Spirit on them. "Simon saw that through laying on of the apostles' hands the Holy Ghost was given." (Acts 8:18.)

11. By the baptism of the Holy Spirit, the apostles were enabled to make known the terms of the remission of sins. "Whose soever sins ye remit, they are remitted unto them; and whose soever sins ye retain, they are retained." (John 20:23.)

12. Spirit baptism gave the apostles the "keys of the kingdom." (Matt. 16:18.) It enabled them to "bind on earth"

what is bound in heaven, and "loose on earth" what is loosed in heaven.

13. By it the apostles were enabled to be "witnesses." (Luke 24:48.) Jesus told them to tarry for this power as witnesses. (v. 49.) Then he said, "Ye also shall bear witness . . ." (John 15:27.) Also with their own eyes they had seen certain things of which they could bear witness.

14. There was a language barrier in their way. In giving the apostles the Great Commission, Jesus had said, "Go ye into **all the world**, and preach the gospel **to every creature**." (Mark 16:15.) They could not do that without divine help, because not every creature in all the world could speak the same language. This humanly-impossible barrier was in the way, and they would be unable to carry out the Great Commission, unless the Lord gave them the power to preach in the various languages. Holy Spirit baptism enabled them to speak in languages they had never studied or learned, and thus get the gospel started among all tongues, by empowering them to preach in the various languages. (Acts 2:1-14.)

15. It was to establish the church. The Holy Spirit came (Acts 2:1-4); the kingdom came "with power" (Mark 9:1) —the power of the Holy Spirit. (Acts 1:8.) Peter said, "The Holy Ghost fell on . . . us at the beginning. (Acts 11:15.) But the Holy Spirit fell on them on "Pentecost." (Acts 2:1-4.) Hence, Pentecost was the beginning—the beginning of the church or kingdom, which came with power. (Mark 9:1.)

16. The apostles were baptized in the Holy Spirit to inspire them. They began to preach the gospel, or speak "as the Spirit gave them utterance" in other tongues (or languages). Peter said the gospel was preached "with the Holy Ghost sent down from heaven." (1 Pet. 1:12.) "All scripture is given by inspiration of God." (2 Tim. 3:16.)

17. In the next place, Holy Spirit baptism was to aid the apostles to carry out the Great Commission. Whatever was required in the matter of revealing and confirming

the great Gospel of Jesus Christ, the Spirit showed them
—even things to come. (John 16:13.) He guided them into
all the truth that the world will ever need. (John 16:13.)
They were the "last" apostles, says Paul. (1 Cor. 4:9; note
marginal reading.) The only current, living 'apostles' on
earth are "false apostles." (2 Cor. 11:13-15.) Jesus said the
Ephesians had "tried them which say they are apostles,
and are not, and hast found them liars." (Rev. 2:2.) So they
had lying "apostles" back then; and there are today lying
"apostles"—"false apostles, deceitful workers, transforming themselves"—as Mormon 'apostles' do—"into the apostles of Christ." They claim to be real 'apostles,' successors
of the apostles of Christ; but the apostles of Christ had
no **successors**! Paul said, "God hath set forth us the apostles last." (1 Cor. 4:9.)—"L-A-S-T!"

### No Successors

One function of an apostle was to be a **witness**; and a
witness cannot have a successor. If a prominent and important witness in a legal case dies, we can't have some
neighbor, or anyone else, come in and take his place, and
testify in his stead. A witness can't have a **successor!** Since
that is one of the prominent functions of an apostle—to
be a witness—it follows therefore that we can  have  no
other apostles. These New Testament apostles are  **our**
apostles tonight. They are on their thrones (Luke 22:30) tonight. They have ruled, and do now rule; they have made
inspired decisions and they are on record. Every decision
necessary, every truth ever to be revealed, has been revealed by them, and has been confirmed. This truth needs no
new **revelation**; and it needs no new miraculous **confirmation**. Thus, my friends, when we follow the apostles' teaching in the New Testament, we  are  being  governed  and
guided by the Holy Spirit through them. The New Testament apostles are **our** apostles—and we don't need any 'living apostles' tonight. This was one purpose of Holy Ghost
baptism for the apostles. (Acts 2:1-4.)

### The Case Of Cornelius

Now, let us briefly turn to the house of Cornelius: Cornelius and his household were also baptized with the Holy

Spirit, but not for the purpose of revealing and confirming the New Testament, as were the apostles. The purpose of the baptismal measure of the Holy Spirit at the house of Cornelius (Acts 10 & 11) differed from the purpose of the Spirit baptism of the apostles on Pentecost. (Acts 2.) Peter said that as he "began to speak" (Acts 11:15) at Cornelius' house, "the Holy Ghost fell on all them which heard the word." (Acts 10:44.) **All** who heard the word—kinsmen, near friends, all those gathered by Cornelius (Acts 10:24) —all who heard the word. It didn't fall on just a few here, and a few there, who were 'seeking' it—nothing of that sort happened! It fell on everybody, seemingly unexpected. This was a great miracle! They could "speak with tongues" (v. 46); this was a miraculous outpouring. Perhaps it came with the noise of a cyclone or tornado, as it did on Pentecost when it was accompanied by the sound "as of a rushing mighty wind;" and "cloven tongues" (Acts 2:2-3) no doubt sat upon these also. There was some visible manifestation of it, so that Peter could say, "As I **began** to speak . ." He knew exactly when it happened! "As I began to speak, the Holy Ghost fell on them, as on us at the beginning." (Acts 11:15.) He did not say that it fell on them as on us last week, last year, or during the 'big meeting' where I was recently preaching!

## Only New Case

Several years elapsed between Pentecost and the house of Cornelius—about eight or ten years, according to Bible scholars' estimates. But Peter could not think of another case like the house of Cornelius between that time, and Pentecost! He had to go all the way back to Pentecost to think of another case like it. "The Holy Ghost fell on them, as on us **at the beginning**." (Acts 11:15.) Well, the apostles received the "baptism" of the Spirit in the beginning—for Jesus said it would be that. (Acts 1:5.) And Cornelius also received the "baptism" of the Spirit—for Peter said, "Then remembered I the word of the Lord, how that he said" (in Acts 1:5) ". . . ye shall be **baptized** with the Holy Ghost." (Acts 11:16.) (Peter left off—did not quote—the "not many days hence" part of Christ's promise, because the "not many days hence" part would fit only the apostles. Acts 1:5 with 2:1-4.) So Peter remembered Christ's promise about the "baptism" of the Holy Spirit, and applied it to the household of Cornelius. Hence, he and his house received a "baptism" of the Spirit, like the apostles did on Pentecost. Luke says that it "fell on all them which heard the word" —at his house. (Acts 10:44.)

### Did Not Save

Spirit baptism to Cornelius' household was not to **save** them—nor did it fall on the **apostles** to save **them**. They had been out preaching under the limited commission (Matt. 10:5-7) for three-and-a-half years before Pentecost, before they received the baptism of the Holy Spirit. (Acts 2.)

It was not to give either Cornelius and his household or the apostles a "second blessing," in the sense of taking the "Adamic nature" out, and making it impossible for them to ever sin any more; because John (one of the apostles) says, "If we say that we have no sin, we deceive ourselves, and the truth is not in us." (1 John 1:8.)

Man could note when the house of Cornelius received the baptism of the Spirit. It was a direct outpouring, like that on Pentecost, in a baptismal measure. (John 1:33.) Christ administered it. Nobody laid hands on Cornelius and his house as Peter started to speak, so that they received this! But it came directly from God. **Christ** was "baptizing" with the Holy Spirit, as had been promised. (John 1:33; Matt. 3:11.) Joel's promise (Joel 2:28) was now being fulfilled: God poured out his Spirit on "all flesh," which includes **Gentile** flesh. There are just two "fleshes" (if you please), **Jew** flesh, and **Gentile** flesh. Jew flesh had received this promise on Pentecost (Acts 2), and now Gentile flesh received it. There is no other "flesh" of man left.

### Purpose Of It

Now, in view of that, we read that the purpose of it on this occasion was to bear witness of the fact that Gentiles can be saved if they obey the gospel—just like anybody else. For fifteen hundred years the Gentiles had been excluded from God's covenant grace and mercy, as revealed to the Jews. (Ex. 31:17; Rom. 3:1-2.) Paul explains: "That at that time ye"—Gentiles—"were without Christ, being aliens from the commonwealth of Israel, and strangers from the covenants of promise, having no hope, and without God in the world. But now in Christ Jesus ye who sometimes were far off"—the Gentiles had been far off—"are made nigh by the blood of Christ. For he is our peace, who hath made both one, and hath broken down the middle wall of partition between us; having abolished in his flesh the enmity, even the law of commandments contained in ordinances; for to make in himself of twain one new man, so making peace; and that he might reconcile both unto God in  one body by the cross, having slain the enmity thereby." (Eph. 2:11-16.) Here is a great mystery which Jesus solved. Even the apostles seemed not to understand the very words of the Holy Spirit. Their prejudice,  established  for  fifteen hundred years, was so great that they couldn't think of any but Jews as being recipients of the blessings of the Great Commission. (Mark 16:15.) So, it took these miracles (Acts 10 & 11) to break down this great barrier, and to get the gospel started to the Gentile world. God planned it all, and executed his plan for us. The mystery was, "That the Gentiles should be fellowheirs, and of the same body, and partakers of his promise in Christ by the gospel." (Eph. 3:6.)

### Before They Heard

But the Holy Spirit fell on these Gentiles **before they heard** the gospel! Peter says, "As I began  to  speak,  the Holy Ghost fell on them." (Acts 11:15.) Thus it was **before they heard** the word. The Spirit did not, nor does he now, have to fall on people to get them to obey the gospel—that is, people who were already understood to be involved in gospel provisions and promises. But these Gentiles did not understand themselves to be acceptable; neither  did  the Jews think Gentiles were acceptable. It took a miracle, in the first place, to get the Gentiles to send for  a  Jew,  a preacher like Peter. The angel said to him, "Send men to Joppa and call for Simon, whose surname is  Peter;  who shall tell thee words, whereby thou and all thy house shall be saved." (Acts 11:13-14.) Cornelius sent for the preacher;

but it took a miracle—the housetop vision—to convince
Peter to go over there! Finally, the Spirit said, "Go with
them, doubting nothing: for I have sent them." (Acts 10:20.)
So it took a miracle to make the Gentile send for a Jew;
and a miraculous work was required on the preacher himself (a Jew) to get him ready to go to these Gentiles. But
when he arrived he said, "God hath showed me that I
should not call any man common or unclean." (Acts 10:28.)
These two miracles were for the purpose of getting the
preacher and the unsaved together.

So the preacher came. As he arose to speak, the Holy
Spirit "fell on all them which heard the word." (Acts 11:15.)
This was God's way of bearing witness to the fact that the
gospel is for all people, Gentiles, the same as Jews. Peter
later said, "God made choice among us, that the Gentiles
by my mouth should hear the word of the gospel, and believe." (Acts 15:7.) Like all others, the Gentiles had to get
their **faith** by **hearing** the gospel preached, and not by direct information or revelation from God. "And God, which
knoweth the hearts"—not 'their' hearts, as you often hear
Peter misquoted as saying, but—"**the** hearts"—God knew
the prejudice in the minds of the **Jews**, in **their** hearts; and
he knew the doubts in the minds and hearts of the **Gentiles.**
So, "God, which knoweth **the** hearts"—the prejudice and
doubt from both sides, Jew and Gentile. "God, which
knoweth the hearts, **BARE THEM WITNESS** . . ." (Acts
15:8.) "Bare them witness"—**How**? and witness to **what**?
To the fact that a Jew has no more chance of being saved
by the gospel than a Gentile; that a Gentile can be saved
through the gospel of Christ the same as a Jew. God "bare
them witness" to this fact. How? Let Peter answer: "God
. . . bare them witness, giving them the Holy Ghost, even
as he did unto us; and put no difference between us and
them." There is **no difference** in the conditions of pardon
to the Jew and the Gentile! (Acts 10:34.) It took several
miracles to convince Peter the gospel is for those who,
under the Old Testament, were "far off." (Eph. 2:13.) So
Peter said the baptism of Cornelius and his household with
the Holy Ghost was to bear them "witness." "God **bare**

**them witness**, giving them the Holy Ghost, even as he did unto us; and put no difference between us and them, purifying their hearts by faith." (Acts 15:7-9.) That simply means that Gentiles can be saved by hearing the gospel, believing and obeying it, so as to be saved by obedient faith —just like Jews and everybody else on earth who will ever be saved in the gospel age.

## Was To Confirm

Thus the purpose of Holy Spirit baptism at Cornelius' house was to **reveal** the fact the gospel is for all people; that God is no respecter of persons; that in every nation— Gentile as well as Jewish nation—"he that feareth God and worketh righteousness is acceptable to him." (Acts 10:34, ASV.) It was also to **confirm** this great truth. But when it was confirmed, it remains confirmed; it does not have to be proved over, and over, again and again, every time somebody wants God's truth. The old truth is sufficient; there is no "new" truth; and there is no new confirmation of the truth. For instance: Christ was raised from the dead to prove, to declare, him to be the Son of God with power. (Rom. 1:4.) Now, he does not have to be raised again and again in order to declare and to prove that fact, nor to keep it established. He was raised one time, nineteen hundred years ago. It proved that fact; and it stays proved! It stays established! It has never been in doubt to anyone who believes the gospel, from that day to this. So also this truth was confirmed in the gospel for all time to come.

## The Report Confirmed Truth

When Peter went back to the church at Jerusalem, they took him to task about his preaching to the Gentiles: "Thou wentest in to men uncircumcised, and didst eat with them." (Acts 11:3.) Peter explained the whole thing "by order," somewhat like I've gone into detail with it here. Hearing about it —**not** seeing it transpire again the second time in their midst, **not** seeing it re-enacted, but just **hearing** about it—convinced the Jewish church, and all people who believe in Christ, that the Gentiles are acceptable. "When they **heard** these things, they held their peace, and glorified God, saying, Then hath God also to the Gentiles granted repentance unto life." (Acts 11:18.) What was the evidence of this fact? Well, the miracles connected here, abundantly confirmed it. If they proved to the Jewish nation that the gospel, as revealed and confirmed, includes Gentiles, then the hearing of it tonight ought to establish that fact in our minds without our wanting a new case of Holy Ghost baptism. Hence, there has not been a new case of it from Cornelius until tonight!

### One Baptism Now

Paul said, "There is . . . one Lord, one faith, **one baptism**." (Eph. 4:5.) That was written in A. D. 64. Cornelius' case of Holy Spirit baptism was in A. D. 41. Pentecost was in A. D. 33. So, by the time Paul said (A. D. 64) there is "one baptism," the baptism of the Holy Spirit had served its purpose in (1) guiding and qualifying the apostles, preparing them for their life's work, and (2) in confirming the fact that the gospel is for Jew and Gentile alike, thus getting the gospel going out to the Gentile world. This was established with proofs which, when anybody else ever hears the gospel message (including these "proofs" in preached form, as revealed), will satisfy all other people to the end of the world. These proofs never need to be repeated in a single case. Hence, there are only two **recorded** cases of the baptism of the Holy Spirit. (I think Saul also was baptized in the Holy Spirit, but there is no **record** stating it, as in these two cases.)

### One Baptism Is What?

Now, in view of this, what is the "one baptism" (Eph. 4:5) that is left? Well, it is whichever one was intended to last, and was for all people. Holy Spirit baptism was not for all. Jesus says, "Even the Spirit of truth; whom the world cannot receive." (John 14:15-17.) It is not for the world, not for everybody; it was intended for only a few, just a few necessary ones. (Acts 2 & 10.) But water baptism is for all people: Jesus said, "Go ye into all the world and preach the gospel to every creature; he that believeth and is baptized shall be saved." (Mark 16:15-16.) Peter, when speaking of **water baptism**, said, "The like figure whereunto even baptism doth also now **save** us." (1 Pet. 3:21.) Salvation is for the world; and so is the baptism (water baptism) upon which it is conditioned. But Holy Spirit baptism is not for the world. Hence the world is not to be "saved" through Holy Ghost baptism—and this was also true of the apostles, and the household of Cornelius.

## Water Baptism

In Matthew's record Jesus says, "Go ye therefore, and teach all nations, baptizing them . . ." (Matt. 28:19.) This baptism is for all men. It is not Holy Ghost baptism, but is water baptism instead. ". . . baptizing them in the name of the Father, and of the Son, and of the Holy Ghost: teaching them"—after you baptize them—"teaching them to observe all things whatsoever I have commanded you: and, lo, I am with you"—with you, in what? In this work of teaching all nations, baptizing people, and then teaching those taught and baptized. But, wait a minute, Lord: how long are you going to be with this work? "And, lo, I am with you alway, even unto the end of the world." (Matt. 28:18-20.) This work of the Great Commission will last "unto the end of the world" or always! This baptism, which can be administered by the disciples, must be water baptism. (Matt. 3:11.) But this baptism—water baptism—will continue always, "even unto the end of the world." Holy Spirit baptism was nowhere promised to last unto the end of the world. Hence, water baptism is the baptism of the Great Commission; it is a condition of salvation, and is for all people of the earth who will accept the gospel and who want to be saved. Therefore, the "one baptism" of Ephesians 4:5 is water baptism.

## Preach The Word

That's sufficient, I think. This explanation is as brief as I can make, yet be sufficiently clear in a time of controversy. Recently I received an eight-page document from a brother in California who has gone off into sectarianism, and now contends for Holy Ghost baptism—including 'speaking in tongues' (?)—for members of the church of the Lord Jesus Christ! Brethren, if we have any true regard, reverence, and respect for the word of God, we'd better get back to preaching the WORD! It seems strange to me that people can't see that it is easy to drift off into error.

The simple things which I have preached here tonight are nothing new in gospel preaching. The old pioneers preached them! And people back there understood and believed the truth about it. But we are producing a generation of preachers who talk **about** the word, and preach **about** the word—instead of telling people what the **word** says, and what the **word** teaches! They don't study God's word; they read after denominational preachers, and denominational commentators; and they fill our hearts with **chaff.** They don't have the **wheat** to present!

I'd like to plead for a return to good, old-fashioned GOSPEL preaching! That is the only kind that will ever convert the world to Christ. Stop this idea of trying to get people to 'hit the sawdust trail' with a little fifteen or twenty minute psychological appeal to get them into (?) the church! Such "converts" will be ignorant of the gospel of Christ, and will be nothing but problems in our midst, to decoy, to lead astray, and to divide us up into little 'tenth-rate' sects and parties! The uninformed and untaught can be nothing but **problems** on our hands!

Teach the truth, preach the word of God. Don't support a man with one copper cent who won't faithfully "preach the word." (2 Tim. 4:2.) Don't stand behind him! He is not a **gospel** preacher if he doesn't fully preach the "gospel of Christ." "Make full proof of thy ministry" is God's exhortation to gospel preachers. (2 Tim. 4:5.) "Prove all things; hold fast that which is good." (1 Thess. 5:21.) "Make all men see" the truth. (Eph. 3:9.) Now, we are not sent to make them believe it; but you are sent to make them see it.

But the time is up for this occasion. After we sing the invitation hymn, you may ask whatever questions you may wish on this subject. Let us sing.

## QUESTIONS AND ANSWERS

**Question:** Since Peter was baptized with the Holy Spirit on Pentecost, as were the other apostles, then why did he exclude himself when he said, "**These** are not drunken as ye suppose, since it is but the third hour of the day!" Acts 2? Why did he not say, **"We** are not drunken as ye suppose . . ."?

**Answer:** I do not know just why that is true. I think about the only way that I could recommend that you could be sure to find out is to just be a Christian and live the Christian life and go to heaven. Then you can ask Peter, and he can tell you exactly why. But there is no argument in it against anything that the Bible says in the scriptures presented. It does not prove that Peter was not involved in the number. In fact, **"These** men are full of new wine," they said. Peter might have been included in that number. And then when he got up, naturally, it would be enough to say that **"these** are not drunken as ye suppose," and refer to the others. Naturally, if it fit them, it fit him, too.

**Question:** Why is it so important to affirm that the Holy Spirit, in Acts 1 and 2, descended upon the apostles only and not on the 120?

**Answer:** Well, for the very reason that if the Holy Spirit came upon the 120, then the doctrine would be established that the baptism of the Holy Spirit on this occasion was for the disciples in general, and would thwart the very purpose of God in revealing it to be the other way—that it was for the apostles. Regardless of the reason for it, we do find, and have shown, that the Spirit fell upon the apostles; and not upon the multitude, that the multitude was not there. Miraculous powers were not to be received by the multitude, nor one hundred twenty. They are just not in it as far as this miracle is concerned. It had to do with revealing the gospel, and was for the Lord's apostles to be the men through which that would be done.

**Question:** Why do not other religions realize that they are doing wrong? They say that they are the right religion, when they do not even go by the Bible?

**Answer:** Well, they need teaching, and we are not doing it as well as we could if we would just get a little more interested in their salvation. Many are taking it for granted that error will save the world the same as truth. We ought to function in our true setting and responsibility, and remember that if we do not preach the gospel to the world, the gospel will never be preached to the world. Other people are not preaching it; they are preaching certain parts of it, and we would not have them change the part that is right, but the gospel as a system of truth is not taught by anybody else on God's earth, than the Lord's people.

**Question:** When you said, "Go ye into all the world and preach the gospel to every creature." Well, what if you do not know about some island, and people who live on it, and you do not know their language? What would you do?

**Answer:** If I wanted to preach to them, I would do like everyone under heaven has to do—I'd study the language, and then go and preach to them. Or I'd take an interpreter. I spoke in Jerusalem at the Church of Christ in 1962, and Brother Henley had to interpret for me. We had the house nearly filled with Jews, about half of them perhaps were not members of the church. They listened while I talked about Abraham, but when I developed the promise that in his seed, which is Christ, all nations would be blessed, then they began to lose interest because I was establishing Christianity in their minds. And they were reluctant, of course, to accept Christianity, and it is hard to convince them. But, anyway, you will have to either speak to them in their own language or use an interpreter or learn the language in some way. But God did not want to wait years and years to get the gospel started to different nations in their own tongues, there on Pentecost. God started it right then in their different languages, and let them take it back to their people in their own tongues. (Acts 2:4-11.) Now we have people who have translated it into the various languages—more than a thousand languages, and dialects.

**Question:** Last night you said, "If you sin against the Holy Spirit, you will never be forgiven." What do you mean by that?

**Answer:** I mean the blasphemy of the Holy Spirit. "He

that shall blaspheme against the Holy Ghost hath never forgiveness, but is in danger of eternal damnation." Those are the very words of the Bible. (Mark 3:27-30.)

**Question:** When you die, do you receive the Holy Ghost, and if you have sinned a lot, will your soul go to hell? If you have not sinned real bad, will your soul go to heaven, or what?

**Answer:** I think I will answer this because it might help some precious soul to obey the gospel and be saved while he can. First of all, we do not receive the Holy Ghost when we die; there is not any proof that you receive the Holy Ghost when you die. Acts 2:38 says, "Repent, and be baptized every one of you in the name of Jesus Christ for the remission of sins, and ye shall receive the gift of the Holy Ghost." Acts 5:32 ". . . so is also the Holy Ghost, whom God hath given to them that obey him." You had better not expect to receive something in death that God has not promised. As for the other, I have already answered.

**Question:** What is really the point in trying to show the pronouns in Acts 1 and 2 are exclusive, and then have to say that Cornelius and Paul also received the baptism of the Holy Spirit?

**Answer:** Because the Holy Spirit is given for one purpose on Pentecost, and that was to reveal through the apostles, and confirm through them, the gospel of Christ. It did not inspire Cornelius. He still had to be told what to do. It was to confirm what had been revealed by the Holy Spirit through the apostle Peter in their preaching and teaching that God is no respecter of persons. That was the revealed truth, but it needed confirmation. And it would show, in the first place, and that is our purpose in it of course, that Cornelius and his household were not inspired like apostles, for they were not apostles and not in that class, and did not need what the apostles needed. The need on that occasion was confirmation of the gospel of Christ, and it confirmed for the Gentile world rather than being for new revelation.

**Question:** You said, "Things that were created in the be-

118 LECTURES ON THE HOLY SPIRIT

ginning were created miraculously, but contend for natural
law today." I missed your scripture reference for the last
part. Please, give it again: that things continue by natural
law today.

**Answer:** Well, in the first place, I do not need to prove
that which is obvious. If you want corn, you know better
than to plant cotton seed. It is because you know that natural law would be violated if you were to plant cotton seed
to reap corn. "The seed is the word of God." (Luke 8:11.)
"The sower soweth the word." (Mark 4:14.) And if you want
Christians, you have to preach the word, the thing that
makes Christians; and then if you want them to remain
Christians, to live the Christian life, continue to preach
the word. If you want man to produce prayer in his life,
sow the seed that produces prayer. If you want him to at-
tend the worship services of the church as God ordained,
preach that part of the word that shows that that is necessary and that is God's will; and so on down the line.

**Question:** Last night you said that we should get out of
our minds the idea that the Holy Spirit is somehow asso-
ciated with an angel. You did say that God had manifested
himself as an angel. Why is the above idea wrong? What
Scripture teaches you to say this?

**Answer:** What Scripture teaches you to say that the Holy
Spirit is an angel? And that is the thing that I called for
last night, and stated that it is not in the Bible. And I am
sure that it is not there now, or you would have produced
it. I stated that God is presented AS an angel, and I have
proof. (Jud. 13.) I gave Abraham and Lot as cases, where
an angel appeared, and God talked to the people through
this angel on the occasion. (Gen. 18-19.) And yet, he looked
like a man, and Abraham did not know any better at first.
And I quoted from Heb. 13:1, "Be not forgetful to entertain
strangers; for thereby some have entertained angels unawares." Unawares means not knowing who they were at
the time. And so I proved my point that God sometimes
presented himself as though he were a man, but yet he
was in the form of an angel, in the form of man, no doubt,

because Heb. 13:1 says the person was an angel. But you have not produced the verse, and you will not produce the verse that says the Holy Spirit is an angel. Angels were created beings; the Holy Spirit is an eternal being, never was created. (Heb. 9:14.) He who "through the ETERNAL SPIRIT offered himself to God." Hence, the Holy Spirit is eternal.

**Question:** I had heard the following argument put forth: On the day of Pentecost, there were more than 12 different dialects represented in the multitude, and if only the 12 apostles were baptized with the Holy Spirit, then a miracle was worked upon the multitude so that all could hear in their own tongue. What is the truth in this matter?

**Answer:** The truth is that the multitude was not present at first. That is the first truth to remember. The multitude was not there when the Spirit came. "When this was noised abroad, the multitude came together." (Acts 2:1-7.) They were not there when the Holy Spirit fell upon the apostles. And in the second place, it has been understood by Bible scholars who have studied these different nationalities, the Parthians, the Medes, etc., that these people spoke less than a dozen languages. Now, the idea that each one of them had a language separate from all the others is not necessarily established at all. And the apostles simply spake in each language or tongue and all heard. I started the first night by referring to 1 Tim. 3:16, "Great is the mystery of godliness." We cannot understand all the mysteries connected with everything and explain all those things, but we are to stay with what is revealed. I want to emphasize that again tonight. (Deut. 29:29.)

**Question:** How do you know that the apostles are on their thrones tonight? Is this their heavenly throne? If so, when were they resurrected?

**Answer:** Their thrones were thrones of power. I stated tonight that they were (figuratively speaking) upon thrones. That they were enthroned with power, and quoted Acts 1:8, "And ye shall receive power, after that the Holy Ghost is come upon you." I referred to Matt. 19:28. He said that, "ye that have followed me," —then there is a comma— "in the regeneration"—well, we are now in the regeneration. We know we are in it because Titus 3:5 says God saved us by "the washing of regeneration." They were in the regeneration nineteen hundred years ago under the apostles' preaching. "Ye that have followed me, in the regeneration, when the son of man shall sit upon the throne of his glory" —you see, this was spoken during the personal ministry, in Matt. 19, while Christ was crucified in the twenty-sixth and twenty-seventh chapters, raised from the dead in the twenty-eighth chapter. And then he was looking forward to Pentecost and the Christian age that would soon be established, and the giving of the Great Commission, and how it was going forth. And he said, "In the regeneration, when the Son of man shall sit upon the throne of his glory; ye also shall sit upon twelve thrones, judging the twelve tribes of Israel." He said that they would be on thrones in the regeneration, and at the same time he was on his throne. In Zech. 6:12, 13, we read that he would sit and rule upon his throne; and Acts 2:29-36 says that he was raised to sit on the throne. So he got on his throne when he started reigning and ruling, was declared to be on his throne on Pentecost, raised to sit on his throne. And they were to be on their thrones at the same time he was to be on his, "when the son of man shall be seated on the throne, ye also shall be seated on twelve thrones." And so, we know by that the thrones of the apostles were for the time of their lives here on earth. And there they exercised the authority and power by functioning as apostles while they lived upon the earth, and there is no evidence that they will get on any apostolic throne hereafter. The apostles are still upon their thrones and judging. Their inspired teachings and decisions for people are now in the inspired New Testament. (2 Cor. 3:6; John 16:13.)

# HOLY SPIRIT AND MIRACULOUS GIFTS

Your presence is duly appreciated by us all. An area-wide meeting like this for the purpose of studying the subject of THE HOLY SPIRIT AND HIS WORK should be a blessing to all here assembled, and to the various congregations from whence you have come.

We want tonight to prayerfully study the **"Miraculous Gifts of the Spirit."** There are two miraculous measures of the Spirit which had to do with the establishment of the church and of Christianity. While they served the divine purpose for them, and were done away, we are Christians tonight as a result of their work—as we shall see in our study.

One night we hope to study the 'Ordinary' gift of the Holy Spirit—the only measure of the Spirit for us today. The subject then will be: **"The Indwelling of the Holy Spirit,"** which, as we shall see, is a non-miraculous measure of the Spirit given unto all true Christians at conversion.

## Measures of the Spirit Given
1. Christ had the Holy Spirit without "measure," as stated in John 3:34.

2. The apostles of Christ, and the household of Cornelius, were "baptized" with the Holy Spirit, as stated in Acts 1, 2, 10, and 11.

3. Those on whom the apostles laid their hands received a miraculous measure of the Holy Spirit, as is seen in Acts 8:18 and 19:6.

4. Then there is, as we have stated, the "ordinary" gift of the Spirit which bestowed no miraculous power, which is for all the children of God.

## The Personality of the Spirit
I would like to remind us that the Holy Spirit is one of

the Godhead. (Matt. 28:19; Rom. 1:20; Col. 2:9.) He is mentioned eight times in two verses (John 16:13, 14) in the masculine gender. The Holy Spirit is a divine person. He is as invisible as God and Christ, or as air, electricity, gravity, the infinity of space, mind, or a thought—or even as is the human spirit in man—and other like things in the world of the unseen.

### The Holy Spirit Is Intelligent

(1) The Holy Spirit "knows." (1 Cor. 2:11.) (2) The Holy Spirit can "strive" with man—is interested in man. (Gen. 6:1-5.) (3) The Holy Spirit could be "vexed." (Isa. 63:10.) (4) The Holy Spirit could be "resisted." (Acts 7:51-53; Neh. 9:30.) (5) He could be "lied" against, or "lied" to. (Acts 5:1-14.) (6) He could be "blasphemed" or "spoken against." (Matt. 12:32-33; Mark 3:27-30; Luke 12:10.) (7) The Spirit could "guide." (John 16:13.) (8) He could "teach" and "instruct." (Neh. 9:20; John 14:26.) (9) He could "speak" by men. (2 Sam. 23:2; Acts 1:16; Heb. 3:7-11 with Ps. 95:7-11; Acts 28:25 with Isa. 6:9; 1 Cor. 2:13; Acts 20:23; 1 Tim. 4:1-3.) (10) The Spirit could "witness" through men. (Heb. 10:15-17 with Jer. 31:31-34; John 15:26; Acts 20:23; Rom. 8:16.) (11) He could move men—inspired men— to "speak." (2 Pet. 1:20-21; Acts 2:4; 1 Cor. 2:13.) (12) He "inspired" the scriptures. (2 Tim. 3:15-17; 2 Pet. 1:20-21.) (13) He "testified against" the wicked by the prophets. (Neh. 9:30.) (14) And the "words" of inspired men were the "Spirit's" words. (2 Sam. 23:2.)

### Holy Spirit's Part in Creation

The Holy Spirit had a part in the creation of this world, and of the universe. **God** created it by **Christ**. (Heb. 1:1-3; John 1:1-3; Col. 1:13-18.) But the **Holy Spirit** also had a part in it. (Gen. 1:1-2.)

"Thou sendest forth thy Spirit, they are created; and thou renewest the face of the earth." (Ps. 104:30.) "By his Spirit he hath garnished the heavens; his hand hath formed the crooked serpent." (Job 26:13.) "The Spirit of God hath made me, and the breath of the Almighty hath given me life." (Job 33:4; cf. Gen. 1:26-27; 2:7.)

### The Work of Creation Finished

The Godhead performed all the miracles of creation in the first chapters of the Bible for our benefit now, as well as for the early peoples of the earth. He has not kept on creating the heavens and the earth, over and over, just to show his power. He has made no more people of the dust as he did Adam, nor of a rib, as he made Eve. Oh, yes: God has as much power as he ever had. It never was his purpose to keep on creating people as he did the first pair. There is no need for it. The vegetable kingdom also was miraculously created; but God does not keep on doing this work over and over. Instead of continued miracles of the sort, he gave us the seed. It would be absurd for the farmer to go into the fields and pray for a miraculous harvest like the first, and ignore the seed. The man of faith plants the seed, while doubters and cranks may expect a miraculous harvest without seed. It seems that the Holy Spirit was God's organizer and law-giver in creation—that he gave laws by which created things are to be governed and perpetuated.

### The Patriarchal Age Began In Miracle

All the miracles of creation were to originate and plan for the perpetual operation of things created. The Patriarchal Age was ushered in by all the miracles of creation. No other miracles were wrought of God except as needed, such as at Noah's flood. (Gen. 6.) God respected and honored his own laws of nature, and man prospered as he also honored them.

When man sinned and fell, it seems that God headed for Pentecost (of Acts 2), and the establishment of Christianity. (Gen. 3:15; 49:10.) His purpose was made known in his promise to bless and save the world through Abraham and his seed, "which is Jesus Christ." (Gen. 12; 18; 26; Gal. 3.)

After about twenty-five hundred years, the Patriarchal Age ended with God still honoring his laws, and keeping the miraculous at a minimum.

## The Jewish Age Came In By Miracles

Then the Jewish Age (or Mosaic Dispensation) was ushered in by all the stupendous miracles of Mount Sinai. (Ex. 20.) But instead of proposing to make man holy and righteous by miraculous power wrought directly upon man, God gave his great law—and again kept miracles to the minimum for more than a thousand years. When that religion was completely revealed, and the Old Covenant finished or fully made known, God said no more directly to man, nor wrought any more miracles, for about four hundred years before the coming of Christ.

## The Christian Age Came In By Power

Just as all things originated in miracles, so all the marvelous miracles in the early part of the New Testament ushered in Christianity—the greatest religion of all ages, and the final system of religion for man on earth. Like the former two, this dispensation also was created in miraculous power. The virgin birth of Christ, his life, and miracles of power were to establish Christianity for all time to come.

Again, God honored and respected his laws of nature, and kept miracles to a minimum. God has always purposed to rule over man by reason and revealed truth, by moral and suasive power, rather than by miraculous power wrought upon man.

## A New Covenant Promised

God had promised that in the establishment of Christianity, he would make a new covenant, and give us the perfect law of the gospel. (Jer. 31:31-34.) He had promised to set up the kingdom of Christ. (Dan. 2:44; Isa. 9:6-7; 2:1-3.) This would call for the greatest miracles of all time, and this power also was promised. (Joel 2:28-32.)

## The Forerunner Sent To Prepare

John the Baptizer was to come and prepare the way for the acceptance of the Lord Jesus. (Isa. 40:3-5; Matt. 3:1-3.) Although John was "filled with the Holy Ghost" (Luke 1:15), he "did no miracle." (John 10:41.) Being the last prophet of the Old Covenant, his main mission was to

get men back to God, whom they had forsaken in the period
between the Testaments.

### Finally The Messenger Came

Finally Christ—the messenger of the New Covenant—
came. He wrought many great and mighty miracles for
the purpose of establishing his claim to be the Son of God.
(John 20:30-31.) He died for our sins (1 Cor. 15:1-4), and
God raised him from the dead the third day. (Rom. 1:1-4.)
He had the Spirit without "measure." (John 3:34.) He cast
out devils "by the Spirit of God." (Matt. 12:28.) He spoke
by the power of Holy Spirit, and "through the Holy Ghost"
he gave "commandments" to his chosen apostles. (Acts
1:2.)

### Would Go Away, And Send The Spirit

Looking forward to his leaving, Christ had chosen the
twelve men whom he named "Apostles," into whose hands
he would leave the task of the great commission, and the
affairs of his kingdom which was about to be established.
(Luke 12:32.) They needed more supernatural power than
any other group of men in the history of the world. The
church was to be built upon the death of Christ for man's
sins, his burial, and his resurrection the third day. (1 Cor.
15:1-4; Rom. 1:4; Matt. 16:13-19; Isa. 28:16; 1 Cor. 3:11.)

### Needed Revelation And Confirmation

What God had planned for four thousand years, and
promised in the Old Testament, and what Christ had come
to execute—the Holy Spirit was to come, reveal and confirm in mighty power, which would shake and shape future
history for all time to come. The great commission (Matt.
28:18-20; Mark 16:15-16; Luke 24:46-47) was given unto
these ordinary men. They were to go and teach all nations,
preach the gospel to every creature in all the world, and
cause the people to believe and obey this gospel. This was,
and is, the world's most colossal program.

### "Power From On High" Promised

1. As his **apostles**, they were commanded, under the
great commission, to tarry in the city of Jerusalem until

endued with "power from on high." (Luke 24:46-49; Matt. 28:19-20.)

2. God, through John had promised them that they would "be baptized with the Holy Ghost." (Matt. 3:11.) The "fire" baptism of this verse was for Judas, who fell away and was lost. (John 17:12.)

3. Just before he ascended to heaven, Christ applied this promise of Holy Ghost "baptism" to his apostles. (Acts 1:1-5.)

4. He said, "Ye shall receive power, after that" (ASV: "when") "the Holy Ghost is come upon you: and ye shall be witnesses unto me both in Jerusalem, and in all Judea, and in Samaria, and unto the uttermost part of the earth." (Acts 1:8.)

5. It was to be "not many days hence." (Acts 1:5.) This was about ten days before it was fulfilled on Pentecost. (Acts 2:1-4.)

6. This miraculous power would make these apostles "able ministers of the new testament" (2 Cor. 3:6)—enable them to give unto us the New Testament, with its glorious gospel of Christ.

7. The Spirit would come in **baptismal** "measure" to "guide" them into all truth. (John 16:7-13; Acts 1:1-8.)

8. He would bring to their memory (John 14:26) all things which Christ had taught them during three and one-half years of association under the limited commission. (Matt. 10.)

9. They would also be comforted by the teaching and revelation of the Spirit through them. (John 14:1-6, 26; Rom. 15:4; 1 Thess. 4:18.)

10. Christ promised them that the Spirit would "teach" them "all things." (John 14:26.)

11. The Spirit would also "show" them "things to come," such as the foretelling of a coming apostasy. (John 16:13-14; 2 Thess. 2.)

12. The Spirit would speak in, and through, the apostles. (Matt. 10:19-20; Acts 2:4.)

13. There was a language barrier in the way: they were to preach to "every creature;" but they knew only one language or tongue. They needed to use all languages. (Acts 2:1-11; Mark 16:14-18.)

14. They needed such miracle-working power as would enable them to "confirm" their preaching. This need was met. (Mark 16:20; Heb. 2:3-4.)

15. They needed to preach the gospel "with the Holy Spirit sent down from heaven." (1 Pet. 1:12; 1 Cor. 2:13; Acts 2.)

16. They needed power to "remit" and "retain" sins, by binding the conditions of remission of sins. (John 20:20-23; Acts 2:38.)

17. The apostles were to "bind" and "loose" for God on earth as he would bind and loose in heaven. (Matt. 16:19; 18:18.)

18. As witnesses of the resurrection of Christ, and of his life and miracles, as well as of his teaching, they needed supernatural power to enable them to infallibly testify. (Luke 24:48-49; Acts 1:5-8; 2:32; 10:39.)

19. It would take great power to bring in and establish the kingdom of Christ. This need was met. (Mark 9:1; Acts 1:8; 2:1-4.)

20. They needed power to write the New Testament Scriptures, and confirm them by signs and wonders. (John 20:30-31; 1 John 2:1; 2 Tim. 3:16; 1 Tim. 3:14-15; Eph. 3:2-6.)

21. The apostles needed supernatural power to make them "ambassadors" for Christ. (2 Cor. 5:17-21.)

22. They needed such power as would establish Christianity and secure the future of the church, so we can have a firm foundation on which to build to the end of time. (Eph. 2:11-22; Rom. 1:5; 16:26.)

23. They needed to be able to do "greater works" than Christ did. (John 14:12; Heb. 2:3-4; Acts 14:1-3.)

24. They needed great divine power with which to make their gospel preaching effective so as to "convict the world of sin." (John 16:7-13.)

### Apostles Received This Power

Let us remember that Jesus promised that his kingdom would come with power —the power of the Holy Spirit. (Mark 9:1; Luke 12:32; 22:29-30.) The promise of the Spirit was made to the apostles. (John 14, 15, 16.) He "showed himself alive," after his resurrection, and gave commandments "unto the apostles, whom he had chosen." (Acts 1:1-3.) Unto them he said, "John truly baptized with water; but ye"—ye apostles—"shall be **baptized with the Holy Ghost** not many days hence." (Acts 1:5.) The last words of the chapter are that Matthias was "numbered with the eleven apostles." (Acts 1:26.) In the next verses we read that "they"—the apostles—"were all filled with the Holy Ghost." (Acts 2:1-4.) The apostles were then qualified to reveal and confirm the gospel, to preach it "with the Holy Ghost sent down from heaven." (1 Pet. 1:12.)

This is called "the beginning." (Acts 11:15.) It was the beginning of the church or kingdom. (Mark 9:1; Matt. 16:18.) It was the beginning of the great commission. (Matt. 28; Mark 16; Luke 24; John 20; Acts 1.) The New Testament had just gone into force. (Heb. 9:14-17.) The apostles had just received "the keys of the kingdom" (Matt. 16:18-19), and were ready to make known the way of salvation through Christ. The multitude came together (Acts 2:6), and the apostles began to speak to every man "in his own tongue." (v. 8.) They could understand the message, for they said, "We do hear them speak in our tongues the wonderful works of God." (v. 11.)

### Peter Stood Up With The Eleven

"Peter, standing up with the eleven, lifted up his voice, and said unto them, Ye men of Judaea, and all ye that dwell at Jerusalem, be this known unto you, and hearken to my words." (Acts 2:14.) He then began to preach the gospel, as commanded in the great commission. (Mark 16:15-16.) He had a great "multitude" (v. 6)—perhaps hundreds of thousands—for his audience.

### The Spirit To Convict The World

We remember that Jesus had promised that when the Spirit should thus come, he would "teach" them all things, "guide" them "into all truth" (John 14:26; 16:13), and that he would "reprove the world of sin," or "convict" the world of sin, as he (through the apostles) would preach the gospel. The Spirit came to the apostles—not upon the multitude—to do this. Jesus had said of the Spirit, "whom the world cannot receive." (John 14:17.)

### What The Multitude Needed

1. The multitude there assembled needed the gospel—needed to hear about Jesus. Peter's subject was **"Jesus of Nazareth"** (Acts 2:22), "approved of God" by "miracles, wonders, and signs" done among them. The Holy Spirit through the apostle Peter "reproved" or "convicted" them of the sin of having murdered the Son of God (v. 23), and declared the good news, however, that God had raised him from the dead. (v. 24.)

2. Paul said the gospel "is the power of God unto salvation to every one that believeth." (Rom. 1:16.) They believed the gospel. (Acts 2:36; 1 Cor. 15:1-4.) They asked what to do, as they, by the Spirit, through the preaching of the inspired apostles, were convicted of their sins.(Acts 2:37.)

3. They received their faith by the preaching of the gospel—not by a direct operation of the Spirit upon them. (Acts 2:36-37; Rom. 10:17; Acts 15:7.)

4. They were to be "begotten" by the gospel (1 Cor. 4:15), or word of truth (Jas. 1:18), and not by a miracle wrought on them. They were to be "born again by the word of God." (1 Pet. 1:22-23.)

### Three Thousand Converted By The Spirit

When many of the multitude believed the gospel which Peter had just preached, were convicted of sin thereby, and asked, "What shall we do?" (Acts 2:22-37), Peter said: "Repent, and be baptized every one of you in the name of Jesus Christ for the remission of sins, and ye shall receive the gift of the Holy Ghost." (Acts 2:38.) "Then they that gladly received his word were baptized: and the same day there were added unto them about three thousand souls." (v. 41.) The Holy Spirit had converted them by the gospel which he preached by the apostles.

### Word Was Confirmed By Signs And Miracles

After his resurrection, Christ had promised his apostles that, if they would believe on him, signs would follow them to confirm the word. (Mark 16:14-20.) So we read in Acts 2:43 that "many wonders and signs were done by the apostles." And, perhaps two years later, we read, "And by the hands of the apostles were many signs and wonders wrought among the people." (Acts 5:12.) "They brought forth the sick into the streets, and laid them on beds and couches, that at the least the shadow of Peter passing by might overshadow some of them. There came also a multitude out of the cities round about unto Jerusalem, bringing sick folks, and them which were vexed with unclean spirits: and they were healed every one." (Acts 5:15-16.) Christ had promised the apostles this very power. It was to confirm, or prove, the word—their preaching. (Heb. 2:1-4.)

### God Worked With Them

Wherever the apostles went preaching the word, the Lord was indeed "working with them, and confirming the word with signs following." (Mark 16:20.) They were establishing Christianity in the earth for all time to come. God broke down one barrier after another to this end.

### A Great Problem Solved

But for several years the apostles had continued to preach only to the Jews—their own people. In giving the great commission, Jesus had said, "Teach all nations," and "preach the gospel to every creature" in "all the world." (Matt. 28:19; Mark 16:15.) But a great wall had been built up between Jews and Gentiles; and the apostles were staying with the idea of the limited commission, previously given, before the cross. (Matt. 10.) This they continued to do for several years since Pentecost.

This was a great crisis in the history of the newly-established church. God determined to solve the problem, and get the gospel unto Gentiles also. The "middle wall" had been broken down in **God's** sight at the cross. (Eph. 2:11-16.) **The Lord's church was not to be a Jewish church, but is** for all nations.

### Cornelius A Test Case

There was a Gentile by the name of Cornelius, who was a devout and religious man in error, who needed to hear the gospel and be saved. (Acts 10:1-3, 22; 11:1-18.) God by an angel directed him to send for Peter, one of the inspired apostles. (Acts 11:13-14.)

Knowing that Peter, who was at Joppa, was prejudiced against preaching to Gentiles, the Lord first of all convinced **him**—by a miracle—that he should go and preach to Cornelius. Aware that among the Jews this was thought a thing unlawful, Peter took six Jewish brethren with him, somewhat in self-defense, and to be witnesses of what might occur. (Acts 11:12-14.) Cornelius sent for Peter, and four days later he arrived. Cornelius had invited his kin and near friends. (Acts 10:24.) He introduced the preacher and said, "Now therefore are we all here present before God, to hear all things that are commanded thee of God." (Acts 10:33.)

### Holy Ghost Baptism Again

As Peter "began to speak, the Holy Ghost fell on them" as on the apostles "at the beginning"—on Pentecost. (Acts 11:15.) This was another case (the only other recorded one) of the mighty outpouring of the Holy Spirit—a "baptism" of the Holy Ghost. It fell on all them which heard the word. (Acts 10:44.) This astonished the six Jews who came with Peter, "because that on the Gentiles also was poured out the gift of the Holy Ghost. For they heard them speak with tongues, and magnify God." (Acts 10:45-46.) This established and confirmed the fact for all time to come that God "is no respector of persons." (Acts 10:34-35.) It proved

to all men for all future history that "God hath put no difference between us"—Jews—"and them"—Gentiles. (Acts
15:7-9.) This was the purpose of Holy Ghost baptism and
the miraculous "tongues" on this occasion.

Holy Ghost baptism (in Acts 10) was God's way of confirming the truth that the gospel is for Gentiles, as well
as for Jews. Peter later said, "God . . . bare them witness,
giving them the Holy Ghost, even as he did unto us; and
put no difference between us and them, purifying their
hearts by faith." (Acts 15:8-9.)

### Holy Ghost Baptism Ceased

This was the last **recorded** case of Holy Spirit baptism
in the New Testament. It had to do with revealing and confirming New Testament truth. It finished fulfilling a part
of the prophecy of Joel (2:28-30) where "all flesh" included
Gentiles.

There was—and is—no more a need for another case of
Holy Ghost baptism. This was also another instance of
God's bearing witness to the apostles that their message
is true. "How shall we escape, if we neglect so great salvation; which at the first began to be spoken by the Lord "—
in the great commission, Mark 16:15-16 —"and was confirmed unto us by them that heard him; God also bearing
them witness, both with signs and wonders, and with divers miracles, and gifts of the Holy Ghost, according to his
own will?" (Heb. 2:3-4.)

### Was Paul Baptized With The Spirit?

While the record does not **say** that the apostle Paul was
also baptized with the Holy Spirit, it does seem that he
was. He certainly needed all the miraculous powers received by the other apostles. (Luke 24:48-49; Acts 1:5-8.)
Later Paul said, "For I suppose I was not a whit behind
the very chiefest apostles." (2 Cor. 11:5.) (I also "suppose"
he was not!) Again he said: "For in nothing am I behind
the very chiefest apostles." (2 Cor. 12:11.) Paul was inspired
(1 Cor. 2:11; 14:37) like the other apostles. He said of his
work, "Truly the signs of an apostle were wrought among
you in all patience, in signs, and  wonders,  and  mighty

deeds." (2 Cor. 12:12.) The "signs" of an apostle are mentioned in Mark 16:14-20. Not **one** of these alone, but **all** of
them, together, are "signs of an apostle." The church at
Ephesus "tried them which say they are apostles, and are
not, and hast found them liars." (Rev. 2:2.) Hence there
was a standard by which they could be tested or "tried."
"For such are false apostles, deceitful workers, transforming themselves into the apostles of Christ. And no marvel;
for Satan himself is transformed into an angel of light.
Therefore it is no great thing if his ministers also be transformed as the ministers of righteousness; whose end shall
be according to their works." (2 Cor. 11:13-15.) Here is the
certain doom of all men who claim to be in the class with
the apostles!

### "One Lord, One Faith, One Baptism"

When Paul wrote the Ephesians (A.D. 64) he said, "There
is . . . one Lord, one faith, one baptism." (Eph. 4:5.) This
"one baptism" is the baptism of the great commission.
(Matt. 28:18-20; Mark 16:15-16.) There are only two cases
which are "called" Holy Ghost **baptism** in the entire New
Testament. Even if Paul were baptized with the Holy Spirit, let it be remembered he was one of the apostles, wrote
nearly half the books of the New Testament, and "turned
the world upside down." (Acts 17:6.)

### There Are "Measures" Of The Spirit

"For he whom God hath sent speaketh the words of God:
for God giveth not the Spirit by measure unto him." (John
3:34.) It is implied in this statement that the Spirit is given
to some "by measure," or sparingly; but not so unto Christ.
The context shows this refers to Christ.

The baptism of the Spirit at the house of Cornelius (Acts
10) is identified by Peter as "the **like** gift" of the Spirit to
the gift received by the apostles on Pentecost. (Acts 11:17;
2:1-4; 1:5.) There is no reason to say it was the "like" gift
unless there were other gifts "**unlike**" it. If all stars were
exactly identical, one would not use superfluous words to
say a certain star was a "like" star to another.

The apostles on Pentecost were "all filled with the Holy

Ghost." (Acts 2:4.) Why say they were "filled"—unless one could have, or may have had, less?

The record says Stephen was "a man full of faith and of the Holy Ghost." (Acts 6:5.) Do all men have the same amount of **faith**? Stephen was "full of faith." Of course, there are degrees of **faith**. "Your faith groweth exceedingly." (2 Thess. 1:3.) Jesus said, "O ye of little faith." (Matt. 6:30.) Why not believe there are differing amounts of the **Spirit** to be possessed, when the record says "full of faith and of the Holy Ghost," (Acts 6:5)? This may refer to a non-miraculous measure of the Spirit in Stephen's case at that time, for this was before the apostles laid hands on him. (v. 6.)

### A Baptismal Measure

The word "baptism" refers to an act which requires "much water." (John 3:23.) Jesus refers to his suffering and death as a "baptism" of suffering. (Matt. 20:20-23.) (Surely no Christian thinks our Lord meant only a little 'sprinkling' of suffering awaited him!) Similarly, when Jesus said unto his apostles, "Ye shall be **baptized** with the Holy Ghost, not many days hence" (Acts 1:5), the very word "baptized" meant an overwhelming measure of the reception of the Spirit. He did not mean a little sprinkling of the Spirit.

### Classic Greek

In classical Greek literature, "BAPTIZO" (the Greek word for baptize) is used to describe one "baptized" in debt. This certainly refers to an overwhelming amount one might owe. We also read of one "baptized" (or drowned) with questions.

It is reckless to go to the New Testament and call every "gift" of the Spirit a "baptism" of the Spirit, and then conclude that we either have all the inspired apostles had, or else we do not have the Spirit at all. If all who receive the Spirit in any sense receive the same amount, or measure, of the Spirit, why did not the Bible writers uniformly say "the gift of the Holy Spirit"? Sometimes they said, "baptized with the Holy Ghost," "the gift of the Holy

Ghost," and the "like gift" of the Spirit. Hence there were different "measures" (John 3:34) of the Spirit given in the New Testament.

### Laying-On-Of-Hands Measure
Having spent all the time available in studying about the baptism of the Holy Spirit, let us now consider those cases where the Holy Spirit was bestowed by the laying on of the apostles' hands.

Let us remember that only Christ was the administrator of Holy Ghost baptism. (Matt. 3:11; John 1:33.) But there was a "measure" of the Spirit which the apostles could administer, and it also was a miraculous measure. But it is never called in the Bible the "baptism" of the Spirit.

### The Case of the Samaritans
The "Samaritans" were expressly excluded from the limited commission. (Matt. 10:5-7.) Of course, the great commission includes them. (Matt. 28:18-20; Mark 16:15-16.)

The evangelist Philip was one of the seven chosen to serve tables in the Jerusalem church. (Acts 6:1-5.) On him the apostles had laid their hands. (v. 6.) He "went down to the city of Samaria, and preached Christ unto them." (Acts 8:5.) Philip also confirmed his preaching by working miracles among them. (vs. 6-8.)

"But there was a certain man, called Simon, which beforetime in the same city used sorcery, and bewitched the people of Samaria, giving out that himself was some great one: to whom they all gave heed, from the least to the greatest, saying, This man is the great power of God. And to him they had regard, because that of long time he had bewitched them with sorceries." (Acts 8:9-11.)

Simon was a deceiver, and had never performed a genuine miracle of any sort. He, like thousands today, was a deceiver of the people. Simon "bewitched" the people "with sorceries." He made high-sounding claims, and they all "gave heed" to him, and said, "This man is the great power of God"—while in fact he was a child of the devil instead.

Such deceivers will no doubt curse the world as long as it stands. Some people prefer a high-sounding deception, rather than the plain truth. They will go off after false doctrines, grabbing at straws.

Simon, and all modern pretended "healers"—fake healers—remind us of Solomon's warning against all such: "Whoso boasteth himself of a false gift is like clouds and wind without rain." (Prov. 25:14.)

### But The Samaritans Were Converted

But be it said to the credit of the Samaritans, they could see the difference between the real "miracles" Philip did, and the pretentions of Simon. The Devil is a copy-cat! As sure as there is a genuine dollar, there is also counterfeit money. But we should know the difference! There are also counterfeit "miracles." Simon was a "counterfeiter."

"But when they believed Philip preaching the things concerning the kingdom of God, and the name of Jesus Christ, they were baptized, both men and women." (Acts 8:12.) They were then saved.   (Mark 16:16.)

However, you should note that the Samaritans were not converted by any sort of miraculous power of the Holy Spirit. Four verses later we read of the Holy Spirit that "as yet he was fallen upon none of them: only they were baptized in the name of the Lord Jesus." (v. 16.)

It follows therefore that one can become a believer without the Spirit "falling" upon him in any miraculous way. They had also been baptized, "both men and women." (v. 12.) So the sinner can become fit for baptism without the Spirit falling upon him to make him fit.

### Spirit By His Word

What had converted these people? what had made them believers? what gave them faith? what brought about their repentance, which is implied in the fact that they wanted to obey the Lord in baptism? It was the preaching of Philip. "It pleased God through the foolishness of preaching to save them that believe." (1 Cor. 1:21.) "Faith cometh by hearing, and hearing by the word of God." (Rom. 10:17.)

Sinners are not converted by a miracle. The miracles of healing, and such like, were miracles wrought on the sick (and others) to confirm the word. A miracle wrought on the body would not necessarily have anything to do with the salvation of one's soul. The Scriptures plainly say that the Spirit "as yet . . . was fallen upon none of them." (Acts 8:16), although they had been baptized. (v. 12.) Sinners are converted by the gospel (1 Cor. 15:1-4), not by the Spirit falling on them. The Spirit converts by his word, not by falling on the sinner. "The law of the Lord is perfect, converting the soul." (Ps. 19:7.) The **gospel**, preached "by the Holy Ghost sent down from heaven" (1 Pet. 1:12) on Pentecost, is now "the power of God unto salvation." (Rom. 1:16.)

But Simon also was converted! Deceivers, and the deceived, alike, can be converted by the true gospel. The gospel is for sinners—all of them. "Then Simon himself believed also: and when he was baptized, he continued with Philip, and wondered, beholding the miracles and signs which were done." (Acts 8:13.) He was then saved (Mark 16:16), just as the Samaritans who had done the same thing. (Acts 8:12.)

### Spirit By Laying On Of Apostles' Hands
Although Philip worked miracles among the Samaritans, and preached the gospel to them, causing them to believe and be baptized (Acts 8:5-13), **he could not lay hands on them and give them the miraculous power of the Holy Spirit.** Only the apostles could do that.

### By Apostles
"Now when the apostles which were at Jerusalem heard that Samaria had received the word of God, they sent unto them Peter and John"—two **apostles**—"who, when they were come down, prayed for them, that they might receive the Holy Ghost"—the miraculous measure—"For as yet he was fallen upon none of them: only they were baptized in the name of the Lord Jesus. **Then laid they**"—the apostles, Peter and John—"**their hands on them, and they received the Holy Ghost.** And when Simon saw"—it was a visible miracle, one that could be seen—"that **through lay-**

**ing on of the apostles' hands the Holy Ghost was given,** he offered them money, saying, Give me also this power, that on whomsoever I lay hands, he may receive the Holy Ghost. But Peter said unto him, Thy money perish with thee, because thou hast thought that the gift of God may be purchased with money. Thou hast neither part nor lot in this matter: for thy heart is not right in the sight of God. Repent therefore of this thy wickedness, and pray God, if perhaps the thought of thine heart may be forgiven thee. For I perceive that thou art in the gall of bitterness, and in the bond of iniquity." (Acts 8:14-23.)

### Apostles' Hands

Note that "through laying on of the **apostles'** hands the Holy Ghost was given." (v. 18.) It was so miraculous that Simon "saw" this. He could see that it was done, and "how" it was done—that it was through the "laying on of the apostles' hands." After the apostles had laid their hands on Philip (Acts 6:5-6), he could work miracles; but he could not himself pass this power on to anyone else by the laying on of **his** hands—for only an apostle could do this. It is obvious, then, that when all the apostles died, and all died on whom they had laid hands, this miraculous "measure" or "gift" of the Spirit ceased. But by the close of the first century they had the complete New Testament written and confirmed by miracles, and this "laying-on-of-hands" measure ceased.

### The Twelve At Ephesus

Paul baptized about twelve disciples at Ephesus, then the record says, "And when Paul had laid his hands upon them, the Holy Ghost came on them; and they spake with tongues, and prophesied." (Acts 19:6.) Here are two miraculous gifts of the Spirit bestowed by the laying on of the apostle Paul's hands: (1) "They spake with tongues," and (2) "prophesied."

These are two of the nine "gifts of the Spirit" mentioned in 1 Cor. 12:1-11. We have just seen that such gifts were bestowed by the "laying on of the apostles' hands." (Acts 8:18; 19:6.)

### Nine Miraculous Gifts Of The Spirit
### By Laying On Of Apostles' Hands

We have showed that the apostles were miraculously endowed with spiritual gifts by the baptism of the Holy
Spirit. But they were only twelve in number, and could
not be in thousands of places all over the world at the
same time, and there was miraculous work needing to be
done for which they themselves would not have the time
and opportunity necessary to do all that was needed.
Hence, the apostles had power to lay hands on others and
give them some spiritual gifts. (Acts 8:18; 19:6; Rom. 1:11;
2 Tim. 1:5-6; Acts 6:6-8.) There were nine of these gifts. (1
Cor. 12:1, 8-10.) They were: (1) "For to one is given, by the
Spirit, the word of wisdom; (2) to another the word of
knowledge by the same Spirit; (3) to another faith (miraculous) by the same Spirit; (4) to another the gifts of healing by the same Spirit; (5) to another the working of miracles; (6) to another prophecy; (7) to another discerning of
spirits; (8) to another divers kinds of tongues; (9) to another
the interpretation of tongues." Let us consider the importance of these gifts at that time, and before any of the New
Testament was written or committed to record.

1. WORD OF WISDOM. 1 Cor. 12:8-10. After the infant
church grew and was greatly enlarged, they needed more
and more men who could speak words of wisdom in the
church, and help to solve the problems that would arise.

2. WORD OF KNOWLEDGE. 1 Cor. 12:8-10. There was
also a great need for men who could speak the truth, and
present gospel facts accurately, as revealed by the apostles,
until the New Testament could be written.

3. MIRACULOUS FAITH. 1 Cor. 12:8-10. So much of this
faith as a grain of mustard seed would enable one to move
mountains. (1 Cor. 13:2.) This was not the common faith
which comes by hearing the word. (Rom. 10:17; Titus 1:4.)
The Corinthians already had gospel faith, and this miraculous faith was not for all, but just as is stated: "To another
faith." (1 Cor. 12:9.) No one of them had all nine of these
gifts. Miraculous faith has now served the divine purpose

for it and ceased, and we have the faith of the gospel. (Phil. 1:27; Jude 3; 1 Cor. 16:13; 2 Cor. 13:5-6.)

**4. GIFTS OF HEALING. 1 Cor. 12:8-10.** They had some in the church who could miraculously heal the sick. Later, we learn that some elders were thus endowed. (Jas. 5:14-15.) This was miraculous healing, and not such healing as now takes place in answer to prayer where the time element must be considered, as God, by means, heals, when death might have come without our prayers. Let us remember that Jesus says the sick need a physician. (Luke 5:31.) And in the days of these very gifts, Luke was a physician, even "the beloved physician." (Col. 4:14.) Paul prescribed a physical remedy for Timothy when he was sick, and the water at Ephesus was not pure. (1 Tim. 5:23.) Even the great apostle Paul who was not lacking in any gift, left Trophimus at Miletum sick. (2 Tim. 4:20.) Miraculous healing would take place only when the word would thereby be confirmed. (Mark 16:20; Heb. 2:3-4.) One of my friends in debate with me boasted that he belonged to a healing church. I informed him that he only belonged to a pretending church, whereas the apostles belonged to a dead-raising church. They were told to: "Heal the sick, cleanse the leppers, RAISE THE DEAD, cast out devils." (Matt. 10:8.) And they did raise the dead, even after the church was established. (Acts 9; Acts 20.) Men have no such power as this today, for all miraculous gifts of the Spirit have passed away, having accomplished God's purpose for them. Of course, we still have false teachers today who remind us of Prov. 25:14 which says, "Whoso boasteth himself of a false gift is like clouds and wind without rain." We still have those like Simon the sorcerer, who "used sorcery, and bewitched the people of Samaria, giving out that he himself was some great one; to whom they all gave heed, from the least to the greatest, saying, This man is the great power of God. And to him they had regard, because that of long time he had bewitched them with sorceries." (Acts 8:9-11.) We have such deceivers today, and some of them make fortunes off the poor and diseased of earth by means of their TV programs. Not one of them could miraculously and instantly heal a briar-scratch on the most faithful member they have. The apostles could raise the dead as easily as they could heal the sick. (Matt. 10:8; Acts 5:15-16.) The apostles had no failures. They "healed every one."

**5. WORKING OF MIRACLES. 1 Cor. 12:8-10.** Christ could still the raging storm with his word, walk upon the waters, turn water into wine, strike the barren fig tree with death by his marvelous power, and raise Lazarus, etc. (John 11.) His apostles could do the works he did. (John 14:12; Mark 16:14-20.) They were called "the signs of an apostle." (2 Cor. 12:12.) Modern apostles are called "liars" and "false apostles." (Rev. 2:1-2; 2 Cor. 11:13-15.) The apostles could lay hands on others and give them miraculous power. (Acts 19:6.) But when they died and all died that they had laid hands on, such gifts ceased. But by that time, the New Testament was written, or revealed and confirmed by miracles and signs, and such were no longer needed, but were like ladders and scaffolding used in the building of a house—laid aside when the building was fully erected and finished. When the church was fully established, and all truth revealed and committed to record about the close of the first century, A. D., then the miraculous passed away. But during the writing of the New Testament, such helps and proofs of the truth were needed.

**6. TO ANOTHER PROPHECY. 1 Cor. 12:8-10.** The apostle could lay hands on disciples and enable them to prophesy. (Acts 19:6.) New Testament prophets were inspired, along with the apostles. (Eph. 3:2-6; 4:8, 11-16.) Mark, Luke, Stephen, and Phillip were, no doubt, among the New Testament prophets. But the time was to come when the perfect New Testament would come into existence and prophets would fail from the church, as no longer needed. (1 Cor. 13:8-13.)

**7. DISCERNING OF SPIRITS. 1 Cor. 12:8-10.** Acts 5:1-14 gives an example of how Peter could discern that Ananias and Sapphira were lying. In those days they could not try lying teachers by the New Testament, for it was not at first written, and so they needed those who could discern spirits, or teachers claiming inspiration. Now, we are to try them by the written word. (1 John 4:1-6; Isa. 8:20; 2 Tim. 3:5-17.)

**8. DIVERS KINDS OF TONGUES. 1 Cor. 12:8-10.** When Christ commissioned his apostles to go into all the world and preach the gospel to every creature, they could not, without divine help, carry out the commission received. The nations and peoples of the world did not all speak the same language. So Christ promised them that they would "speak with new tongues." (Mark 16:15-20.) The Lord did not want to wait forty or fifty years after Pentecost till the New Testament could be written, and have it translated into all languages before getting the gospel started to all nations in their own languages. The barrier in the way was overcome by the baptism of the Holy Spirit enabling the apostles to speak in other tongues or languages. (Acts 2:1-11.) Then the apostles could lay hands on others and enable them to speak with tongues. (Acts 19:6; Acts 8:18.) This would enable them to teach foreigners who might come into their assemblies. (1 Cor. 14.) And if a foreign gospel teacher came into an assembly, they could use him, for they had interpreters.

**9. INTERPRETATION OF TONGUES. 1 Cor. 12:8-10.** Not only would the gift of tongues, and the interpretation of tongues be of great service in the congregation, as we have suggested, but such gifts would prove to all unbelieving men and sinners that God was back of the truth being taught. (1 Cor. 14:21-25.) Furthermore, if a brother who was a foreigner came into an assembly and they knew not his language, and if there was no interpreter he had to hold his peace, and speak to himself and to God only—he was not to be permitted to address the audience. (1 Cor. 14:26-28.) And this would be equally true of one having the gift of tongues. Now, all religious teachers alike in going to some foreign country of another language have to study the language, or use a natural interpreter. I preached to the Hebrews in Jerusalem, but Brother Ralph Henley had to interpret for me, for he knew their language. No one can do anything now but speak his own known language or languages. Those who claim to speak in other tongues today by the power of God, do nothing but jabber. I heard one of them saying "Glory, glory, glory," and finally he started muttering "Glo, glo, glo, glo." Those deceived by him said, "Now he is talking in tongues." But he was not, he was only trying to say "glory" without saying it, and was deceiving himself and "the hearts of the simple." (Rom. 16:17-18.)

Brother Joe S. Warlick published in his paper, the Gospel Guide, an instance of such deception. One of such preachers arose and claimed to speak in a tongue, and had another to interpret. Then a gospel preacher arose and started quoting John 3:5 in the Bulgarian language, and asked them to interpret for him. They gave some strange and wild ideas about what he said. Then he rebuked them sharply for their trickery and told them he had quoted from the Bulgarian translation of the Bible, John 3:5.

### "Spiritual Gifts" Have Ceased

There are no living apostles to lay hands on men and give them "spiritual gifts." Paul said such gifts would "fail . . . cease . . . vanish away . . . be done away—when that which is perfect is come." (1 Cor. 13:8-13.) We have the perfect law of liberty. (Jas. 1:21-25.) The New Testament, which was given a book at a time, was finally completed, or perfected, or became a perfect revelation, and "then" that which was "in part" was "done away." By that time the Spirit had guided inspired men "into all truth"—the complete New Testament truth—all truth the world will ever need—as Jesus promised would take place by the time the last apostle died. (John 16:13.)

### These Three—Abide

After saying spiritual gifts would be done away when revelation was complete, the apostle said, faith, hope and charity, or love, would "abide." (1 Cor. 13:8-13.) Neither one of the three is miraculous, but they are enough to save the souls of men. He did not say miracles abide.

### Let Us Remember

The work of revealing and confirming Christianity has been finished for nearly nineteen hundred years, and the ladders and scaffolding needed in its revelation and con-

firmation are removed—no longer needed. All things originated in miracle, and are carried on by divine law. The
first man originated in miracle, but God is not making men
that way today. Christ was born of a virgin, rose from the
dead, baptized the apostles in the Holy Spirit, but he is not
doing these things over and over today.

### Great Need For It

In the early church they had no part of the written New
Testament for several years after the church was established on Pentecost day. (Acts 2.) They not only had no
written copies of the new covenant, but also had no record
of miracles, which was needed to confirm the oral teaching
and preaching of the gospel.

They also needed more and more teachers; hence by the
laying on of the apostles' hands some would be able to
"prophesy" or teach. (1 Cor. 12:10; Acts 19:6.) These prophets were also inspired. (Eph. 3:2-6.) This was needed in the
infant church to safeguard the correctness of doctrine. Also
a great effort was made to train uninspired teachers (Acts
2:42; 2 Tim. 2:2) in anticipation of the time when these miraculous gifts would cease.

### To Establish the Cause

Paul wrote to the Romans, "I long to see you, that I may
impart unto you some spiritual gift, to the end ye may be
established." (Rom. 1:11.) This "spiritual gift" was not
something which the apostle could send in his Roman epis-
tle. He would have to "see" them, for (as we have seen)
these spiritual gifts were bestowed by the "laying on of
the apostles' hands." (Acts 8:18; 19:6.)

### Paul Imparted Some Gift To Timothy

To Timothy Paul said, "Stir up the gift of God, which
is in thee by the putting on of my hands." (2 Tim. 1:6.) The
eldership also laid hands on Timothy, probably to
formally set him apart to mission work: "Neglect not the
gift that is in thee, which was given thee by prophecy,
with"—not "by"—"the laying on of the hands of the pres-
bytery." (1 Tim. 4:14.) But the "gift of God" was in Timothy "by" the laying on of Paul's hands—an **apostle's** hands!

### Formal "Laying-on-of-Hands"

Hands of certain brethren were laid on Paul and Barnabas (Acts 13:1-4) to set them apart to their first missionary journey. But this was not to give them the Holy Spirit, for both Paul (2 Cor. 11:5; 12:11) and Barnabas (Acts 11:24) were already "full" of the Holy Spirit. This laying-on-of-hands was a method of setting them apart to their work. (Acts 13:2.) Men like Philip could not bestow the gift of the Spirit by laying on of hands. (Acts 8:5-18.) Apostles alone could do that.

### Miracles Were To Cease

Paul wrote, "Whether there be prophecies, they shall fail; whether there be tongues, they shall cease; whether there be knowledge, it shall vanish away. For we know in part, and we prophesy in part. But when that which is perfect is come, then that which is in part shall be done away." (1 Cor. 13:8-10.) Of the nine "gifts" of the Spirit listed in the previous chapter (12:4-11), some are mentioned here as examples of spiritual gifts; and they were to "fail," "cease," "vanish away," and "be done away"—all **"when that which is perfect is come,"** when the "perfect" (or complete) revelation is culminated in the written New Testament or gospel of Christ. Remember that it required nearly fifty years to get all the New Testament in writing, for it was given in installments, as it were.

But "that which is perfect"—the finished revelation—came into existence by the close of the first century. **"Then"**—not two thousand years later—but **"then** that which is in part"—the segments or portions of the whole (or complete) revelation—"then that which is in part shall be done away." (1 Cor. 13:10.)

This occurred about the same time the other scriptures have logically pointed us to—when the apostles, and all they had laid hands on, died. From either point of view, miracles ceased after the days of the apostles.

### Purpose Of Such Gifts Fulfilled

Paul says such gifts were, "for the perfecting of the saints, unto the work of the ministry, unto the edifying of the body of Christ: till we all come in the unity of the faith, and of the knowledge of the Son of God, unto a perfect man, unto the measure of the stature of the  fulness  of Christ: That we henceforth be no more children, tossed to and fro, and carried about with every wind of doctrine, by the sleight of men, and cunning craftiness, whereby they lie in wait to deceive; but speaking the truth in love, may grow up into him in all things, which is the head, even Christ." (Eph. 4:12-15.)

### Last Till

"The unity of the faith" (v. 13) is the complete revelation of the faith for which we are to "earnestly contend." (Jude 3; 1 Cor. 16:13; 2 Cor. 13:5.) It is the "faith of the gospel." (Phil. 1:27.) The miraculously-endowed teachers and "gifts" were to last "till"—yes, **"till"** the "part" of the faith not then revealed would be given and united with the "part" already written. These gifts were to last only "till" that time. (v. 13.)

### Till Completed New Testament

Paul further says these gifts were to last **"till** we all come in the unity . . . of the knowledge of the Son of God." (v. 13.) This (like the other) refers to the time all "knowledge" which would ever be given from the Son of God would be revealed. This was when the New Testament was finished.

He also says these things were to continue **"till**  we  all come . . . unto a perfect man." (v. 13.) The church then was in its infancy, and was called "one **new** man." (Eph. 2:14-16.) When the New Testament was all revealed and confirmed, the church had matured, or become a "perfect" (full-grown) man.

### Time Fulfilled

Remember, by the time the last apostle died, man had received **all** truth—a complete or "perfect" revelation. The Spirit guided the apostles "into all truth." (John 16:13.)

As revelation increased, miracles decreased. When all the apostles died, and all died on whom they had laid their hands, these gifts naturally ceased. But we lost nothing:

the message which was first in the **inspired man**, is now in the **inspired Book**—the written New Testament. The miracles which they witnessed are written that we might believe. (John 20:30-31.)

Remember that each of the Bible dispensations—the Patriarchal Age, the Jewish Age, and the Christian Age—began in great miracles—and, that God has always purposed to keep the miraculous at a minimum, and to respect his own laws, natural and spiritual, so we will honor them.

Please remember that everything began in miracle, but is perpetuated by the non-miraculous. The first crops were not from seed; the first oak was never an acorn; the first man and woman were never babies. But God did not keep on making people of the dust of the ground, as he did Adam. He did not keep on miraculously creating vegetables, as he did the first. If God were to begin now to inspire men, as he did the apostles, the Bible would soon be discarded. Man would rather be inspired than to study; but study is best for man. Sinners would rather be converted miraculously, than to learn and obey the truth. Man would rather pray and get well instantly, than to discipline himself and obey the laws of nature, seeking to discover remedies, and let God's will be done.

### Ladders And Scaffolding Not Needed

The "house" of God has been built. (1 Pet. 2:5.) On the divine side, it has been finished. We have all divine truth—religious truth—which we shall ever need in this world. When a building is finished, we remove the ladders and scaffolding. Who would want Christ to come back and be born of a virgin again, just because he once did it? Who would want him to be crucified again, and be put to an open shame a second time? Who would contend for new apostles now? Who wants to renew the miracles of the New Testament period, which had to do with the **establishment of** Christianity, and have served their purpose, and passed away, as God said they would? **Who would want God to continue in the future to do all he has ever done?**

Christianity in all its grandeur and beauty remains. The

gospel plan of salvation remains. The New Testament church remains. The worship remains. Prayer remains. God and Christ are the same. Heaven remains. Providence remains. God still answers prayer, and cares for us. But he does not raise the dead today, nor do any other miracles today.

Holy Spirit baptism (Acts 2 and 10) has served its purpose, and has ceased. The miraculous measure of the Spirit, imparted by the laying on of the apostles' hands, has served its purpose, and has ceased. But the ordinary "gift of the Holy Ghost" (Acts 2:38) remains, and will be our study at another night. Suffice it now to say that this measure of the Spirit is for all who will "repent, and be baptized" in Jesus' name "for the remission of sins," for Peter promised: "and ye shall receive the gift of the Holy Ghost." (Acts 2:38.)

## QUESTIONS AND ANSWERS

**Question:** What is meant by the phrase, "The Spirit does not operate separate and apart from the word of God" and "only through the word of God upon the sinner, or upon the children of God?"

**Answer:** It doesn't seem to me that the statement needs any further explanation. It is explained in the statement. A farmer produces his crop through seed, not separate and apart from seed. If a farmer produces his crop through seed, he does not produce the crop separate and apart from seed, by detouring around seed. That's as simple as can be, it seems to me. And yet the Bible says, "The seed is the word of God." (Luke 8:11.) And it says, "The sower soweth the word." (Mark 4:14.) "If anyone heareth the word of the kingdom." (Matthew 13:19.) "Receive with meekness the engrafted"—the ASV says 'implanted'—"word which is able to save your soul." (Jas. 1:21.) Now, if the word is able to do it like seed is able to produce a crop, then we can't produce a crop without seed. Now if you think you can, you just get out here and try it sometime. Some of you city folks try to produce a wheat crop without using wheat seed. You will be showing disregard for God's law. When

God made the first vegetable creation, it wasn't produced from seed. But it bore seed. And then, those seed are necessary for reproduction. A man who wants to produce an oak tree and plants an acorn, has a  thousand-fold  more faith in God, than the fellow who will get out here and pray for God to give the tree separate and apart from an acorn.

Every idea which God Almighty reveals for the human race is in the seed, the word of God. He does not want us to believe anything except what he has said to  us,  and taught us. (Rom. 10:17.) And to preach that word is to sow that seed. If in the last hundred years, every preacher had preached nothing but the word of God, we would have no religious product except Christians. There wouldn't be a denomination on earth. You can't find denominations and factions, in the word of God approved. They are  not  a product of the seed. They are a product of human creeds, and human wisdom, and man's ideas, and man's imaginary revelation and human books of guidance and the like.

**Question:** Can God or Christ or the Holy Spirit help a Christian any other way than through the word?

**Answer:** Yes, but he doesn't work any miracle upon us in doing it. It's not miraculous. There is no miraculous revelation through any Christian and there is no miraculous something done to us. It's all done through the word of God, and through worship and service to God. Christian growth and development come  through the word. "Desire the sincere milk of the word that ye may grow **thereby**." (1 Pet. 2:2.) It is not by something else that is imaginary and yet miraculous and directly given. Every effort made to try to defend some other sort of revelation other than through God's word is just some sort of atheism and infidelity. It is just advertising unbelief in the all-sufficiency of the word of God as a revelation from God. (2 Tim. 3:16-17.)

**Question:** When the Christian prays for wisdom, James 1:5, how does the Godhead help in supplying this wisdom?

**Answer:** In the first place, James 1:5 says, "If any of you LACK WISDOM." That's not knowledge, but wisdom. Wisdom is the skill and ability to properly use the tools of knowledge. Information is the tools, and we need to know how to use the tools. Just like a surgeon needs to know how and when to operate. That would be skill and wisdom and is given of God through experience and observation. Elders of the church need to WISELY govern and guide the church. First of all, people would have to have a great deal of wisdom before they should be chosen for service. We read in Acts 6, "Look ye out seven men full of the Holy Ghost and WISDOM." (v. 1-7.) They could have already had wisdom without the apostles' hands being laid upon them, because wisdom comes through observation and experience and wisely considering all the facts and trying to exercise and use mature, well-balanced judgment.

Yes, God helps us, but there is no miracle wrought on us. If so, a man who is silly and ridiculous in judgment and has no wisdom, would have to do nothing but just pray for wisdom and then he would be suddenly a great wise man. Why it is not so. That is not the way it's done. THERE IS NO MIRACLE CONNECTED WITH IT. (Jas. 1:5-7.) What God does for us in living the Christian life involves no miracles on us. It's not a miraculous operation upon us.

Providence is not a present miracle. God's present operations are not upon man in a miraculous way.

**Question:** Do you think Romans 8 implies the Holy Spirit helps in providence? (Romans 8:26-28.) Does God provide only through the word?

**Answer:** The Holy Spirit helps, but how does he help? Does he help by working for us in some miraculous way? The passage says that he helps our infirmities by making intercession for us to God. Notice, he is interceding to God up in heaven. "Maketh intercession" to God. (Romans 8:25, 27.) And so up in heaven he is working with God for us. And still again, I say I don't see how in the world any man can get the idea here the Spirit is operating

ON US in some miraculous way, like he inspired the apostles. (1 Cor. 2:13.)

**Question:** Should we pray to God to give a preacher a "ready recollection?" Is this providential, miraculous, or what?

**Answer:** That's all borrowed from the Apostles in John 14, where Jesus promised them that the Spirit would inspire them to reveal Christianity, to reveal the Gospel. He said, "He shall bring to your remembrance all things whatsoever I have said unto you." (John 14:26.) Jesus did not want them to go out and preach without knowing exactly what he had taught, without any perversion whatsoever. He would not let them preach until they had received that power.

In Luke 24:48, he said, "Ye are witnesses of these things." And then in v. 49, "Tarry ye in the city of Jerusalem until ye be endued with power from on high." It is error for a man to claim that same power tonight, when he is not even an apostle, not in the same class they were, when the world is not in the same condition. (Acts 1:8.) They had no New Testament at that time, not a line of it. And I say again, it is a pity for people to reason in circles and ignore the facts that make the difference.

**Question:** When did Paul receive the power to convey the miraculous power of the Holy Spirit by the laying on of hands?

**Answer:** The Bible doesn't tell us exactly when he received it. The gift of the Holy Spirit was received when he was baptized. Peter said, "Repent, and be baptized, everyone of you in the name of Jesus Christ for the remission of sins, and ye shall receive the gift of the Holy Ghost." (Acts 2:38.) One might have the ordinary gift of the Holy Spirit without having miraculous power. Take for instance, the Ephesians, in chapter one, verse 13: "After ye believed, ye were sealed with the Holy Spirit of promise." They had the Holy Spirit. (1:13.) Then in 4:30, "Grieve not the Spirit of God whereby ye have been sealed until the day of redemption." So they had been sealed by the Holy Spirit. But in the next chapter (5:18-19) he said, "Be filled with the Spirit." That does not mean they did not have the Spirit at all. And so one could have the ordinary gift of the Holy Spirit, and be sealed by it, and still not have the Spirit in another sense.

Verse 18 is not miraculous power considered. "Be not drunk with wine wherein is excess." The heathen in their Bacchanalian feasts would drink wine, strong drink, and get intoxicated and then dance in a drunken fashion round about their idols. Paul said, "Don't get your excitement and religious enthusiasm from strong drink like that, but you be "FILLED WITH THE SPIRIT." In other words, drink in great draughts of the Holy Spirit. But that is the subject for tomorrow night, and I will further discuss those things at the appropriate time then. The Spirit by his word in us gets us excited about our religion.

**Question:** How can we be certain that the Holy Spirit given to the Samaritans by Peter and John was not the one promised in Acts 2:38. The one baptized is promised the Holy Spirit, but not told how soon it would come after baptism.

**Answer:** Of the laying on of hands, it does tell how soon. "When Paul had laid his hands upon them, the Holy Ghost came on them; and they SPAKE WITH TONGUES AND PROPHESIED." (Acts 19:6.)

And in Acts 2:38, that belongs to tomorrow night, but I'll answer it now. There is no statement indicating they received miraculous power in Acts 2:38. It just says, "Repent, and be baptized every one of you in the name of Jesus Christ for the remission of sins and ye shall receive the gift of the Holy Ghost." And there is not a word about their receiving any miraculous power. These are the people who obeyed the gospel and became Christians after the apostles had preached the gospel on that occasion. Not a word about their performing any miracles.

But Acts 2:43, that same chapter, says, "Many signs and

wonders were done by the apostles,"—and all those who had repented and been baptized and received remission of sins and the gift of the Holy Ghost? No. A thousand times no—as if they were all in the same class. Some people scramble religion like vegetable soup. The first year or so, the **apostles only** wrought miracles. (Acts 5:12.)

**Question:** How many men had miraculous power by the laying on of hands?

**Answer:** I don't know, but there is no proof that all Christians had apostles' hands laid on them. (Rom. 1:11.) Yet all Christians had the Holy Spirit. (Rom. 8:6-12.)

**Question:** Explain apostle and disciple.

**Answer:** The word disciple means "learner" and the word apostle means "one sent." The apostles were disciples, but not all disciples were apostles. The sheriff is a citizen, but not all citizens are sheriffs.

**Question:** You quoted a passage naming nine miraculous, special gifts. One of them was "miracles." (1 Cor. 12:8-11.) Some one said this word could have been interpreted, "inworking of miracles." That is, that those not apostles could impart miraculous gifts by laying on of hands, as the apostles did. Please explain. If this were true, there could be a continuation of miracles.

**Answer:** Can you do this? Who can? Only Mormons claim to do this. Not a word of proof for it in the New Testament! The interpretation is fantastic. Acts 8:18 says, "Through the laying on of the APOSTLES' hands the Holy Ghost was given." Just any one could not do this. (Rom. 1:11.)

**Question:** Last night you stated that the Holy Spirit has never appeared in the form of angels because angels are created beings. But he, the Holy Spirit, is eternal. The Father and Son are eternal beings. Does either or both of these appear in the form of an angel at any time. What about Gen. 18? Exo. 3?

**Answer:** I have already explained Gen. 18, and Heb. 13:1, last night. The Holy Spirit and Angels are not identical.

There are many angels, but "one Spirit." (Eph. 4:4.)

**Question:** You said Tuesday (using 1 Pet. 1:10-12), that the Holy Spirit was the one that revealed the prophecy in the words of the Old Testament. Would you explain who the person is, if possible, who appeared to Manoah and his wife, Judges 13:2-20, and told them of the future. Is this the Holy Spirit? If not, couldn't you somehow amend your lesson of Tuesday night?

**Answer:** The Bible says it was an angel of God. Why not be satisfied with that? Why quibble? There is only "one Spirit." (Eph. 4:4.) But, there are many angels as all know. They are not identical, and God may speak by an angel as in Judges 13.

**Question:** Would it be wrong to think, or to consider the possibilities, of having a very early lesson about the Godhead being three, presented to us in Gen. 18:1-19, 29. Several of these verses seem to state that the three are God. In Gen. 13:3, Abraham said, "My Lord" and in v. 9, they spoke together, and in chapter 19:12, Lot bowed to the two and called them Lord, and in 19:9, one is called a judge, and in 19:13, he said, "We will destroy," and in 19:29, God is described as bringing out Lot and destroying the city, yet the account says the two did it. If this reasoning is wrong, please explain why.

**Answer:** The Holy Spirit is not actually an angel. I quoted last night Heb. 13:1, that it was an angel. It says: "Be not forgetful to entertain strangers, for thereby some have entertained angels unawares." Your interpretation is speculative and far-fetched. We need to stay with the plain passages of the Trinity, such as Mt. 28:19. God often spake by angels. (Acts 7:30-40.) But God is not an angel. The Holy Spirit may have spoken by angels, but the Spirit is not an angel. Angels were spirits, but the Holy Spirit is not an angel. Paul says, "There is one Spirit." (Eph. 4:4.) Was there just one angel? No, but many angels. (Heb. 1:13-14.)

Let us stay with things revealed. (Deut. 29:29.)

# INDWELLING OF THE SPIRIT

Let us prayerfully study the subject of "The Indwelling of the Holy Spirit." In the outset we must confess that there are various and conflicting opinions, even among brethren, concerning this subject. Whatever the Bible teaches on the subject is not contradictory. We should all be certain that we teach only what God says about the Holy Spirit and his work, as well as upon all other Bible topics and doctrines.

All positions should be charitably viewed on most controversial religious subjects. Especially should this be true concerning the "Indwelling of the Holy Spirit" in the Christian.

The Holy Spirit either (1) really and truly dwells in us—faithful Christians—in a **personal manner**, or (2) he dwells in us in some **other manner**, or (3) else he **does not dwell in us at all**. This latter position would force one to make void many plain and easily-understood scriptures; so we dismiss it at once, and turn our attention to the first two views.

## No Need Of Strife

I see no reason for disturbance among us over this question so long as all believe and teach that the Holy Spirit **does** dwell in faithful and obedient children of God in some way. The honest but misguided interpretations which may be made in trying to show how the Spirit dwells in us should not, by those on either side, disrupt brotherly love and unity, and ravage our brotherhood. There are many reasons why one's position as to how the Holy Spirit dwells in us should never be made a test of fellowship. The only reason which needs to be stated now is, that to all who obey the gospel from the heart, the promise will be fulfilled as God planned it, whether or not we understand "how" the Spirit dwells in us.

## Consider Our Spirit

We believe and teach that each man has a soul or spirit in his body. Without understanding much about it, we accept by faith the fact—and the Bible doctrine—of the human spirit. Certainly such understanding is not essential to the **possession** of a soul or spirit. Well do I remember when I learned—I must have been four or five years old —that I have a soul. I had not read such Scriptures as Matt. 10:28; 16:26; Mic. 6:7; Dan. 7:15; Jas. 1:21; 1 Pet. 3:1-4; Acts 7:59; Rev. 6:9-11; 2 Cor. 4:16-18; 5:6, 8; Eccl. 12:7; and Heb. 12:9.

I have been preaching the gospel for fifty years, and I still do not claim to fully comprehend the glorious doctrine of the human soul, or spirit. I could not prove that I have a soul or spirit in any way other than by the Bible. I can not prove it by my feelings, for my spirit does not dwell in me in any miraculous manner. I have the word of God for the fact of it, and that is good enough for me. So far as I know a heathen might hear and obey the gospel and be saved, before ever hearing that he has a soul. **Our ignorance of the human spirit does not exclude us from having a spirit.** This matter is over on the divine side, and God will look after the mysteries connected therewith.

Factious men could cause strife and division over almost anything, or nothing, if permitted to do so. Free and full discussion should be had by sincere men on all matters thought to merit discussion. Of course, there are certain errors which are more dangerous than others.

## Things Not Revealed

"The secret things belong unto the Lord our God: but those things which are revealed belong unto us and to our children." (Deut. 29:29.) There are some things which God has not revealed, and we should be content with revealed things. We should leave all else to Him who doeth all things well.

### Does The Holy Spirit Dwell In Us?

"Then. Peter said unto them, Repent, and be baptized every one of you in the name of Jesus Christ for the remission of sins, and ye shall receive the gift of the Holy Ghost." (Acts 2:38.)

"And we are his witnesses of these things; and so is also the Holy Ghost, whom God hath given to them that obey him." (Acts 5:32.)

"But ye are not in the flesh, but in the Spirit, if so be that the Spirit of God dwell in you. Now if any man have not the Spirit of Christ, he is none of his. And if Christ be in you, the body is dead because of sin; but the Spirit is life because of righteousness. But if the Spirit of him that raised up Jesus from the dead dwell in you, he that raised up Christ from the dead shall also quicken your mortal bodies by his Spirit that dwelleth in you." (Rom. 8:9-11.)

"Know ye not that ye are the temple of God, and that the Spirit of God dwelleth in you?" (1 Cor. 3:16.)

"Know ye not that your body is the temple of the Holy Ghost which is in you, which ye have of God, and ye are not your own?" (1 Cor. 6:19.)

"He therefore that despiseth, despiseth not man, but God, who hath also given unto us his holy Spirit." (1 Thess. 4:8.)

"These be they who separate themselves, sensual, having not the Spirit." (Jude 19.)

"In whom ye also trusted, after that ye heard the word of truth, the gospel of your salvation; in whom also after that ye believed, ye were sealed with that holy Spirit of promise." (Eph. 1:13; cf. 4:30.)

These are a few of the scriptures which teach that we, as Christians, have the Holy Spirit dwelling in us. Upon this fact we should all be united, as we have been ever since I have been a member of the church. However, there are some who hold theories which logically would deny that the Holy Spirit now dwells in us at all, that is, in any real sense.

## A False Impression

Before we examine some of those theories, I relate a story told by a Mr. Scott, Ph.D., of Chattanooga, in our debate at Carbon Hill, Ala., many years ago. He said a foreigner came to America, met one of our gospel preachers, from whom he learned the truth. He was baptized, as was the Ethiopian, upon a simple confession of his faith in Christ, then went on his way rejoicing. (Acts 8:35-39.) Later he urged the preacher to go to his native country to teach and baptize his beloved parents—for he was confident that they, too, would be converted by the example of the Eunuch, if he would go teach them. The preacher could not go, but insisted that his new convert return home and teach his parents. The hopeful man returned, and read to them the story in Acts 8. Sure enough, they wanted to be baptized immediately. The son had never baptized anyone—in fact, he had never witnessed a baptizing except his own; he distrusted his ability, but fearfully agreed to baptize his parents, as they urged. In the water, he lifted his hand to say a few words, a sort of ceremony, stating that he was baptizing them "in the name of the Father, and of the Son, —" but forgot the other person in the Godhead! Finally, after much embarrassment, he said, "—Lord, I can't think of the name of the other one just now, but I'm sure it will make no difference, for he has not been on earth since Pentecost in the first century." Of course, this story misrepresented me and my understanding of the Holy Spirit and his work. I believe the Holy Spirit dwells in Christians today.

## Our Subject and Acts 2:38

Let us take Acts 2:38 for a text on the subject of the indwelling of the Holy Spirit. I shall examine some of the theories which I have heard and read in my fifty years as a preacher. Read carefully the text: "Then Peter said unto them, Repent, and be baptized every one of you in the name of Jesus Christ for the remission of sins, and ye shall receive the gift of the Holy Ghost." (Acts 2:38.)

### I. "Gift Is The Baptism Of The Holy Ghost"

Mr. C. J. Weaver (in the Nichols-Weaver Debate) contended that the "gift" of the Holy Ghost in Acts 2:38 is a promise of "Holy Ghost Baptism." He claimed Holy Ghost Baptism would bring a "second blessing" called "sanctification," and might be received years after baptism in water, or might never come, to one who is saved.

1. What Peter called the "gift of the Holy Ghost" was promised to all who would repent and be baptized for the remission of sins. It is not easy to see how this promise might not be fulfilled at all!

2. Another objection to this theory that the "gift" in Acts 2:38 is Holy Ghost baptism, is the fact that in A. D. 64 there was only "one baptism." That year Paul wrote, "There is . . . One Lord, one faith, one baptism." (Eph. 4:5.) The theory would have **two** baptisms in force ever since Pentecost. Peter promised the gift of the Holy Ghost **after** repentance, **baptism**, and the remission of sins. (Acts 2:38.) The "one baptism" is water baptism, as in the great commission. (1) It was to be performed by those doing the "going" and the "teaching." (Matt. 28:19.) But only Christ could baptize with the Holy Spirit. (Matt. 3:11; John 1:33-34.) (2) It was in the name of the Father, Son, and Holy Spirit. (Matt. 28:19.) This shows that the baptism of the great commission is water baptism, since Spirit baptism would not be in the name of the Spirit. (3) It was to continue "always, even unto the end of the world." (Matt. 28:19-20.) Since there was only "one baptism" (Eph. 4:5) in A. D. 64, and that was water baptism, it follows that Holy Ghost baptism had served its purpose of qualifying the apostles and confirming the word at the house of Cornelius, and ceased.

3. Again: **Holy Spirit baptism**, in every case called such in the divine record, was accompanied by speaking in foreign languages or tongues. (Acts 2:4; 10:44-46.) But there

was no speaking in tongues connected with receiving the "gift" of the Holy Spirit in Acts 2:38-41.

4. When the apostles were baptized with the Holy Spirit early on Pentecost, and before the multitude came together, they were inspired to preach the gospel "with the Holy Ghost sent down from heaven." (Acts 2:4; John 16:13; 1 Pet. 1:12.) But no such inspiration was bestowed on those baptized in obedience to Peter's sermon on Pentecost. (Acts 2:38.) They rather "continued . . . in the apostles' doctrine" or teaching. (v. 42.) This again shows they did not receive what the apostles did early that day.

5. Furthermore, nobody except the apostles is said to have performed any miracles following Pentecost for perhaps two years or more. "Many wonders and signs were done **by the apostles**." (Acts 2:43.) "With great power gave the **apostles** witness of the resurrection." (Acts 4:33.) Why does it not say, "And by those they baptized?" Again we read: "And by the hands of the **apostles** were many signs and wonders wrought among the people." (Acts 5:12.) Then it says, "And of the rest durst no man join himself to them." (v. 13.) No man among the disciples would dare claim to be in the class with the apostles, or join them, by claiming their miraculous powers. "But the people magnified them." (v. 13.) All this shows that those receiving the "gift" Peter promised were not "baptized" with the Holy Spirit, as were the apostles.

6. Some have contended that since the "baptism" of the Holy Spirit is called a "gift" (Acts 11:15-17; 10:45), and Peter promised the "gift of the Holy Ghost" (Acts 2:38), that therefore Peter promised the "baptism" of the Holy Ghost to those whom he commanded to be baptized in water. This is a very weak argument: one might as well argue that because a sprinkle of rain, and a cloud-burst of rain, are both gifts of rain—therefore a sprinkle is a cloud-burst or a downpour!

7. If Holy Spirit baptism is the only "gift" of the Spirit, and Holy Ghost baptism has ceased (as we just showed), then it follows that this theory of Acts 2:38 would leave no

gift of the Holy Ghost for any people this side of A. D. 64. (Eph. 4:5.) Is this where Mr. Scott got his story? I believe I have the "gift" promised in Acts 2:38, the "ordinary" gift of the Spirit.

## "Holy Spirit Baptism Is Part Of The New Birth"

I have met other modern 'Holiness' debaters who contended that the "gift of the Holy Ghost" is the "Baptism of the Holy Spirit," but that it is a part of the new birth— not a "second blessing"—and is necessary to the remission of sins.

However, Peter promised the "gift of the Holy Ghost" **after** remission of sins. He said, "Repent, and be baptized every one of you in the name of Jesus Christ for the remission of sins, and ye **shall receive** the gift of the Holy Ghost." (Acts 2:38.)

## II. "Laying-On-Of-Hands Measure"

Another theory is that Peter meant that if his audience would "repent, and be baptized . . . for the remission of sins" they would receive the "gift of the Spirit"—that is, the apostles would lay hands on them and bestow the Spirit on them, as in Acts 8:18; 19:5-6.

1. But according to this theory, Mr. Scott's story would be true, and the Spirit has not been on earth since the last apostle died, about the close of the first century! For it was "through the laying on of the apostles' hands the Holy Ghost was given" at Samaria. (Acts 8:12, 16, 18.) This was not the "baptism" of the Spirit, which only Christ could administer. (Matt. 3:11; John 1:33-34.) But the apostles had power to lay hands on some and bestow miraculous gifts of the Spirit. Paul "laid his hands on them, and they received the Holy Ghost, and spake with tongues and prophesied." (Acts 19:6.) This is the gift which would cease at the death of the apostles, and not the "ordinary" gift of Acts 2:38. There is not a word said on Pentecost, nor for two or three years afterward, about the apostles' laying hands on any to bestow upon them the miraculous gift of the Spirit. (Acts 6:6 is the first recorded instance.)

2. Again: the laying-on-of-hands measure of the Spirit be-

stowed miraculous gifts. (Acts 19:5-6.) But there is no mention of miraculous gifts bestowed by the apostles in  the
Jerusalem church for perhaps two or three years after Pentecost. Instead of the Spirit's ceasing from the earth (after
there would be no more apostles to lay on  hands), Jesus
said the Spirit would "abide with you forever." (John 14:16.)
And Peter promised the "gift" of the Spirit, and in the next
verse added, "For the promise is unto you, and  to  your
children, and to all that are afar off, even as many as the
Lord  our  God  shall  call." (Acts 2:38-39.)  Instead of  the
promise of Acts 2:38 only being for **some** Christians,  and
only during the lifetime of the apostles, Peter says, (1) "the
promise is unto you"—the Jews on Pentecost who would
obey the gospel; (2) "and to your children"—this included
their infants when they later in life obeyed the gospel, even
in old age; (3) "and to all that are afar off"—this takes in
the Gentiles all over the world; (4) "even as many as the
Lord our God shall call." This takes us in, for Paul says we
are "called" by the gospel. (2 Thess. 2:14.) Again he says we
are "called in one body." (Col. 3:15.) Therefore the
promise of Acts 2:38 is for "as many as the Lord our God
shall call" into the one body, the church, by  the  gospel.
Surely this did not also cease at the  death  of  the  last
apostle!

3. Again: Since only the apostles wrought any miracles
in the Jerusalem church at that time, and for two or three
years after Pentecost (Acts 2:43; 5:12), and since the laying-
on-of-hands by the apostles was  to  bestow  miraculous
power, it follows that the "gift" of the Spirit promised in
Acts 2:38 was not the temporary "gift" bestowed  by  the
laying on of the apostles' hands.

4. Disciples at Rome had  the  'ordinary'  gift  of  the
Spirit (Rom. 8:9-11) without the laying on of an apostle's
hands. Later Paul wrote them, "I long to see you that I may
impart unto you some spiritual gift to the end ye may be
established." (Rom. 1:11.) They had repented, been baptized
for the remission of sins, and had received the  promised
"gift" of the Holy Spirit, which was non-miraculous, prior
to Rom. 1:11.

5. The scriptures at the beginning of this lecture show clearly that all Christians had the "gift" of the Holy Spirit in New Testament times. But not all had had apostles' hands laid on them to bestow a miraculous gift of the Spirit. (Rom. 1:11; 8:9-11.) All had the "gift" promised upon the conditions of repentance and baptism for remission. (Acts 2:38.) There were many Christians in many countries who never saw an apostle so as to receive the Spirit by laying on of his hands.

6. The "ordinary" or non-miraculous "gift" of the Spirit as promised in Acts 2:38 was found among the disciples two or three years after Pentecost when the seven were appointed. They were "full of the Holy Spirit" before the apostles laid their hands upon any of them. The apostles said, "Look ye out among you seven men of honest report, **full of the Holy Ghost** and wisdom, whom we may appoint over this business." (Acts 6:3.) "And they chose Stephen, a man **full of** faith and of **the Holy Ghost** . . ." (v. 5.) They brought the seven to the apostles, and "they laid their hands on them." (v. 6.) Then "Stephen" (one of the seven) did "great wonders and miracles among the people." (v. 8.) Another one of them (Philip) did miracles in Samaria. (Acts 8:5-13.) They first had the Spirit—were chosen because already they were "full of the Holy Ghost" (v. 3)—before the apostles laid hands on them. (v. 6.) Miracles followed the laying on of the apostles' hands. (v. 8.) **We** have **now** what **they** had **before** the apostles laid hands on them —the ordinary "gift" of the Spirit, the non-miraculous "gift."

7. We have the same measure of the Spirit that all who then obeyed Acts 2:38 received. Peter said, "We are his witnesses of these things; and so is also the Holy Ghost, whom God hath given to them that obey him." (Acts 5:32.) Christ "became the author of eternal salvation unto all them that obey him." (Heb. 5:9.) But the Holy Ghost is "given to them that obey him." (Acts 5:32.) Therefore, all the saved had the Holy Spirit dwelling in them. But not all the saved did have the miraculous gifts given by laying on of the apostles' hands.

8. Do you, my friends, believe that Acts 2:38 is good scripture now? this year? Remember; according to this theory, no one since the days of the apostles has received the "gift" of the Holy Spirit promised to all Christians. Is Acts 2:38 applicable to sinners now, when they ask what to do to be saved? If some were to come now, and ask, "What shall we do?" should I say in reply, as Peter did then, "Repent, and be baptized every one of you in the name of Jesus Christ for the remission of sins, and ye shall receive the gift of the Holy Ghost"? Or, should I water it down, and say, "Repent, and be baptized every one of you in the name of Jesus Christ for the remission of sins, and ye shall **NOT** receive the gift of the Holy Ghost—for he has not been on earth since the days of the apostles, nineteen hundred years ago"???? Would I be honest to quote Acts 2:38 to sinners today, without explaining that (according to this theory) some part of this answer to sinners in the first gospel sermon is not good now? Then how would I deal with the next verse, which says the promise is to all who are called by the gospel of Christ? This "promise" is to all who are "called" into the one body! (Acts 2:38-39; 2 Thess. 2:14; Col. 3:15.) O! yes, I have obeyed Acts 2:38, and by faith claim its promise, as in v. 39 also. I believe it is still "good" scripture today!

### III. "Must Be Miraculous If In Us"

Another theory is that if the Holy Spirit is really in us as Christians, he must be in us "miraculously." Those who hold this view remind us that when Paul laid his hands on the twelve disciples at Ephesus, they received the Holy Spirit in a MIRACULOUS degree, for "they spake with tongues and prophesied." (Acts 19:5-7.)

1. We have just called attention to the fact that this was a miraculous measure of the Spirit, and not the "ordinary" measure common to all Christians. (Acts 2:38; 5:32; 1 Cor. 3:16; 6:19-20; 1 Thess. 4:8.)

2. To say one could not have the Holy Spirit without having miracle-working power is to contradict the Scriptures. John the Baptist was "filled with the Holy Ghost

from his mother's womb." (Luke 1:15.) Yet we read, "John did no miracle." (John 10:41.) Here is a man "filled with the Holy Ghost," and yet he "did no miracle."

3. The human spirit came from God at birth, and returns to God at the death of the body. (Eccl. 12:7.) God is the "Father" of our spirits. (Heb. 12:9; 1 Cor. 2:11; Dan. 7:15; Matt. 10:28.) "What is a man profited, if he shall gain the whole world, and lose his own soul? or what shall a man give in exchange for his soul?" (Matt. 16:26.) Now my point is this: this spirit, or soul, dwells in man—in a natural way—not miraculously. It is just man's own idea that the Holy Spirit could not dwell in him unless in some miraculous degree. We cannot "feel" the human spirit in us, as we might feel and observe a growing tumor in the body. It seems that God has sought to do as many things as infinite wisdom thought best in an ordinary way, and in harmony with the laws of nature. He does not trifle with his miraculous powers, as a child might play with toys. God knows that if he does not honor his own laws of nature, he will create on man's part distrust in these laws, and man would soon distrust all natural laws. This would mean ruin and havoc to the human race. If God were to unnecessarily feed us with manna for a few years, we would not farm and work, and at the end of his miraculous care there would be famine and starvation in the earth. Man's extremity is said to be God's opportunity. God does not do for man that which man can do for himself. Man had rather be inspired than to study the Bible to know the truth. Man had rather be miraculously healed than to live wisely and seek natural remedies. Man would have thought that the soul must be in us in some observable and miraculous manner, for it will mean nothing to be merely told in the Scriptures that man has a soul, or spirit. So of the "gift of the Holy Ghost." Man does not want to walk by faith; he wants something visible, and for display. If you doubt all this, read 1 Corinthians 14.

4. Some say they cannot comprehend the Holy Spirit's being in all faithful Christians. It is a matter of faith. I cannot comprehend the soul, or spirit, which dwells in me,

any more than I can the idea of any such Being as the Holy Spirit—but I believe it. I cannot comprehend the infinity of space, nor gravity, atoms, the wind, a thought, and other things invisible. But I believe! I am not a naturalist, nor a materialist.

5. Some say they see no reason for the Holy Spirit to be in us in any real sense, unless he is to be in us "miraculously." However, this question is not to be settled by what man thinks, or can understand in his fleshly mind; but the question is, "What saith the Scripture?" (Gal. 4:30.) If God's word is regarded by you as having weight, then read again Acts 2:38 and see if you are accepting what it says.

### IV. "Representatively—By The Word"

Still another theory of the manner in which the Holy Spirit dwells in true Christians, is that the Godhead (or Trinity) dwell in us only "representatively." It is thought that God (the Father, 1 John 4:12, 15; 2 John 9), and the Lord Jesus Christ (Col. 1:27; 2 Cor. 13:5), dwell in us—but that they do so only in the person of the Holy Spirit;—and that only the Spirit dwells in us. He is in us to "represent" the Father and the Son; then they claim the Trinity or Godhead—all three: Father, Son, and Spirit—dwell in us "representatively" by the word's dwelling in us. Those who hold this view claim that the **word** is really and actually in us. But by the time they are through talking, it is clear that they do not think the Holy Spirit is in us in any real sense, like the word is in us, actually, and in fact.

1. Peter promised unto all who would repent and be baptized for the remission of sins, "the gift of the Holy Spirit." (Acts 2:38-39.) Peter spake of the **"Holy Ghost, whom God hath given to them that obey him."** (Acts 5:32.) "Know ye not that your body is the temple of the **Holy Ghost which is in you,** which ye have of God, and ye are not your own?" (1 Cor. 6:19.) "Know ye not that ye are the temple of God, and the **Spirit of God dwelleth in you?**" (1 Cor. 3:16.) (This very question indicates that they might not know by their own reasoning that the Spirit was in them.) If God had wanted to tell us that the Holy Spirit is really and actually

in us, as Christians, how could he have chosen words more effective for the purpose than he has used?

2. Peter uses the word **"receive"**—"ye shall   receive   the gift of the Holy Ghost." (Acts 2:38.) Remember: this was a "gift" to be "received" after repentance, after baptism, and after remission of sins. (Acts 2:38.) And it was to be "received" because they had obeyed the commands  of  Acts 2:38. Remember the words: "The Holy Ghost, whom God hath given to them that obey him." (Acts 5:32.)

Now, this was after they had   received   the **word.** They had already "received" the **word**, but they had **not** "received" the "gift of the Holy Ghost." (1) They asked what to do, (v. 37.) (2) "Then Peter said . . . Repent, and be baptized every one of you in the name of Jesus Christ for   the   remission of sins." (3) "And ye shall receive the gift of the Holy Ghost." (Acts 2:38.) Here the "gift of the Holy Ghost" was to be **after** repentance, and **after** baptism. But the receiving of the **word** came **before** baptism. "Then they that gladly **received** his **word were baptized**: and the same day there were added unto them about three thousand souls." (Acts 2:41.) It follows, therefore, that receiving the "word" was not the same as receiving the "gift of the Holy Ghost" promised by Peter.

3. Furthermore, the Spirit was promised **after** repentance, baptism, and remission of sins (or salvation). (Acts  2:38.) But the "word" was to be received **before** salvation or remission of sins. Christ put salvation **after** baptism (Mark 16:15-16), and Peter put the "gift of the Holy Ghost" **after** baptism. (Acts 2:38.) But Luke says, "They that gladly **received** his **word** were baptized." (Acts 2:41.) So  they  received the "word" **before** they were baptized  and  saved— before remission of sins. James put the  receiving  of  the "word" **before** salvation when he said, "Receive with meekness the engrafted **word**, which is **able to save** your souls." (Jas. 1:21.) So we have (1) "Receive" the "word" **before** salvation, and in order to salvation, and (2) again, "Received" the "word" **before** baptism (Acts 2:41, 38); but (3) "ye. shall receive the gift of the Holy Ghost" subsequent to your re-

pentance and baptism. (Acts 2:38.) Therefore "receiving" the "word" was **not** the same as receiving the "gift" of the Spirit, which is after baptism.

4. Peter promised the "gift of the Holy Spirit" to those who repented, were baptized, and had remission of sins—promised the Spirit to **saved** people. (Acts 2:38.) He speaks of the "Holy Ghost, whom God hath given to them that obey him." (Acts 5:32.) Of course, those who "obey him" are saved. (Heb. 5:9.) But the "word" is for **sinners** at first —for those not saved, and is essential to their salvation. (Jas. 1:21; Rom. 1:16; Mark 16:15-16.) Hence, the reception of the "word" by the sinner is not "the gift of the Holy Ghost" promised by Peter. (Acts 2:38.)

5. If the gift of the "word" is the same as "the gift of the Holy Ghost" promised by Peter (Acts 2:38), why did he not say what he meant? Why did he not say, "And ye shall receive the gift of the holy **word**?"—No, he did not say this, for they received the word (v. 41) before baptism, before remission of sins, and before the reception of the Spirit. (Acts 2:38; Jas. 1:21.)

6. It is argued that to "Let the word of Christ dwell in you richly" (Col. 3:16), and to "Be filled with the Spirit" (Eph. 5:18), mean the same thing—and that, hence, the Spirit dwells in us by the "word's" dwelling in us. The context here shows that this refers to being "filled" with the influence of the Spirit. The Ephesians already had been "sealed with that Holy Spirit of promise." (Eph. 1:13.) They had the gift of the Spirit **promised** by Peter (Acts 2:38) to all who would by faith repent and be baptized for the remission of sins, and promised to "all that are afar off." The Ephesian Christians who were Gentiles had been "afar off." (Eph. 2:11-18; Acts 2:38-39.) Then in Eph. 4:30 we read: "Grieve not the Holy Spirit of God, whereby ye are sealed." They already had the "gift" of the Holy Spirit as promised in Acts 2:38, so now Paul is saying, "You partake of his influence through his word which you are to let dwell in you richly." "Be not drunk with wine . . . but be filled with the Spirit." (Eph. 5:18.) The heathen would fill up on wine, and

depend upon strong drink for his religious enthusiasm and religious excitement; but Paul exhorted the Ephesians to get **their** enthusiasm and religious excitement from the Holy Spirit as they were to let his word dwell in them richly and partake of his exciting and revolutionizing divine thoughts and truths. But they **already** had the gift of the Holy Spirit. (Eph. 1:13; 4:30.) The Spirit had been given unto them when they obeyed the gospel. (Acts 5:32.)

7. In summing up these reasons, with additional ones, let us note that the "hearing of faith" of Gal. 3:5 has reference to the Christian system of faith, and does not mean that the Spirit is given when one hears the gospel. One translation says, "Obedience of faith." This passage (Gal. 3:5) is in a context which speaks of the Spirit as "ministered" by the one who wrought miracles among them, obviously some apostle. (Acts 8:18; 19:6.) This is, therefore, not the ordinary gift of the Spirit promised in Acts 2:38, but the miraculous measure which passed away after the days of the apostles.

8. "Hearing" comes before faith (Rom. 10:17), but the ordinary gift of the Spirit promised in Acts 2:38 comes after faith. "After that ye believed, ye were sealed with that Holy Spirit of promise." (Eph. 1:13; Acts 2:38-39.)

9. The mere "**hearing**" of the word enters into the heart before faith, and often without faith following it at all. "Those by the way side are they that **hear:** then cometh the devil, and taketh away the word out of their hearts, lest they should believe and be saved." (Luke 8:12.) Surely, **these did not have the Holy Spirit** in their hearts, just **because they had the word** in their hearts, and before and without faith and salvation. (1) Christ said they were "they that hear." (2) He says the word was in their hearts but the devil took it "out of their hearts lest they should believe and be saved." (Luke 8:12.) The "promise of the Spirit," in Acts 2:38-39, was to saved people, not to unbelievers, and lost sinners.

10. The word of the Holy Spirit is first of all for those unsaved. James says, "Receive with meekness the engrafted word, which is able to save your souls." (James 1:21.) Here

the sinner, the unsaved or child of the devil, is to "receive" the implanted word before salvation, and in order to salvation. But the gift of the Holy Spirit, promised in Acts 2:38-39, is to be received after remission of sins.

11. **The word** is received **before baptism,** and **before salvation.** (Acts 11:13-14; James 1:21; Luke 8:12.) Salvation comes **after baptism.** (Mark 16:15-16; 1 Pet. 3:21.) "Then they that **gladly received his word were baptized.**" (Acts 2:41.) But the Spirit was not received by them until after repentance, baptism and remission of sins. "Then Peter said unto them, Repent, and be baptized every one of you in the name of Jesus Christ for the remission of sins, **and ye shall receive the gift of the Holy Ghost.**" (Acts 2:38.) Note: (1) They heard the word. (Acts 2:22, 36-37.) (2) They gladly received the word and asked what to do. (Acts 2:41, 37.) (3) Peter told them to repent and be baptized for the remission of sins, and urged them to be saved. (v. 40.) (4) He promised that if they would "Repent and be baptized . . . for the remission of sins," they would **"receive the gift of the Holy Ghost."** (Acts 2:38.) (5) He said this gift or promise would include **"as many** as the Lord our God shall call." (Acts 2:39.) (6) We are called **by the gospel.** (2 Thess. 2:14.) **"Called into one body"**—the church. (Col. 3:15; Col. 1:18; Eph. 1:22-23; 2:16; 5:23.) Hence, the promise of the gift of the Holy Spirit in Acts 2:38-39 is to all who obey the gospel call, and by obedience come into the one body of Christ, the church—is to all those who are saved.

12. The gift of the Holy Ghost was not promised in Acts 2:38 **to sinners and unsaved persons before baptism,** and **before remission of sins.** But it says, "Repent, and be baptized . . . for the remission of sins, and **ye shall receive** the gift of the Holy Ghost."

13. But **they received the word,** in Acts 2, before they were baptized, and before they received the gift of the Holy Spirit. It says, **"Then they that gladly received his word were baptized."** (Acts 2:41.) Note: (1) They "received" the word before baptism. (v. 41.) (2) They were promised the

gift of the Holy Spirit after baptism and remission of sins. (Acts 2:38.)

14. Since the sinner **is unsaved before he is baptized,** (Mark 16:16; Acts 22:16; 2:38), but **"gladly received the word" before baptism,** therefore, the sinner receives the word, and that before he is saved—while he is a sinner— while he is a child of the devil—and before he is baptized, before he receives remission of sins, and the gift of the Holy Spirit. (Acts 2:38-39.) O yes, the record says, "Then they that **gladly received his word** were **baptized."** (Acts 2:41.) If the "gift of the Holy Spirit" promised here is in the word like the medicine in a capsule, as is true of the teaching and converting power of the Spirit, then the sinner, un- saved person, actually a child of the devil, receives the "gift of the Holy Ghost" before baptism, and before remis- sion of sins, by receiving the word gladly before these things. (Acts 2:41, 38-39.)

15. The word is received to make one a child of God. The sinner is to be born again "by the word of God." (1 Pet. 1:23; Jas. 1:18; 1 Cor. 4:15.) Then after the new birth, and because one is already a son, or a child of God, he is given the Spirit to dwell in his heart. (Gal. 4:6.)

16. **The sinner receives the word before baptism.** (Acts 2:41.) **But he receives the Spirit after he is baptized** into Christ. (Rom. 6:3.) Speaking of Christ, Paul said, **"In whom also, after that ye believed,** ye were sealed with that Holy Spirit of promise." (Eph. 1:13.) This means after they be- lieved obediently, after they by faith were baptized into Christ. (Gal. 3:26-28.) **"IN WHOM"**—they were sealed with the Holy Spirit of promise—made in Acts 2:38.

17. One is a child of God because he has been baptized into Christ. (Gal. 3:26-28.) And **"Because ye are sons,** God hath sent forth the Spirit of his Son into your hearts, crying Abba, Father." (Gal. 4:6.) But the word is received before they are baptized into Christ. (Acts 2:41; Rom. 6:3.) Therefore, the word is received before one is a son, or a child of God, and while he is a child of the devil. The Holy Spirit, by the word, operates upon the sinner from with-

out.—until he by the Spirit is led far enough to be baptized into Christ the Spirit does not dwell in him. The Holy Spirit does not dwell in the unsaved, does not dwell in the children of the devil. (John 8:44; 1 John 3:10; Acts 13:10.) But the Spirit first makes us sons of God, and then dwells in us "because ye are sons." (Gal. 4:6.)

18. The gift of the Holy Spirit comes immediately after we obey the imperatives in Acts 2:38, as promised in that verse, and in verse 39. Peter said, "And we are his witnesses of these things; and so is also the Holy Ghost, **whom** God hath given **to them that obey him."** (Acts 5:32.) Note: (1) the sinners must obey the Lord, as in Acts 2:38; Acts 5:32 (2) After they **"obey him"** they are given the Holy Spirit himself to dwell in them, and (3) all who obey the gospel thus have this gift of the Spirit himself. He is given to all them that obey him. (Acts 5:32.) They have the Spirit, whether or not they realize it.

19. One is not a child of God for months, and years without the Spirit dwelling in him, in the ordinary gift of Acts 2:38. **"If any man have not the Spirit of Christ, he is none of his."** (Rom. 8: 9.) "The Spirit of Christ" is the Holy Spirit, as in the context. It says, "But ye are not in the flesh, but in the Spirit, **if so be that the Spirit of God dwell in you."** (Rom. 8:9.) **"But if the Spirit of him that raised up Jesus from the dead** (Spirit of God), **dwell in you,** he that raised up Christ from the dead (God) shall quicken your mortal bodies **by his Spirit that dwelleth in you."** (Rom. 8:9, 11.) The Spirit of Christ is the Holy Spirit which inspired the prophets. (1 Pet. 1:10-11.)

20. All Christians drink in or partake of the Holy Spirit, after they are led by the teaching of the Spirit to be baptized into the church—the one body. (1 Cor. 12:13; Rom. 8:14; John 16:13.) The Holy Spirit dwells in the church—the temple of God. (1 Cor. 3:16-17.) He dwells in our bodies. (1 Cor. 6:18-20.) Those who do not have the Spirit are sensual and lost. (Jude 19.)

21. But the only way we can know we have the Spirit is to know we have obeyed the gospel. (Acts 2:38-39; 5:32.) All

who do this are saved, children of God, and have the Spirit, unless they are backsliders. (Psa. 51:11.) They may not know this, like some of them do not know that man has a soul dwelling in him. (Matt. 10:28; 16:26.)

## V. " 'Gift' Is 'Salvation' Or 'Remission Of Sins' "

Another theory, and one which I often heard when I was a young preacher, is that "salvation" or "remission of sins" is the "gift of the Holy Spirit" promised in Acts 2:38.

1. We have already seen that Peter promised this "gift" of the Holy Spirit **after** remission of sins—after salvation. The order of the events is: (1) Repent. (2) Be baptized. (3) Remission of sins. And (4) "Ye shall receive the gift of the Holy Ghost." (Acts 2:38.)

2. Furthermore, is "salvation" for the **children of God**? or, for **alien sinners**? Christ came to save the "lost." (Luke 19:10.) He came to save "sinners." (1 Tim. 1:15.) Salvation is for the "world." (John 3:17; 12:47; 1 John 4:14.) But, the "gift of the Holy Spirit" is promised **after** remission of sins, after salvation. (Acts 2:38.) The Spirit was given "because ye are sons," and not to sinners to make them sons. (Gal. 4:6.) **Salvation** was given to make them sons, and "remission of sins" was a gift to **sinners.** But the Spirit was given **after** remission (Acts 2:38). Salvation is not the "gift" of the Spirit here meant by the Lord.

3. The Holy Spirit is a "gift" to those **in the church**, while salvation is for the **lost.** "Know ye not that ye are the temple of God, and that the Spirit of God dwelleth in you?" (1 Cor. 3:16.) The church is now God's temple, built by Christ. (Zech. 6:12-13.) It is not the salvation that dwells in this temple which makes it holy (1 Cor. 3:16-17), but the Holy Spirit.

4. Then, it is not "salvation" which is called "the gift of the Holy Ghost" (Acts 2:38), but the Holy Spirit himself as a "gift." "So is also the Holy Ghost, whom . . ."—the Holy Spirit as a divine Being . . .—" **whom** God hath given to them that obey him." (Acts 5:32.) Paul speaks of "the Holy Ghost which is in you, which ye have of God." (1 Cor. 6:19.)

It is not just "salvation" given us of God, but Paul says, "He therefore that despiseth, despiseth not man, but God, who hath also given unto us his Holy Spirit." (1 Thess. 4:8.)

5. "By one Spirit"—by his teaching and leadership (Neh. 9:20, 30; Rom. 8:14)—"are we all baptized into one body ... and have been all made to drink into (ASV: 'of') one Spirit." (1 Cor. 12:13.) Referring to this reception of the Spirit, Paul says this was true of all Christians. This gift of the Spirit is in the one body, the church. As the human spirit really dwells in the human body, the Spirit of the Lord really dwells in his body, the church.

### VI. "Is The Gift Of Eternal Life"

It is claimed by some that the "gift" of the Holy Spirit is "eternal life," which is finally to be given to the Christian who is faithful.

1. This is another theory which logically means that we do not have the Holy Spirit in this life at all. For the Bible plainly teaches that "eternal life" is "in the world to come." (Mark 10:30.) "In the world to come, life everlasting." (Luke 18:30.) "Shall inherit everlasting life." (Matt. 19:29.) At the end of this life we are to "reap life everlasting." (Gal. 6:7-9.) From the judgment we are to go "into eternal life." (Matt. 25:46.) Here we have eternal life out before us as a hope: "in hope of eternal life." (Tit. 1:2.) "Hope" is what we "wait for." (Rom. 8:24-25.) Timothy, a gospel preacher and true disciple, did not have. hold of eternal life, for Paul wrote him: "Fight the good fight of faith, lay hold on eternal life." (1 Tim. 6:12.) In contrast with "now," Paul said in "the end everlasting life." (Rom. 6:22.)

2. But the following scriptures teach that we have the "gift of the Holy Spirit" here and now in this life as Christians: Acts 2:38; 5:32; Rom. 8:8-11; 1 Cor. 3:16; 6:19; 1 Thess. 4:8; Gal. 4:6; Jude 19. Now, since eternal life is "in the world to come," and the "gift of the Holy Spirit" is here and now in this life, it follows that the "gift of the Holy Spirit" as promised by Peter (Acts 2:38) was not eternal life, but the Holy Spirit himself as a gift.

## VII. "Is The Influence Of The Spirit"

It is contended by some that the "gift" of the Holy Spirit promised to Christians is the "influence" of the Holy Spirit, something given by the Spirit. As the "two mites" was the "gift" of the poor widow (Mark 12:42), so the "gift" of the Spirit is something given by the **Spirit**—his holy influence.

1. Already we have seen that the Bible says of the Spirit: "**Whom** God hath given to them that obey him." (Acts 5:32.) The gift of "two mites" is two mites; the gift of a thousand dollars is a thousand dollars; and the "gift of the Holy Spirit" is the Holy Spirit.

2. It is true, that as Christians study the word of the Lord and worship and serve God, they are under wonderful spiritual influence. But is this what Peter promised in Acts 2:38? Would we not be perverting this passage to make it read, "Repent, and be baptized . . . for the remission of sins and ye shall receive the gift of **a holy influence**?" Peter did not say, "And so is also **a holy influence**, which God hath given to them that obey him." But he said, "And **so is also the Holy Ghost, whom God hath given to them** that obey him." (Acts 5:32.)

3. One of the holiest of all influences is to believe that the Holy Spirit as really and truly dwells in our bodies as do our own spirits. Paul said to the Corinthians, "Know ye not that ye are the temple of God, and that the Spirit of God dwelleth in you?" (1 Cor. 3:16.) A temple where deity dwells is a sacred place, a place to be respected and held in reverence. Since the Holy Spirit dwells in the church, and therefore in each member's body, Paul reasons that the fact of the indwelling Spirit should keep the Corinthians from defiling the temple of God by sin. "If any man defile the temple of God, him shall God destroy; for the temple of God is holy, which temple ye are." (1 Cor. 3:16-17.)

4. The indwelling Spirit should influence us not to sin; that is, the very belief that the Holy Spirit dwells in us should clean up our lives, somewhat as if Jesus had lived across the street, or in our homes with us, during his personal ministry. Well, the Holy Spirit dwells in us. (1 Cor.

3:16-17.) Paul argued that belief of this fact should keep the Corinthians from adultery and idolatry. "Flee fornication. Every sin that a man doeth is without the body; but he that committeth fornication sinneth against his own body. What? know ye not that **your body is the temple of the Holy Ghost which is in you, which ye have of God**, and ye are not your own?" (1 Cor. 6:18-19.)

The man who does not think the Holy Spirit has really been on earth since the days of the apostles has, by such thinking, robbed himself of a great and powerful influence to live close to God. Does it not help you to remember that you have a **soul**? (Matt. 16:26.) How much more to remember that the **Holy Spirit** dwells in us? It is a sobering thought! I believe the Holy Spirit dwells in me, really and actually, just as I believe my human spirit or soul dwells in me in truth and fact. Neither is miraculous. I can't "feel" either one, nor can either be found in a laboratory. Neither **works any miracles through me. All I know of either of them is through the word of God. Neither inspires me with new revelations from God. Neither gives me a single idea of religious truth not found in the scriptures.**

5. Since the scriptures so abundantly teach us that the Spirit dwells in us, is it all too good to be true? Is that sort of thinking dangerous? How could it be? To have Deity living in us is not too great for God, if he has willed it to be so. (Of course, God does not do all he could do: he could destroy this world in the next minute; but he may not.) Still, let us not limit God so that he can't do what he has promised. One of the sins which ruined ancient Israel was, "They turned back and tempted God, and limited the Holy One of Israel." (Ps. 78:41.)

6. As to the "influence" of the Holy Spirit, Peter's audience was under the influence of the Spirit through his word, when they asked what to do. (Acts 2:36-37.) They were about to be baptized because the Spirit had by his word (which is sharper than a sword, Heb. 4:12) cut them to the heart, pricked them in their consciences. But they did not have remission, nor the gift of the Holy Spirit as yet.

They had to obey to receive the "gift" of the Holy Spirit. (Acts 2:38-41.) The influence of the Spirit through the word is **not** what Peter promised in v. 38.

### VIII. "Human Spirit Made Holy"

Another theory of the "gift of the Holy Spirit" promised by Peter (in Acts 2:38) is, that if they would thus obey the gospel, their "human spirit" (soul) would be made "holy" —they would receive the "gift" of a "holy" **human** "spirit."

1. Acts 2:38 promised that they would receive "the gift of **the Holy Ghost.**" Where in all the Bible is the **human** spirit ever called "**the Holy Ghost?**"

2. Does not this theory hereby teach that they had a wicked spirit, or **un**holy spirit, until after they were baptized? and after they received the "remission of sins?" (Acts 2:38.) Is this altogether true? Does not one in repentance give up all wicked purposes? Has he not given up the love of sin? Is he not dedicating his life to God? Does he need anything more than his past sins to be forgiven, and the "gift of the Holy Spirit?" It seems that Paul teaches that the human spirit is sanctified in order to salvation.

### IX. "Is A 'Gift' Given By The Holy Ghost"

Some think that the "gift" of the Holy Spirit is just "something"—they do not know what—which is to be given by the Holy Spirit.

1. Remember the apostle Peter says it is the Holy Ghost "whom" God gives—not merely "something" given by the Spirit. (Acts 5:32; 1 Cor. 3:16; 6:19.) "Whom" is a personal pronoun.

2. Just what could it be that the Spirit is to give? He did not directly give them the **gospel**. They afterward had to learn from the apostles. (Acts 2:41-42.) It could not be **remission** of sins, for that came before the "gift" of the Spirit in Acts 2:38; hence they already had that, prior to the reception of the "gift" of the Spirit. It was not **inspiration**, for they still had to study under the apostles. (Acts 2:42.) The gift of the Holy Ghost was not **miraculous power**; for this gift is for all Christians—for all who will

repent and be baptized for remission of sins, for all time
(Acts 2:38-39)—but this is not true of miraculous power.
(1 Cor. 13:8-13.)

### X. "Spirit Dwells In The Church"

Another theory is that the Holy Spirit dwells in the
**church** (1 Cor. 12:13; 3:16-17), but not in any individual
member of the church.

1. While 1 Cor. 3:16-17 teaches the Spirit dwells in the
**church**, this is true only because of the fact that he dwells
in each faithful member of the church. How could he be in
the **church**, yet be in none of its members? Is he only in
the meeting-house? Is he in the air, just floating around in
space? It seems that some think the Holy Spirit can dwell
just about anywhere—except in the Christian! (1 Cor. 6:19.)

2. If the Spirit is upon this earth at all, in any real and
actual sense, then he is in the saints of God. (Acts 2:38.)
One preacher who denies that God, Christ, or the Holy
Spirit (either one) dwells in us in any real sense, waxed
eloquent in a sermon on the "Greatness of God," telling
how he fills infinite space, and dwells on the earth as his
footstool. Yes, just anywhere,—**except in man**—where the
**belief in his presence** would sanctify us and work wonders
in us!

3. One man waxed eloquent, and said "God dwells in us."
(Eph. 4:6.) But this was "interpreted" to mean that God
sent the Son to dwell in us for the Father. (2 Cor. 13:5.)
Later this turned out to mean the Son sent the Spirit—and
finally the Spirit simply gave us the word; and **only**
through the **word** is the Godhead in us.

4. While it is true that the word of God is the word of the
"Spirit," and is full of divine power, the **word** is not one of
the Godhead, not one of the Trinity. (Matt. 28:19.) As we
have shown, the word is received before the Spirit. (Acts
2:41, 38; Jas. 1:21.) The word is not the Holy Spirit, though
it does partake of the nature of the Spirit in thought and
content.

5. The way the Holy Spirit dwells in the **church** is to

dwell in the "body" of each faithful Christian. "Know ye not that your body is the temple of the Holy Ghost which is in you, which ye have of God?" (1 Cor. 6:19.)

## Some Extremes To Be Avoided

1. Some seem to think that if the Holy Spirit really dwells in us, then we are obligated to accept for ourselves miracles, tongues, miraculous divine healing, and all the miracles done by the apostles. This is not true. Those who had only the "ordinary measure" (John 3:34) of the Spirit in the days of the apostles could not do these things. For all Christians to have supernatural power would be like having "all Chiefs and no Indians."

2. Some argue that if the Spirit dwells in us without miraculous power, then he is in us in vain. I have shown that this is not true.

3. Some claim that the Spirit cannot intercede for us (Rom. 8:25-27) unless he can work miracles in us. But he intercedes **to God,** not within us; and to intercede to God **for us** is not to work a miracle in us.

4. Some argue that the Spirit must work miracles in us, else God cannot answer our prayers. **Providence** is **not** the "indwelling of the Spirit." They are two separate subjects. I believe in divine providence; but I do not believe the Spirit works miracles in us.

5. Some think God cannot work for us, and take care of us, unless we can also work miracles by the Holy Spirit. This conclusion is false.

6. Others think that if the Spirit strengthens us "by his might . . . in the inner man" (Eph. 3:14-21), he must do it miraculously, and independent of his word. The Spirit can do this without a miracle, and **dwell in us** at the same time, as easily as he can do it all without a miracle, and **not** be in us at all, as some seem to think.

7. Some argue that unless we have the miraculous power of the Spirit working in our behalf, God cannot do anything for us except what nature does for us without divine

aid. This does not follow. God is at the steering-wheel of the universe; and what he does through nature is not a miracle, but providential. If you mean he does nothing, you are wrong! (Rom. 8:32.)

8. Another extreme is to think the "indwelling of the Spirit" is a mere disposition, or influence, or attitude. Just the presence of the Spirit in our hearts is enough to, by faith, cause us to praise and serve the Lord with all our hearts. (Gal. 4:6.) The greatest truth in all the world will not properly affect us unless we believe it. Do we really believe Acts 2:38?

9. The tendency to dismiss the whole subject of the Spirit because there are "mysteries" connected therewith, is an extreme to be avoided. There are "mysteries" (1 Tim. 3:16) everywhere.

10. We should avoid all contention and unnecessary pressing of any issue to the disturbance of the church, unless it has to do in some way with the faith and obedience of the church—with its growth and development. Hobby-riding will not strengthen the church.

11. We should not go to the extreme of refusing to preach and teach whatever God says about all things, if we know the truth and can present what he says in its true setting and light. "Preach the word." (2 Tim. 4:2.)

12. Remember there are some borderline subjects which (by the very nature of them) are more or less shrouded in mystery. Let us not be dogmatic where God may not have seen fit to reveal all the facts concerning something in which we may be interested. (Deut. 29:29.)

13. Let us study the word of God, for it is perfect and all-sufficient. There is no further revelation for us.

"What more can he say, than to you he hath said? Ye who unto Jesus for refuge hath fled?"

14. Remember the three great dispensations began in miraculous power, just as a great building when being constructed has about it ladders and scaffolding. But when the

building is finished, these are no longer needed, and are removed. Christianity began in miraculous power. But when the church was built, and all truth revealed to it, and confirmed, the things necessary to establishing it are no longer needed, and are laid aside. (1 Cor. 13:8-13; Eph. 4:9-16.)

15. The Spirit, through the apostles, has given us all truth that we shall ever need. (John 16:13; 2 Tim. 3:15-17.) Let us contend earnestly for this truth "once" **for all time to come** "delivered unto the saints." (Jude 3.))

16. The word of God is the "seed" of the kingdom. (Luke 8:11; Mark 4:14; Matt. 13:19.) The whole of Christianity is embraced or "wrapped up" in this seed. There is not a **true** religious idea today which is not in the word of God.

May God bless you, every one.

## QUESTIONS AND ANSWERS

**Question:** After the Dallas lectures, I received the following question by telephone: "Please give us a fuller discussion of the theory that the Godhead dwells in us representatively by the word of the Spirit."

**Answer:** Christ built the church through the instrumentality of the Holy Spirit to be a "habitation of **God**." (Eph. 2:18-22.) The kingdom came with the power of the Spirit. (Mk. 9:1; Acts 1:8; 2:1-4.) The church is the "temple of **God**." (1 Cor. 3:16-17; 2 Cor. 6:16.) God dwells in us. (Eph. 4:6; 1 Cor. 6:18-19.) "God" means Deity, the Godhead in some instances. **Christ** also dwells in us. (Col. 1:27; 2 Cor. 13:5.) And the **Holy Spirit** dwells in Christians. (Acts 2:38; 5:32; Rom. 8:9-11; 1 Cor. 3:16-17; 6:18-19; 1 Thess. 4:8; Jude 19.)

The idea that neither member of the Godhead, or Trinity, **really** dwells in us, but that only the "word" of Deity (which is not a member of the Godhead) dwells in us, can not be harmonized with scripture. The Father dwelt in the Son while here on earth in a fleshly body. (John 14:10-11.) Who are we to say God cannot dwell in his people? (Psa. 89:41.) Did he dwell in Christ only **representatively** through his word? Was Christ in God only **representatively?** Are we in Christ only **representatively?** (2 Cor. 5:17; Rev. 13:14.) "If a man love me, he will keep my words: and my Father will love him, and **we** will come unto him, and make our abode with him." (John 14:23.) Does this mean Deity will only send the "word" which is not one of the Godhead? We are said to partake of the "divine" nature (same Greek as in "Godhead"). (2 Pet. 1:4; Rom. 1:20; Acts 17:29; Col. 2:9.)

After one has obeyed the gospel and received the Holy Spirit (Acts 2:38; 5:32) he may then partake more and more of the divine nature, and of God, Christ, and the Holy Spirit. The Ephesians received the Spirit. (Eph. 1:13.) Later they were promised that Christ would dwell in them on the condition of proper faith. (3:16-17.) Though Christ is in all Christians from the very first, he is to dwell in them more and more till "formed" in them. (Col. 1:27; 2 Cor. 13:5; Gal. 4:19.)

After the Ephesians **received** the Spirit (1:13), they were later to **"be filled** with all the fullness of God" as they would grow and become more Godlike. (3:19.)

And after the Ephesians received the Spirit (1:13; 4:30) they were to "be filled with the Spirit" by partaking more and more of his will and nature, through the word. (Eph. 5:18-19; Col. 3:16.)

But there need be no disfellowship nor confusion among us as to **how** the Spirit dwells in us. God will look after the divine side of our salvation. Let us obey. (Acts 5:32.)

# THE FRUIT OF THE SPIRIT

I want to thank each one of you for the interest that you have already evidenced in this simple series of Bible studies in which we are trying simply to present the Word of the Lord concerning the work as well as concerning the very nature and the personality of the Holy Spirit.

## "Works Of The Flesh"

This morning I would like to lead us in a study of the "Fruit of the Spirit." In the Galatian letter, the 5th chapter, we read of the **works** of the flesh, but of the **fruit** of the Spirit. "The works of the flesh"—works of the flesh do not have to be planted, they do not have to be cultivated. There is no need to have men to come in and to lecture for weeks and weeks and to plead with people earnestly and in tears to get them to follow the flesh—to get them to curse, swear, be profane, dance, revel, drink strong drink, commit adultery, steal and practice fraud and deceit. There is no need for such help. Satan does not need to have anyone come in and lecture to the people and plead with them to practice such things. The works of the flesh spring up from the soil of the heart itself. They just flourish like briars and weeds and bushes and whatever obnoxious thing there is that may grow to hinder the production of a crop. They are just works of the flesh, and do not have to be planted, do not have to be cultivated. They do not have to even be wanted, they do not have to be desired on the part of the individual. They are his enemy and still they grow, and in spite of his best efforts. They are always present.

## "Fruit Of The Spirit"

But the fruit of the Spirit has to be planted. Its fruit has to be cultivated. It is like our crops which have to be planted and nurtured and in some sections, irrigated, and all of this in order that we might have a harvest. I would like for us to keep in mind the distinction between **the works**

**of the flesh**, and the **fruit of the Spirit**, and I am reading of both. "Now the works of the flesh are manifest"—they are obvious. It is obvious as to their source. It is manifest as to where they came from. "Now the works of the flesh are manifest, which are these; adultery, fornication, uncleanness, lasciviousness, idolatry, witchcraft, hatred, variance, emulations, wrath, strife, seditions, heresies, envyings, murders, drunkenness, revellings, and such like: of the which I tell you before, as I have also told you in time past, that they which do such things shall not inherit the kingdom of God." (Gal. 5:19-21.) "But"—now right over against that—"but the fruit of the Spirit is love, joy, peace, longsuffering, gentleness, goodness, faith, meekness, temperance (or self control, A. S. V.): against such there is no law. And they that are Christ's"—those who belong to Christ and are really Christians—"have crucified the flesh with the affections and lusts." (Gal. 5:22-24.) They don't practice the works of the flesh. They are new creatures. They are different. "If we live in the Spirit, let us also walk in the Spirit"—let us be consistent—"Let us not be desirous of vain glory, provoking one another, envying one another." (Gal. 5:25, 26.) The fruit of the Spirit is fruit which springs forth, comes forth from the Spirit. The Spirit is back of this fruit. He produces it.

### Fruit From Seed

The Spirit begets this fruit **through his seed, the word of God.** In Luke 8:11 Jesus said of the parable of the sower, "Now the parable is this: The seed is the word of God," and in verse 14 of Mark 4 he said, "The sower soweth the word." And in Matthew 13:19 he said, "When any one heareth the word of the kingdom." The word is the seed, it is the word, it is the word of the kingdom, in the light of these three different explanatory passages. And so the word of God is the seed of the kingdom.

We pointed out the fact last night that the Holy Spirit created, that the Holy Spirit garnished the heavens, that the Holy Spirit made man, that he was our maker. O yes, God did it, and Christ did it, but the Holy Spirit had a part in it. "Let **us** make man in **our** image, after our likeness." (Genesis 1:26, 27.) The Holy Spirit was back there when God was creating, when Christ was creating. "In the beginning was the Word, and the Word was with God, and the Word was God. The same was in the beginning with God. All things were made by him; and without him was not anything made that was made." (John 1:1-3.) And the same is true of the Holy Spirit. (Gen. 1:1-3.) So the Holy Spirit made man, as we showed last night from several passages. The Trinity all had a part in the great creation of this wonderful, beautiful world. And when things were created, the Holy Spirit's special work seems to have been to garnish the heavens and to give laws to all things. He gave the law of reproduction and the command to multiply and replenish the earth to Adam and then again to Noah. And when the vegetable kingdom was made by him, he had the plants produce seed, every one after its kind. When planted, it would in turn reproduce it's kind upon the earth, and God saw that it was that way and that it was good.

## Spirit Makes Christians

The Holy Spirit, in giving the spiritual law, produces Christians. The Spirit makes people Christians. He makes people to be faithful Christians, if they are led by the Spirit, **by the teaching of His word**, by this seed as planted in their hearts and cultivated properly, and if they weed out these foreign growths which naturally spring up (the works of the flesh). Keep them down, keep them out, give the fruit of the Spirit a chance to grow without being choked. Let us give it a good deep planting, as in the parable of the sower, instead of trying to grow fruit on a rock where the plant has little root and lacks moisture, or where it is trying to grow among the thorns, to be choked out. Many of us are being choked, more or less, by the things of the world. "Cares" of the world—making a living—being able to meet our financial obligations and our general obligations everywhere, choke many. These pressures come down upon us and if we are not careful, they will choke the word out. They will choke down the little plant and it will not produce fruit, as wheat growing under a big thorn bush, which springs up when the warm spring rains come. Hot sunshine comes down upon it, and instead of growing slowly like the little plant, sometimes these obnoxious things grow very rapidly in the lives of people and they go astray and become terribly wicked in a very brief period of time.

### Spirit Works By His Word

And so we have the word of the Spirit. David, one of the prophets said, "The Spirit of the Lord spake by me, and His word was in my tongue." (II Sam. 23:2.) And Peter said, "Men and brethren, this scripture must needs have been fulfilled, which the Holy Ghost by the mouth of David spake." (Acts 1:16.) New Testament writers often quoted the Old Testament Scriptures as the words of the Holy Spirit. In Hebrews 3:7-11, the Hebrew writer said, "As the Holy Ghost saith," and then he begins the quotation: "To-day if ye will hear his voice, harden not your hearts," and quotes from Psalms 95:7-11 and stated the Holy Ghost said what is quoted. Hence, the Bible is not the Holy Ghost, the Holy Spirit; but he said what is in the Bible.

### Bible Is True

Now I want to shock you a bit—and then I'll get you over it—so you will be better off when I get through with you. There **are lies** in the Bible! And there are **no lies** in the Bible! There are **false** statements in the Bible. There **are no false** statements in the Bible. You say, "You are contradicting yourself." O, no. No, I'm not. **Every word of the Bible** is the word of God and some words of the Bible are not the word of God. When a man lied in the Bible and God tells us the man lied, God is telling the truth—the man did lie. But the lie the man told is not the truth; though God tells us that the man told the lie, the lie is still a lie. For instance, in Psalms 14:1, we read, "The fool hath said in his heart, **There is no God**." Now it is true that the fool said that; but what the fool said is not true—is not the truth or any kin to the truth. He said there is no God, and that's not true. There is a God. And so God tells the truth when he says the fool said that, but the fool did not tell the truth at all when he said there is no God. What he said is not so.

And so every word in the Bible is true—"as silver tried in a furnace of earth, purified seven times." (Psalm 12:6.) The Bible is the word of God—the word of the Holy Spirit. The Spirit spoke and wrote the Bible, the entire Bible, every word of it was guided, directed, by the Holy Spirit, and is the truth. **When God says a thing happened, it happened!** Now when men talk in the Bible, they don't always tell the truth; but God tells the truth when he tells us what they said and what they did. **So, on the divine side, the Bible is, every word of it, true.** The human element in it is not always right.

### No Error By Inspired Men

Men make mistakes but God gave the Holy Spirit to keep men from making any mistakes in writing the Bible. "All scripture is given by inspiration of God." (2 Tim. 3:16.) "Holy men of God spake as they were moved by the Holy Ghost." (2 Pet. 1:20-21.) Hence, the Holy Spirit is the author of the Bible, and if the Spirit did all of the talking, there wouldn't be any errors in the Bible, there wouldn't be any lies in the Bible, but when uninspired men talk, and the Holy Spirit through inspired men tell us what uninspired men said and did, then through these uninspired men, there are false statements in the Bible.

**So, we need to know who the speaker is. Is he inspired or is he uninspired? If he is inspired, every word he speaks is the truth. If he is uninspired**—now don't jump to conclusions, don't go on and say it for me, you'll miss it if you do. You thought I was going to say if uninspired, then everything he says is a lie. That isn't so. Uninspired men in the Bible often tell the truth without any guidance from the Holy Spirit. When the blind man, who was not inspired, in John 9, after he had been healed, said, "We know that God heareth not sinners," he told the truth, but he wasn't inspired. John was inspired when he tells us that the blind man said that. The blind man was not inspired, but he told the truth anyway. He didn't say, "I know it," but he said, "we know it"—you know it the same as I do. "We know that God heareth not sinners: but if any man be a worshipper of God, and doeth his will, him he heareth." (John 9:31.) He knew it because the Old Testament taught that truth and he knew it and so did the rest of his Jewish brethren know it and understand it.

## Word Bears Good Fruit

So then, the seed is planted as we preach the word of God. We sow the seed of the kingdom (Mark 4:14 and Matt. 13:19) and this gospel—this word when preached—produces fruit. In Colossians 1 and beginning with verse 5, Paul thanks God for the hope, he says, "which is laid up for you in heaven, whereof ye heard before in the word of the truth of the gospel; which is come unto you, as it is in all the world and bringeth forth fruit." That would be the fruit of the Spirit, wouldn't it? In 1 Peter 1:12, Peter tells us that the gospel was preached "with the Holy Ghost sent down from heaven." Whatever the gospel produced, the Holy Spirit that preached it through inspired men produced, and hence the "fruit of the spirit." The Spirit therefore, being the author of the seed, having revealed it and having confirmed it and having given it to us, with the law of reproduction after its kind, has commanded that we are to preach the word or be lost. We are to sow the seed of the kingdom unto others, or we ourselves will not be Christlike and Christians.

All fruit is not alike. There is good fruit and bad fruit. Jeremiah, in prophesying, spoke of the fruit in Jeremiah 24:1, 2: "The Lord showed me, and, behold, two baskets of figs were set before the temple of the Lord, after that Nebuchadnezzar King of Babylon had carried away captive Jeconiah the son of Jehoiakim king of Judah, and the princes of Judah, with the carpenters and smiths, from Jerusalem, and had brought them to Babylon. One basket had very good figs, even like the figs that are first ripe:" —choice figs—" and the other basket had very naughty figs, which could not be eaten, they were so bad." So as there is good fruit and bad fruit, no doubt, Jesus had that in mind when he said in Matthew 7:15 beginning, "Beware of false prophets, which come to you in sheep's clothing, but, inwardly they are ravening wolves. Ye shall know them by their fruits. Do men gather grapes of thorns, or figs of thistles? Even so every good tree bringeth forth good fruit; but a corrupt tree bringeth forth evil fruit. A good tree cannot bring forth evil fruit, neither can a corrupt tree bring forth good fruit. Every tree that bringeth not forth good fruit is hewn down, and cast into the fire. Wherefore by their fruits ye shall know them." In other words, a man is just what he is. He is not something different to what he is. He is whatever he lives in his life. He is what he thinks. **Or in other words, he is what he thinks all the time every day.** Proverbs 23:7: "As he thinketh in his heart, so is he." And if you want good fruit, you have to sow down the garden or the field of your heart and mind in good seed.

### Must Have True Doctrine

Some people say, "Oh, it doesn't make any difference what people teach, you are obligated to let everybody in the country sow your field down in 'tare seed' or 'Johnson grass' or something of the sort." That isn't so. In Mark 4:24 Jesus said, "Take heed what ye hear." I am not only obligated to hear but I am obligated to select what I hear. I have no obligation unto God to go to hear a false teacher preach. I have no obligation whatsoever to read his writings. I may do it and I will if I can get any benefit from it —can be better informed and know how to refute his false doctrine—but I am not going to permit the soil of my heart to be sown down in false seed—tare seed, and the like. We know what it will produce. It will always produce after its kind. **We are now what we have been thinking and doing. We are what we are today because we were what we were yesterday**. Largely, very few have made any change since yesterday. **So we are what we are each day because of what we were the day before**. Ninety-nine percent of the people are in a rut and it is hard to get them out. They are satisfied to go on in the same old way, and keep the status quo. And so we must have the right environment in which to plant the seed—we must have the proper soil, the proper climate. You can't grow the finest fruits in a country where they have no proper season for it. And so we have to see that our hearts are right. The man is the farmer and his heart is his soil, his field.

## Man Responsible

I was preaching once on the parable of the sower and a man who was a denominational preacher held his hand up. He had a little piece of paper in his hand. He said, "Could the wayside soil keep from being wayside soil? Could the thorny ground soil have made itself some other kind? Could the good ground have kept from being good ground?" He was a Calvinist in belief. Well, I scratched my hair then (I have to scratch my head now), but I scratched my hair a bit and I was a little confused at first. I had never thought of that myself. But in a moment I happened to think of James 4:8: "Cleanse your hands, ye sinners; and purify your hearts, ye double minded." If the mind is the soil and I am the farmer I am to cleanse it from rocks and thorns and the like—fix up my soil so it will bear the right kind of crop. And I thought of Ezekiel 18:30-33 where he said, "Make you a new heart and a new spirit: for why will ye die, O house of Israel?" This makes a man the farmer and his mind his soil. And King Hezekiah prayed, "Pardon every one that **prepareth his heart** to seek God." (2 Chron. 30:18-19.) There is the idea, prepare your soil. Don't blame it off on God if your field is full of rocks that never have been gathered and hauled off. If there is timber growing there, don't blame God with it. If you want to grow a crop, prepare the soil. Make preparations. "Prepare your hearts to seek God," as we just quoted.

## Cultivation

And then, in the cultivation of the crop, or of trees if you are thinking of fruit trees, the tree must be properly planted. We read in Psalm 1: "He"—this good man it describes —"shall be like a tree planted by the rivers of water." That is in contrast to one planted on the mountain top. In Palestine you look up on some of those old mountains as though you were looking at the moon. Way up yonder, miles high, and not a thing growing up there! The soil has been neglected and it is washed off and there is nothing but subsoil —just clay or solid rock. Not a sprig of grass growing up there. If you were to plant a tree up there you would have no fruit. But this good man who meditates on his law day and night, is "like a tree planted by the rivers of water," way down where the soil lodged when it came from up there. "Down by the river side" where there is plenty of moisture, plenty of fertile soil. Give the word of God a chance in your heart and in your life—in your soul. Give it a good planting, plant it where it has an opportunity to grow properly. "If we have been planted together in the likeness of his death, we shall be also in the likeness of his resurrection." (Romans 6:5.) He had just said, "Therefore we are buried with him by baptism into death; that like as Christ was raised up from the dead by the glory of the Father, even so we also should walk in newness of life." So plant it, plant it in obeying the gospel. And plant it in Christ, root it, and ground it in love. "As ye have therefore received Christ Jesus the Lord, so walk ye in Him." (Col. 2:5-7.)

## Good Environment

We received him by obeying the gospel and that left us in Him for we were baptized into Christ. (Rom. 6:3; Gal. 3:26, 27.) And thus grow in Christ! Grow in the environment of prayer. Grow in the environment of a good happy home. Give your children that opportunity. Grow in the environment of a good congregation. My heart almost bleeds when I think of so many boys and girls who don't have a chance to be Christians, in the kind of home they have and the kind of a congregation they have. They grow up in a fussing, wrangling, worldly, godless congregation, where the gospel is not permitted to be preached in all of its rebuking, condemning, encouraging, exhorting, transforming power! Select a good environment for yourself and your family. Don't pitch your tent toward Sodom like Lot did, choosing a bad environment, and lose your family and almost your own soul and have it vexed from day to day as in Genesis the 13th and 19th chapters.

## Cultivation Required

Cultivate the plants, prune the trees, do what you can to cultivate in such a way as to have the maximum amount of the best possible fruit. We read in Matthew 3:10 where John the Baptist said, "Now also the axe is laid unto the root of the trees." When I was a young man, I remember, I used a blackboard in preaching. Sometimes I do now, but not often. It is a very effective way to preach. I would draw a tree. You couldn't tell much about what it was (I would tell them what it was) and then I had an axe drawn at the root of it. The audience would sit there and look at the axe while I preached. The axe was lying there, ready. "The axe is laid unto the root of the trees: therefore every tree which bringeth not forth good fruit is hewn down, and cast into the fire." That sounds like going to hell, doesn't it. In John 15, "I am the true vine, and my Father is the husbandman. Every branch in me that beareth not fruit he taketh away: and every branch that beareth fruit, he purgeth it, that it may bring forth more fruit." There he is with his pruning knife just ready to clip those branches off, of which I am one, if they do not produce fruit. He is clipping off all these old fruitless branches, and we are going to hear a great wailing at the judgment, of brethren who have been deceived and disappointed, when they meet God in judgment to find that they bore no fruit.

### Be Fruit Tree

They have been nothing but shade trees, ornaments. They didn't bear any fruit. God says bear fruit or burn. In John 15:8 he says, "Herein is my father glorified, that ye bear much fruit; so,"—adverb of manner—"**So shall ye be my disciples.**" If you don't bear fruit, you are going to hell. That is what Jesus said. We have the opportunity to bear fruit and there is a great crying need for it. And if we don't produce it, we will burn, as sure as there is a God.

God is the husbandman and he prunes off the old fruitless branches. He may have had some of us cut off until we are almost withered beyond being re-grafted. You can't properly graft an old dead branch. It's gone forever if it once dies. It can be cut off and can come back in a reasonable and proper manner and time.

### The Fig Tree

And then again, we read of the fruit trees. In describing them in Luke the 13th chapter, Jesus gives us some fine things concerning the fig tree. There has to be patience exercised in connection with this fruit-bearing proposition. "He spake also this parable; A certain man had a fig tree planted in his vineyard; and he came and sought fruit thereon, and found none. Then said he unto the dresser of his vineyard, Behold these three years I come seeking fruit on this fig tree, and find none: cut it down; why cumbereth it the ground?" He had become a little too much impatient with it! But listen: "And he answering said unto him, Lord, let it alone this year also, till I shall dig about it, and dung it: and if it bear fruit, well: and if not, then after that thou shalt cut it down." (Luke 13:6-9.) Give it a chance. Some of them have not had much of a chance. When you find many backsliders in the church and a lot of indolent, fruitless members, there is usually a real cause back of it. The church isn't what it ought to be. Many times the leaders are not what they should be. The preacher is not what he ought to be. And the homes are not what they ought to be. We are not making our environment what it should be. And the seed of the kingdom is not being sown like it ought to be. We need therefore to be patient. We read, "Warn them that are unruly, comfort the feebleminded, support the weak, be patient toward all men." (1 Thes. 5:14.) So there is good and bad fruit, and it is essential that we bear the good fruit, or we will be lost.

## Fruit Not Miraculous

Notice, too, that this fruit is not miraculous fruit. He did not say the fruit of the Spirit is speaking in tongues, healing the sick miraculously, raising the dead, casting out devils. No, but the fruit of the Spirit is "love, joy," etc. Don't you see the difference? The miracles were temporary like the ladders and scaffolding round about this fine meeting house. They were essential at one time but when the building was finished, they were all removed and would have been in the way had they left them there. Miracles are not needed today. No miracle is needed today. It would upset the whole scheme of God in redemption to start working miracles now. It would create distrust in his laws and nature. If he were to feed us with manna just one year, the next year we wouldn't plant any crops and the chances are we would have a famine and would starve, because he didn't work miracles again the second year. It would create distrust, upset the whole scheme of nature. It is a blessed thing that we don't have miracles today, but it is wonderful that we can have the fruit of the Spirit.

### Take Heed To Soil And Seed

We can plant the seed. Now the first harvest came without seed. Of necessity, it had to be thus and to produce the first seed. But we don't have any harvest this side of that without seed. A man who plants his seed and prays for a harvest has a million-fold more faith than the man who would ignore planting seed and pray, "Oh God, give me bread, give me a harvest." So, bear the fruit. Be the right kind of tree properly planted in Christ. It is the nature of the tree that produces the right fruit. It's the nature of a bad tree to produce bad fruit. It's the nature of a bad man to produce a bad life, bad fruit. It's the nature of a good man to produce good fruit. It just comes out from the inside. Out of the abundance of heart, the mouth speaketh and life flows. "Keep thy heart with all diligence for out of it are the issues of life." (Prov. 4:23.) "Issue" means to flow forth and hence the flowing of life, like a stream from a fountain, comes from the heart, comes from within.

### Love

As we think about this fruit of the Spirit, we find **love** is first. (Gal. 5:22, 23.) Maybe it's first by divine choice, and not by accident or chance. Because out of love must come forth everything. Galatians 5:13: "By love serve one another." All of our service must come out of it. And by love the whole gospel scheme of human redemption from God came forth out of the fountain of love. "God so loved the world that he gave his only begotten son." (John 3:16.) God loved. God did not love this world because it was lovable. We wait to love people until they are lovable—that is, if we are following the flesh. Christians don't. They are like God, they love people whether they are worthy of it or not. They love unlovable folks. They will even love their enemies. There are two ways of loving—God's way of loving and man's way of loving. "If ye love them which love you, what reward have ye?" (Matt. 5:46-48.) And if you salute those that greet and salute you, what thanks have you? What have you done worthy of any commendation? Just nothing. The publicans, the sinners, would do that. Christians ought to give more and live on a higher plane than other folk. We receive more and we ought to give out more. Freely we received, freely give. (Matt. 10.) And because God has loved us we should reciprocate his love. We should love much in return, and love like God loves. He loved us while we were yet sinners, and unworthy of it. (Romans 5:7, 8.) He "commendeth his love toward us, in that, while we were yet sinners"—unworthy—"Christ died for us." That is the way we are to love. We love him because he first loved us; that is, because we first found out he loved us, because the seed has been sown in our hearts, telling us about his love. (1 John 4:19.) And then we are to love God with all of our heart, soul, mind and strength. (Matt. 22:37.) It will correct our lives Godwardly, if we will love God with all of our heart, with all of our soul, with all of our mind and with all of our strength. (Mark 12:29, 30.)

And then it says, "Love thy neighbor as thyself." That will control his conduct toward his neighbor and his life will be all right neighborly-wise, also. And God-wise it will be all right if he loves God supremely and then loves his neighbor like he loves himself. Did you ever know of a man that would get out and tell lies on himself and try to ruin his good name until nobody would credit him and believe him? Did you ever know a fellow who would destroy himself like that? Well I'm 74 years old and I have never known of a man who did that. I think one ought to be in the insane hospital if he goes to doing that. So man is good to himself. He doesn't tell the bad on himself. He lets the folks find out if they can; but otherwise, he will just fix it with God and leave it there. There is no use to advertise one's sins. And so he doesn't try to destroy himself and his standing with the people. Well if he loves his neighbor like that, he won't hurt his neighbor. Don't you see? He will treat him right. He will be good to his neighbor. He wouldn't steal from himself. Did you ever know of a fellow stealing out of one pocket and putting it over in the other pocket? Why people don't do that, because they love themselves. And if we love our neighbor as ourselves, we would no more steal from him than we would  steal  from  one pocket and put it in the other pocket. And if we love our neighbor's husband or wife as we love ourselves, we would no more think of committing adultery than we would think about destroying ourselves. One is doing that in committing sin like that, destroying his own soul.

**"Love suffereth long and is kind."** (1 Cor. 13.) Love does that; it is personified. Love is spoken of as a person there, as a being, a personality. "Love" does so and so. He means a person actuated by love does that. You can put God there and say God "suffers long and is kind," and the like, and it will make good sense, all the way through. You  can  put Jesus in there and say Jesus "suffers long and is kind," it still makes good sense. And you can put the word Christian in there and say a Christian "suffers long and is kind," and it still makes good sense. But if you put your  own  name down there, how do you feel? "I suffer long." About the first thing you know you are ready to  start  commenting and just leave off making the application any further. We are such poor specimens of it. God and Christ were good examples. I wouldn't be ashamed to put Paul down there, but when I put Gus Nichols of  Jasper,  Alabama,  down there, well, I get embarrassed before I go very far, and I feel like having a prayer instead of preaching a discourse.

We also need to consider the sacrifice that  God  made. (John 3:16.) **Love sacrifices.** "God so loved the world that he gave"—and love always gives. Love is liberal. I overheard a mother and her daughter talking just before "Easter" in an adjoining room to mine, when I was away in a meeting.  The daughter said, "Mother what are we going to be able to do for Easter?" She said, "Darling, your daddy and I have already talked it over." (They were just poor people, like most of us.) She said, "We  have  talked  that over and I am going to re-do my hat and my old suit and we are going to buy you a new outfit." I thought  that  is just like a mother to say we will re-do my old outfit and we will get Mary a new outfit for Easter. That is just like love, and oh, how this old world does need it! It is crying out for it! And there are so few people responding to the call, and the cry of great need.

That's not all, but **love bears our burdens** and makes them light. It is said in Genesis 29:20 that when Jacob worked seven years for Rachael, they "seemed unto him but a few days, for the love he had for her." Love made seven years of slavish toil to seem like a few days. That's what love can do. It can make our burdens light. While a nurse sits there bored to death at the long hours of night waiting upon a little child walking through the valley of the shadow of death, the mother sits there way in the small hours of the morning going into her seventh week. It's a joy that she can serve. She moistens the parched lips, administers a few drops of water, gives the medicine. She doesn't watch the clock. The nurse may watch the clock. There is a difference in the conduct of people who love and those who are serving for money—a world of difference there. And without love we are going to be ruined. We need to love to serve. I quote from Galatians 5:13, "By love serve one another."

I used to have on my desk a motto from the International Harvester Company which I kept for eight years. It said, **"I will love to do my work each day."** And I saw that thing so much all day long for eight years, that it became a part of me. And I believe that, God being my witness, I can say that I really love my work. I have even reached the point where I love for the brethren to criticize me. If they get any pleasure out of it and if they think it will do any good in the world, just let them go to it. Love makes the whole schedule a heavenly program, instead of being bored to death by it, eaten up by it, and becoming nervous wrecks and going to the hospital. We are becoming a nation of tranquilizer addicts because people don't love to do what God wants them to do. They are bored to death by their work. "All things work together for good to them that love God." (Romans 8:28.) To love God, we will do what he said and then everything will work for our good. That which was calculated to be evil will be turned into good.

"Old John" was the blind mule about the old home and the father had said to the boys that he wished Old John would die. He was blind and had been turned out to die. They didn't want to kill him. They loved Old John. He had been a faithful old mule all of his life. One day while the father was away, Old John fell into a deep pit about the place and the boys said this was their opportunity to get rid of Old John. "We are going to bury him alive." And they got their shovels and started shoveling dirt on him and as it would fall in on his back, he would shake it off. He would tramp around and stay on top, just like a Christian always wants to stay on top of his problems, instead of being subdued by them, overcome instead of being overcome by the world. And **when they got him buried alive, Old John went walking off!** The thing that they had calculated would destroy him had turned out to be the only way in the world that they could have gotten him out. And so I thank God that when everything sometimes seems to be headed toward my destruction, that everything is actually working like it did for Joseph to get him out of the pit and make him food administrator to save his people. With that sort of faith and love, nothing can keep us from succeeding.

Love is not just a sentimental feeling, either. It is a strong attachment to someone because of the worthwhileness, the worthy characteristics of that someone. And God is worthy, and when we do our best, we haven't loved him enough. He doesn't require us to do more than we can; but he is worthy of more, worthy of better preaching than we can do, better singing, better praying, better worship. He is worthy of more liberal giving than we can do. He doesn't demand any more of me than I can do, but he is worthy of more. "He that hath my commandments, and keepeth them, he it is that loveth me." (John 14:21.) And the golden rule is a matter of love. (Matt. 7:12.) But I only have time to touch these other points.

### Joy

"Joy in the Holy Ghost." (Romans 14:17.) "Rejoice . . .

and again I say, rejoice," said a man while in jail for preaching the gospel. (Phil. 4:4.) My wife and I were in that old pit, that old dungeon in Rome. Tradition says it is the same one just across the street from the old court house, and pretty close to the block where they cut Paul's head off. He wrote and said, "Rejoice in the Lord alway: and again I say, rejoice." In every chapter of the Philippian letter, he used the words joy, or rejoice in some form or other. And he was right then being persecuted, unjustly—was in jail and on the way to death and likely knew it. Moses chose to suffer affliction with the people of God rather than to enjoy the "pleasures of sin." (Heb. 11:24-27.) There may be pleasure in bank robbery, in robbing lovely wonderful young people of their virtue, robbing people of their good name and the like. There may be some joy to a totally-depraved person in that; but there cannot be any pleasure in that if you have a pure heart—if you love God and love people. Sin has its pleasure for sinful people, people whose hearts are wicked. But it also has a stinger in it. A mother's little child was being cared for by a maid. Little Johnny was crying and the mother told her to give him whatever he wanted. Little Johnny cried out again in a moment. The mother said, "I said give little Johnny what he wants" and the maid gave it to him about that time. And then little Johnny screamed even louder. The mother said, "I said give little Johnny what he wants." The maid said, "That's the trouble, he wanted this yellow jacket that was crawling here on the floor and when he got it, he found out he didn't want it." It had a stinger in it! And that is true of sin. Millions of people have been stung nearly to death by their sins. They are all swollen up. You know sometimes a sting can kill a man. I had a friend out near our town sometime ago, and had it not been for a nurse, one of our girls in the congregation there, who was out at the house when he got stung by just one bee, a honey bee, she said he would have died. Just one sting can kill certain people. They are allergic to it. Sin has its sting. "Be sure your sin will find you out." (Num. 32:23.) And, "The way of transgressors is hard." There is the stinger. (Prov. 13:15.) And then again, "whatsoever a man soweth,"—and if it's to the flesh, he will reap "corruption"—another stinger. (Gal. 6:7, 8.) It does not pay to sin. Not only does crime not pay, but no sin pays. Even the most innocent sort of an evil thought has a stinger in it. You may not feel it at first, but it will poison your soul eventually.

**Joy** is the fruit of the spirit. God wanted us to be the happiest people in all the world. He didn't want us to go around all the time like we were just back from the funeral of our whole family buried at one time. He wants us to be able to say, like Job, "The Lord gave and the Lord hath taken away. Blessed be the name of the Lord." (Job 1:21.) And like David. When his baby died, he went and washed his face and took food and was cheerful, and said, "I shall go to him, but he shall not return to me." (2 Sam. 12:15-23.)

### Peace

Isaiah 26:3: "Thou wilt keep him in perfect peace, whose mind is stayed on thee." Hebrews 12:14: "Follow peace with all men, and holiness, without which no man shall see the Lord." Romans 14:19: "Let us therefore follow after the things which make for peace, and things wherewith one may edify another." Romans 5:1: "Therefore being justified by faith, we have peace with God." Obeying the gospel, being at peace with God makes for peace. And then again, in Isaiah 9:6 Christ is called "the Prince of Peace." Ephesians 2:14 says, "He is our peace." He is the source of it. The angels, in Luke 2:13, 14, sang, "On earth peace, good will toward men," when he was born and they ushered him in. They introduced him, as it were, to the world. Thank God for the Prince of Peace. Had he not come we would have long ago destroyed one another by our inhumanity one toward another. It is too bad like it is, in spite of his influence. What would it have been had he never come? "As much as lieth in you, live peaceably with all men." (Rom. 12:18.) Be content with such things as you have. (1 Tim. 6:6-12.) All of this makes for peace. "I have learned in whatsoever state I am, therewith to be content." (Phil. 4:11.) Matthew 10:34 teaches us not to have peace at any price. "I came not to send peace"—that is at any price, at the compromise of truth. We are to be aggressive and take the sword of the spirit and put sin down in this world. Attack it. Attack it everywhere, beginning in the church, and in our homes and in our own lives.

### Longsuffering

Longsuffering means to suffer a long time. Those two words got married and became one word. Longsuffering. (Gal. 5:22-23; Eph. 4:1-3.) And that may mean in order to attain some worthy goal, like educating the children, getting them through college—suffer and suffer and suffer hardships that they might get by, get through somehow. Find a way or make one. Longsuffering love does that. It took Noah Webster thirty-six years to write his dictionary of the English language. He suffered a long time to accomplish what he did. It took Adam Clark forty-three years to write his commentary on the Bible. Forty-three years of longsuffering. It took a long time to get the job done. But it was worth it.

I was preaching in a meeting and a lady came forward with a large number of others—enough to make twenty-three to be baptized in the entire meeting. Only a few came that morning to be baptized, the most of them were restorations. But when Sister Barnwell came right behind her husband and was seated, I was surprised. She had the reputation of being the best woman in town—the best woman in that church, at least. They lived three miles out and when nobody in the family cared enough about the Lord to worship, she still cared and she would walk in to town three miles in bad weather, and worship, and walk back and then cook dinner for the rest of them. What a godly, wonderful woman she was. And when I got to her to see why she had come, I said, "Sister Barnwell, why have you come?" She was crying and she said, "I don't know, Brother Nichols, why I came. The first thing I knew I was down here. You see, this is my husband, and I have prayed forty-one years to see this." That is longsuffering. Sometimes it takes a long time to get a big job done—converting a husband or a wife. You could move a mountain and you wouldn't do anything comparable to that. Miracles are out. This is so much better than miracles. Miracles never have converted anybody directly; they were not for that purpose. Also, long suffering in persecutions (2 Tim. 3:12; Matt. 5:9-12) is another fruit of the Spirit.

## Kindness

We should show kindness to the brethren. (1 John 3:17-19.) Add to your faith virtue, knowledge, temperance, patience, godliness, **brotherly kindness** and charity. And that gives you the admission into the everlasting kingdom. (2 Pet. 1:5-11.) Eph. 4:32: "Be ye kind one to another, tenderhearted, forgiving one another, even as God for Christ's sake hath forgiven you." A Christian is kind in the use of his tongue. If a man doesn't bridle his tongue, his religion is vain. (James 1:26.) Even a dog likes kindness. He will leave his home if it is not a kind environment and then he will come over and live at your house if you are kind to him. Our son-in-law who lives at Jasper took our old tom cat away from us. We were away from home often and the first thing I knew Old Tom wouldn't stay at our house at all. He was down with Rile and Bertha. And so even lower animals respond to it. There is tremendous power in it. It is more powerful than miracles. Kindness will cause us to actually engage in benevolence. (James 2:14-18.) Don't say, "Depart in peace," but do something about it. Stand for it in the church and from the church treasury. (1 Cor. 16:1-3.) At the judgment that will come up as the main subject. "I was sick and you did something about it." (Matt. 25:31-46.)

## Faithfulness

"Be thou faithful unto death." (Rev. 2:10.) Matthew 25:14-30: "Well done, thou good and faithful servant." They had done something and had done it well. **"Thou good"**—they were good, morally good and then they were "faithful." Faithful is another married word. These two words, faith and full got married. They became one word. And hence the word faithful means what both words mean. It simply means full of faith to the end. Even young people can be faithful. "I have written unto you, young men, because you are strong, and the word of God abideth in you, and you have overcome the wicked one." (1 John

2:14.) We need to be faithful to the church. We need to be faithful to its eldership and its deacons—cooperate with them 100 per cent plus. We need to be faithful to the song leader. We need to be faithful to the janitor. We need to be faithful to one another. We need to be faithful to God. We need to be faithful to the outside world and render proper service and respect our obligations to the outside world. Be a good example at least. And be faithful to the Lord.

### Meekness

"Meekness" is the very opposite of pride. Meekness is **strength suffering**. It is not weakness. It is not an inferiority complex either. People are no account in the church who have an inferiority complex. They never undertake anything worthwhile, because they always imagine they cannot. They are just about as harmful in the church as those who are full of pride, and have themselves over-rated. In Romans 12:3, 4, Paul says man ought not to think of himself more highly than he ought, and he ought to think highly of himself. He is a child of God most high. His heavenly father owns it all, and he is heir to it. We don't need to go around imagining that we are nothing. I think the Israelites did themselves a disfavor and a discredit when they said, "We were in our own sight as grasshoppers." When a man gets a grasshopper complex, he is no account. (Num. 13:33.) No wonder they didn't go over and take the land. They said it is worth it, it is wonderful and it is fine; but we are grasshoppers, and they are giants. We have to deal with folks like that in the church. They hinder the work of the church. They are always saying, "We can't." "It is impossible for us to reach the budget, and thus and so." Galatians 6:1: **"In the spirit of meekness**, considering thyself." That is when you are restoring the other fellow. "I beseech you by the meekness and gentleness of Christ." (2 Cor. 10:1.) I want you to think about his meekness and his gentleness and then be influenced by that to live likewise. That is the idea.

### Temperance

This is the same as self control. (Gal. 5:22, 23.) Man needs to control himself. There are those who would like to un-

dertake to control the world; but they cannot control themselves. They would like to control a family; but they cannot control themselves. They would like to control the
church, but they cannot control themselves. And a man
who cannot control himself cannot control anything properly. When Adam fell and when sinners fall, they bring
down everything in the world under them. Every thing
that is under them comes crashing down with them. That
is why it is so bad for somebody to fall. They do not fall
alone. They bring others down. Paul said, "I keep under my
body, and bring it into subjection: lest that by any means,
when I have preached to others, I myself should be a cast-
away." ( 1 Cor. 9:25-27.) "If you live after the flesh, ye shall
die." (Rom. 8:13.) Learn to control yourself. Christians do
control themselves. They cease to be Christians when they
cease to control themselves. They who are Christ's "have
crucified" the flesh. They have already accomplished it,
every last one of them. "They that are Christ's have crucified the flesh with the affections and lusts." (Gal. 5:24.)

Strong drink, cigarette smoking—we have a brother that is
going to the grave smoking cigarettes; no doubt he has lung
cancer and he still will not stop. How on earth can a man
learn to be Christ-like and go around sucking a cigarette?
He is taking money away from the family, sometimes, that
is needed in the family budget. How can a man do that, the
echo answers back, "How?" and be a Christian? And then
we are to eat and drink to the glory of God. (1 Cor. 10:30,
31; 6:20.) "Glorify God therefore in your body, and in your
spirit, which are God's." This body belongs to God, he has
bought it and I am not honest if I don't deliver it. If I go
down and buy a brand new automobile and the man says,
"We are going to service it and I'll send it out. I'll present
it in the afternoon." And I wait and night comes and still
he hasn't delivered the car. I wait and the next day passes
and he hasn't delivered it. Weeks and weeks pass and he
hasn't delivered it. And months and months go by and he
hasn't delivered it. What do you think of a fellow like that?
I bought it, I paid for it. It's mine. He is supposed to present it. He is supposed to deliver it and he hasn't done it.
Is he an honest man? Is he a man of integrity? Is he a

worthwhile type of a citizen? He is a thief. He may be out of jail but he ought to be inside—a man that would do that. And that is some of my brethren. Not relative to automobiles, but God has bought their bodies, and paid for them, and their spirits, and they won't deliver the goods. "Present your bodies a living sacrifice, holy, acceptable unto God, which is your reasonable service." (Rom. 12:1, 2.) And they won't do it. They don't do it. They won't let God have the body. They won't let God have the spirit. Although they won't let God have it, he has bought it, he has paid for it. He paid a tremendous price for it. If all the wealth of the world were converted into gold, and that whole sum offered for one man's spirit and body, it wouldn't be comparable to the price that God paid for my soul and spirit. No wonder Paul said, "Thanks be unto God for his unspeakable gift." (2 Cor. 9:15.) You can't speak it s worth! You can speak a billion. You can't comprehend it perhaps. And you can speak a trillion, but you can't comprehend that, of course. **You can't even speak the value of the Son of God to a man. A billion worlds like this would not equal the value of the Son of God**. "Thanks be unto God for his unspeakable gift." (2 Cor. 9:15.)

Let us stand and sing the hymn of invitation.

# UNITY OF THE SPIRIT

Let us read concerning the Holy Spirit and the subject of "Unity." "I therefore, the prisoner of the Lord, beseech you that ye walk worthy of the vocation wherewith ye are called, with all lowliness and meekness, with longsuffering, forbearing one another in love; endeavoring to keep the unity of the Spirit in the bond of peace. There is one body, and one Spirit, even as ye are called in one hope of your calling; One Lord, one faith, one baptism, one God and Father of all, who is above all, and through all, and in you all." (Eph. 4:1-6.)

## Be Filled With The Spirit

These Ephesian Christians had received the Holy Spirit. "After that ye believed, ye were sealed with that Holy Spirit of promise." (Eph. 1:13.) They had received the Holy Spirit as "promised" in Acts 2:38. God had the apostle Peter, who was guided and spoke by the Holy Spirit, to say, "Repent and be baptized every one of you in the name of Jesus Christ for the remission of sins, and ye shall receive the gift of the Holy Ghost." (Acts 2:38.) The "gift of the Holy Ghost" is the "promise" to them. Then again, we read: "Grieve not the holy Spirit of God, whereby ye are sealed unto the day of redemption." (Eph. 4:30.) They had been sealed by the Holy Spirit. The Holy Spirit had been given them as a "seal," as a pledge of God's further fulfillment of great and gracious promises. And so, they had the Holy Spirit.

Yet, in the next chapter, Paul said, "Be not drunk with wine, wherein is excess; but be filled with the Spirit." (Eph. 5:18.) He mentions their worship. (v. 19.) So, those who have the Spirit as they had the Spirit (Eph. 1:13; 4:30) could still "be filled with" the Spirit. It follows therefore, that the reception of the Holy Spirit is not limited to one reception, to be through with it, with no other case in which we could receive more of the Holy Spirit. We are to partake more and more of his nature—the divine nature—as we drink in the Spirit: "For by one Spirit are we all baptized into one body . . . and have been all made to drink into one Spirit." (1 Cor. 12:13.) Drink in it! Partake of it! We partake of **Christ** more and more, as we read in Gal. 4:19: "My little children, of whom I travail in birth again until Christ be formed in you." Christ was already in these Galatian Christians, for of course one could not be a Christian without Christ dwelling in him. But yet, they were to partake more and more of Jesus, until he is more fully formed in them—"until Christ be formed in you." Earlier, Paul wrote, "That ye, being rooted and grounded in love, may be able to comprehend with all saints what is the breadth, and length, and depth, and height; and to know the love of Christ, which passeth knowledge, that ye might be filled with all the fulness of God." (Eph. 3:17-18.) This shows that we may be filled more and more with all "the fulness of God." The Ephesians had received the Spirit (1:13), were sealed by it (4:30), and yet were to "be filled with" it. (5:18.) The trouble is that most of us are too empty! We are driving on a tea-cup full of gas (as it were). We need to "fill up!" "My cup runneth over." (Ps. 23:5.) So we need to fill up until we preach, and sing, and pray, and work, and serve out of the "overflow" of all "the fulness of God." (Eph. 3:19.)

### Prerequisites To Unity

What Paul said preceding verse 3 is as essential to "the unity of the Spirit" as what he says following that verse. Many good sermons have emphasized the fact that there are seven planks in the platform of divine unity. But there is more to stress than merely the seven "ones." (Eph. 4:4-6.)

### "I Beseech You"

Paul said, "I therefore the prisoner of the Lord beseech you . . ." (Eph. 4:1.) Even in this there is a principle which promotes unity. First of all, Paul was an apostle, an inspired man. As an apostle he had divine authority. He could have said, "I command you." On some occasions he did write, "I command you, brethren . . ." (2 Thess. 3:6.) So, at times he did command, but only when it was essential to do it. He was not "drunk" on authority. Nor did he find some special type of joy and pleasure in **exercising author-ity** over brethren. One thing that is essential to unity is the spirit of humility, the spirit of meekness. Paul, in Eph. 4:1, did not say, "I command you brethren . . ." He did not even say, "I ask," or "I request you, brethren "—as he could have said. Instead he wrote, "I . . . **beseech** you." What is the difference? It is not a mere technical distinction; there is much difference between "I command" and "I beseech" you. To say, "I command you" puts the one in authority above the other; he looks down on the other; they are to be submissive and subservient to him, and to his will, in the matter. They were to be under his authority, and his "command" would remind them of this.

"I **request** you, brethren," would have been putting them upon the same level with him, and would have made them equals. Any one of us could say to the rest, "I want to make a request of you." (A brother did that at this service: he gave me an envelope with his address, and "requested" —he did not command, but "requested"—that I reply by letter to a certain matter.) Any of us may make a "request" of the rest. To treat each other as equals is a lovely spirit, isn't it? But for one on our same level to issue "orders" or "commands" would be entirely different, and would grate on our sensitive nerves—at least a little! So, there is a great deal of difference. Our attitude toward one another has much to do with unity.

But Paul did not even make a "request" of the Ephesians —as an equal: he became an **inferior**! He got down below them on his knees, and looked up at these brethren, saying, "I . . . beseech you." (Eph. 4:1.) He was beneath them, en-treating them. That beautiful spirit is a challenge for our consideration, isn't it. There is nothing in the Bible amiss, nothing just to fill up space and make a larger book out of what would have been a smaller book; but every word of God is "profitable," some for doctrine, some for reproof, some for correction, some for instruction in righteousness.

(2 Tim. 3:16-17.) All of it is for some good purpose. "The words of the Lord are pure words: as silver tried in a furnace of earth, purified seven times." (Ps. 12:6.) There is no impurity in it, nothing amiss, nothing superfluous about the word of God. So, Paul said, "I . . . beseech you that you walk worthy of your vocation." (Eph. 4:1.) This is as essential to the "unity of the Spirit" as what follows verse 3.

## Must Agree

". . . that ye walk . . ." (Eph. 4:1.) We can't walk together without agreement. We can't have unity without walking in the same direction. The prophet asked, "Can two walk together, except they be agreed?" (Amos 3:3.) That rhetorical question simply means they can not. If two are going to walk together, they must agree on a starting place. Where are we going to get together? Shall we meet at the public square? Or at what particular place? Where shall we meet in order to start walking together? We must have a starting place. This must be agreed upon.

And we must agree upon a time. If one says, "I am going to walk today," and the other says, "I can't walk until next week," they can't walk together! If they walk together, they must agree upon a time to walk. But if they agree upon a place to start, and a time to walk, they still are not sufficiently agreed. Suppose one of them says, "I am going to walk west," while the other says, "That doesn't suit me; I'm going east." They can't walk together, can they? They are not agreed. Suppose one of them says, "I'm going to walk at the rate of four miles per hour," while the other says, "That is too fast for me; I think two, or two-and-one-half miles an hour will be sufficient." The first thing you know, they would not be walking together, because they are not "agreed" upon the speed. So they must agree. "Can two walk together except they be agreed?"

## A Worthy Walk

It is essential that we walk worthily of our "vocation;" and if we do not, but are unworthy of our calling as Christians, there will be a lack of Christian unity among us because some are not walking worthy of their calling. God "called" us by the gospel (2 Thess. 2:14), and we are to "walk worthy" of our vocation or calling.

## Your Vocation

The Christian life is our "vocation." It is not an "avocation," or side-line. For example, the vocation of a physician is the practice of medicine. Day or night, when he is urgently needed, he lays aside everything else (which he makes to be nothing but an avocation) in the interest of his "vocation." If someone has been in an accident, and is bleeding profusely, and needs medical attention immediately, the doctor may be working in his flower garden (which may be his avocation) but he would lay all of that aside, and leave it, putting his "vocation" ahead of and before all else. We must put living the Christian life ahead of every other thing in the world.

## A Hindrance To Unity

One hindrance to the unity of the Spirit is that we are living in a secular age. We see everything through the spectacles of "dollar-marks." We are materialistic, we think of values in terms of money, and houses, and lands, and things of that sort. We forget that one little child to be reared and trained for the Lord, can rear and train others, and they others, and they others (Ps. 78:5-6), until in a thousand years there may be thousands of souls in heaven—all because we took time out to train **one**. Or, it may be the other way: if we fail, it may be that this **one** will fail, others under like influence will fail, and others still under those influences will fail—and there may be thousands of souls burning and suffering in hell forever, a billion years from now, all because we put money, and other things, ahead of the spiritual—because we failed to train a child, failed to put the kingdom first. (Matt. 6:33.) This is important and basic; it is fundamental, and must not be relegated to the background. When we put the kingdom and the work of the Lord in the background, and put the world and everything of this life ahead of it, we are not going to be the type of people that can get along with others. We will be so materialistic, until it will be like tying a cat and dog together. They will not get along very well. The first thing you know they will be in a fight! If you tie up the right kind of person with a terribly bad and wicked person, they won't get along very well!

## Not Compromise

The "unity of the Spirit" does not mean that Christians are to compromise and go along with error, and compromise the truth. Jesus said, "I came not to send peace, but a sword." (Luke 12:51-53.) Oh, yes, Jesus wants unity, but he does not want it at just any price. He does not want peace where his people must give over to the devil and his cause. A farmer can ease away from the fence, and from the ditch, and from the hedge-rows; as the briars grow, he can just back off, and give over to them, until—the first he knows, he is cultivating a few acres right out in the middle of the field, while briars are taking the rest of the field! The devil can take this world, and he is taking it over more rapidly than we imagine. Communism (which is a form of Atheism) can so take over as to finally get at the steering-wheel. It may be a thousand years, if the world stands, before we can ever get it back out of the control of Atheism, so that we can have the liberty to function as Christians only. We need to be careful, put the kingdom first, and "walk worthy"—not in some avocation, or side-line, but in the "vocation wherewith we are called, with all lowliness, and meekness, . . ." (Eph. 4:1-2.) Then we can get along with one another, and promote the "unity of the Spirit in the bond of peace."

## Forbearance

Paul further says, "Forbearing one another in love." Suppose I have mistreated you, and you know how you could hurt me. You have the law on your side, and I don't have the law in my favor at all. You have advantage of me, and you know it. Forbearance says, "Don't use it. Wait awhile! Give God time to work it out. Give the word of God time. Give all heaven time to work in us, and through us, to solve our problems for us. Don't be too hasty when you don't know what to do. Don't rush on without investigation." "Stand ye in the ways, and see, and ask for the old paths, wherein is the good way, and walk therein . . ." (Jer.

6:16.) Stop, if you don't know what to do. Investigate; find out before you act at all. I think Balaam did a wonderfully fine thing when he did not know what to do, and he went to the Lord about it. "Shall I curse those people, or not?" (Num. 22.) The Lord said, "No." That should have been the end of all controversy. But Balaam did the most foolish thing of his life: after he already had God's decision on the matter, he went back to the Lord, to try to get God to change his mind. That is like a man who finds the truth in the Bible, but does not like it: he goes careering around through the Bible, looking for something he likes better— looking for a delusion—and he always gets one. That is the kind of person to whom God sends "a strong delusion," that he might "believe a lie and be damned." (2 Thess. 2:10-12.) He **wants** to believe a lie, anyway; he does not want the truth.

### God Loves Man

God never aids nor assists in his error a man who wants the truth, and wants to turn from his wickedness and get out of it. But he will "send a strong delusion" to the man who is seeking some pretext or excuse to get to go on and do what he wants to do, regardless of God's will. When a man is determined to do that, he is lost anyway. And God will send him a "working of error" (ASV), a strong—not a little, weak—"delusion," that he might believe a lie and be damned. (2 Thess. 2:10-12.)

We have certain tests that we must go through in this world before we can be developed into mature Christians. If we are not going to accept these tests, then God will aid us in going in the other direction—not because he wants us to be lost, but we would be lost anyway. He just separates us from his people and their fellowship, by giving us a delusion of some sort. That will bring out the wickedness that is already in our hearts. The sunflower keeps its face toward the sun all day long. When the sun rises, the sunflower turns its face toward the east, with its neck bowed over in that direction. Then, at noon, it still has its big face turned toward the sun. And at sunset, it is turned toward the sun. When God sees a man with his face turned toward heaven, toward God and his word, he never sends a delusion of any kind—not even a **weak** one—to that person, because he wants God. He hungers and thirsts for God. As David said, "My soul thirsteth for God, for the living God." (Ps. 42:2; cf. 63:2; 143:6.) A man in a parched desert, where there is no water, would give a dollar—perhaps much more —for just one little swallow of water! Likewise, when we yearn for God, long for—"hunger and thirst after righteousness" (Matt. 5:6)—God will help us to find it. He will "fill" that person with righteousness.

### Longsuffering

To attain the unity of the Spirit, in addition to "lowliness and meekness," we need "longsuffering." It takes time to get big things done. A giant oak tree is not made overnight. We have to be patient if we are going to grow to be big trees. If you want to grow great men and women in the church, you have to be patient in working with them. You will have to remember that none of us was strong at first when we were little sprouts or saplings. Exercise good judgment and wisdom in dealing with each other. Do not provoke one another to sin and evil, nor aggravate and stir up trouble or strife. Instead, "seek peace and ensue it." (1 Pet. 3:8-11.) Take off after peace, and run after it, like a dog after a fox. Chase it! Run it down and catch it, and you will have it and possess it. That is exactly the idea.

"Longsuffering" means to suffer a long time. It means altogether the opposite of a fickle spirit that will act upon the spur of the moment, and then regret and repent (maybe forever) some decision made in a fit of temper, or under stress, strain, or provocation of some sort. One who is "longsuffering" takes time to pray about it. And yet, people can be too slow, at times when they should decide and act quickly. We should never act until we have decided, and until we have decided in the light of divine truth.

### Forbear One Another

"Walk worthy of the vocation wherewith ye are called. with all lowliness, and meekness, with longsuffering, **forbearing one another** . . ." (Eph. 4:1-2.) You could hurt some fellow. You know something you could tell about him that would hurt him, but you "forbear" to do it. You restrain yourself. This will promote unity! It will go a long way toward having unity. Overlook the faults of others—actually forget them. Someone reminded me of a man in our congregation (where I have been preaching since Jan. 1, 1933), who was guilty thirty years ago of a flagrant sin. Although I had a part in bringing him to repentance, I had forgotten it. Honestly, for 15 or 20 years I had not even thought about the fact that he had to be restored! When we forbear one another, we will soon forget. We will not talk about it—not to our companions in the home, nor to anyone else. If you want to talk about it so that it won't hurt, talk to **God** about it! There is no limit to the amount of time you could spend talking to him about it. You will probably be very careful what you say if you are talking to God! These are some simple, common-sense, basic facts (which are often overlooked); but they have to do with "Unity." And this is the "unity of the Spirit," as you will see later.

### Love

Paul next says, "**forbearing** one another **in love**." (Eph. 4:2.) There are different ways of forbearing. One may "forbear" on the ground that he is afraid of retaliation. He is afraid to hurt the other fellow, because of the fear that he will be hurt in return. And so, not having on "the breastplate of righteousness" (Eph. 6:14), he is afraid to stab, because he is afraid he will be stabbed! That is not "forbearing **in love**," but is forbearing **in fear**. Let us love people, and love them so much that we won't hurt them. I have always respected Joseph, the husband of Mary. God tells us that Joseph was going to put Mary away "privily." (Matt. 1:18-20.) He could have been severe with her, for it was a death penalty to have a child out of wedlock. (Deut. 22:23-24.) Joseph was thinking that this baby was to be born out of wedlock, but he knew he was not the father of it; he felt Mary was not a good woman—so he resolved to legally terminate his engagement to her. But he said he was going to do this "privily," or secretly. (Matt. 1:18-20; cf. Luke 1:26-35.) Joseph was not going to let anybody know there was anything wrong. He was going to keep it under cover. He thought, "I know something about you, Mary— but I'm not going to publicize it, I am not going to advertise it; I am going to handle it in the way that it will hurt the least." Don't you admire Joseph?

Paul said, "I beseech you by the meekness and gentleness of Christ." (2 Cor. 10:1.) I love Paul's expression! If a doctor has to cut on me, I don't want him to see just how painful and hurtful he can make it! I want him to be as gentle as possible.

Perhaps I have had more experience than any other man in the South in dealing with church problems and church troubles. Once some elders had to reprove and admonish a guilty man. One of them (his kinsman) said, "I feel for you, because when I was about your age, I know how weak I was. I just happened not to get in the clutches of the law; but I could have been, had they caught me. I would have been guilty before the law, just like you are. I feel for you. I want you to know that you are not in the presence of enemies; we are your friends. We want to go to heaven, and we want you to go with us." The man broke down and cried like a little child. Tearfully he said, "I want to go, too," and confessed his wrongs, and penitently sought forgiveness. That is "forbearing . . . in love."

Many times the operation is successful because the doctor didn't see just how much he could hurt, or how much he could cut! He didn't get any joy out of hurting. So we, likewise, need to have love back of all these things. We need to love one another as brethren. (1 Pet. 3:8; 2:17.) We can know that we are Christians, not just because we have believed, repented, confessed Christ, and been baptized! These things are essential, but we may have done all that through formality. We may not have done these things "from the heart." (Rom. 6:17-18.) How may I know, then, whether I was sincere in it, or not? The Bible gives us a rule. "We know that we have passed from death unto life, because we love the brethren " (1 John 3:14)—not just because we have been baptized! We do not know it was acceptable unless we love the brethren. Now, if we don't love the brethren, if we had rather be anywhere else rather than with the brethren, I just wonder if we have been born again??? How could we be children of God, and not love one another? It's natural for normal children under normal environment to love one another. (John 13:34-35.)

### Unity Is "Of The Spirit"

Next Paul says, **"Endeavoring to keep the unity of the Spirit."** (Eph. 4:3.) How do it? By doing those things just emphasized, as well as what follows. The unity "of the Spirit" is the unity into which the Holy Spirit **leads** us. Paul says, "As many as are **led** by the Spirit of God, they are the sons of God." (Rom. 8:14.) So the Holy Spirit **leads** us who are children of God. Paul was not here talking about alien sinners. He wrote this to the church, to Christians. "To all that be in Rome, beloved of God, called to be saints." (Rom. 1:7.) He was writing to children of God, and this needs to be understood. "As many"—as many of you who are addressed, you Christians in Rome—"As many as are led by the Spirit of God . . ." This means, "As many members of the church, as many Christians, as are led by the Spirit of God, they are the sons of God." What about those members who are not led by the Holy Spirit, but are led by the spirit of the devil? Though they may have been baptized, they have the spirit of the devil in them. Well, they will cause division and strife and trouble in the church. Like the rotten apple in a barrel, they will cause others to rot and perish. They are **not** led by the Holy Spirit. They can't go to heaven.

### Holy Spirit Leads Us

How does the Holy Spirit "lead" us? He leads us through his word. David said, "The Spirit of the Lord spoke by me, and his word was in my tongue." (2 Sam. 23:2.) When they heard David speak as an inspired prophet, and followed his teaching, they were being led by the Spirit. It was the Spirit doing the teaching. Nehemiah (9:20) said, "Thou gavest also thy good Spirit to instruct them." He said God "testifiedest against them by thy Spirit in thy prophets." (v. 30.) So God gave the Spirit to the prophets, to testify against those people at that time though they were wicked, and to "instruct" them in behalf of their doing right.

When we follow the **instruction** of the Holy Spirit, we are following the Holy Spirit. If you follow the instructions in a letter from a friend, you are not just following the instructions of a piece of paper—you will be following your friend's instructions. So it is, when you follow the instruction of the Holy Spirit, you are not just following the instruction of a book, or a piece of paper; you are not following the instruction of printer's ink. You are following the instruction of the Holy Spirit. The Holy Spirit is guiding and directing you. "He will guide you"—apostles—"into all truth." (John 16:13.) How would he do that? By teaching the truth to them, and through them presenting it to others, the Spirit guides people by the truth which they taught. "He shall teach you"—apostles—"all things." (John 14:26.) And hence, we follow the Holy Spirit when we follow his word.

### Led By Word

Now, if we turn up our noses at his word, and take off after some "feeling," after some sort of "hunch," that is not following the Holy Spirit. We must "hear what the Spirit **saith** unto the churches." (Rev. 1:7.) The Spirit was saying his directions through the letter that he had written through the apostle John to those people. When we hear the letter, we hear what the Spirit **"saith"** to us as members of the church. He guides Christians by talking to us through inspired men. This is the only way in the world we can follow the Spirit. You will be following superstitious ideas, and you will go astray, if you begin to follow imaginations and the like.

One denominational preacher says that he has been directly called of God to preach a certain doctrine. Another contradicts that by saying the Spirit called him to preach **against** that doctrine. One preacher claims he was called by the Spirit to preach "once in grace, always in grace" (or the impossibility of apostasy). Another says he was called by the Spirit, that same Spirit, to preach that one **can apos-**

**tatize**—that a child of God can so live as to finally be lost in hell. They are contradicting one another! Somebody is not following the Spirit. Somebody has missed it.

Why not follow the "call" of God **in the Bible?** Concerning becoming a Christian, Paul said, "He called you by the gospel." (2 Thess. 2:14.) Why not follow that gospel? It was preached with the "Holy Ghost sent down from heaven." (1 Pet. 1:12.) By that same gospel men are "called into one body." (Col. 3:15.) So if we follow the Holy Spirit, we will all enter one body, be called into the same body, says this verse. The Holy Spirit never called anybody into a sect, or a party, or a faction, or a denominational church.

Men get into denominations, sects, or factions by following their "hunches" or their imaginations, feelings and dreams, or by following their own wishes. Some feel obligated because their parents, or other kin, belonged to it. "Loved ones"—people who died a generation ago—"would 'turn over in their graves' if I did not follow their example." Well, I know, because I was once like that; I have had that experience. I was the first one of my relatives to ever obey the gospel of Christ as it is in the Book. I know what a tremendous "pull" these other things can have against one who has heard the gospel. One seems to be living between two worlds, hardly knowing which way to turn! I had to make a grave decision that will determine where I will be a billion, trillion, years later! People like that need sympathy from us. But those who reject the very words of the Holy Spirit, and turn off to something else, need reproving, and rebuking. (2 Tim. 4:2.)

### One Body
Paul then said in our text, "There is one body." (Eph. 4:1-4.) He starts with "one body." As long as there are two bodies, or three bodies, or 1,200 bodies, there is no "unity of the Spirit." Division is among those who compose those different bodies. They are not united. Jesus prayed that his disciples might all be one. (John 17:20-21.) He gave a perfect standard of unity, or a standard of perfect unity at which to aim. Though we may never fully reach it, we

should always aim at it. He prayed for such perfect unity "as thou, Father, art in me, and I in thee, that they also may be one in us: that the world may believe that thou hast sent me." (John 17:21.) He added, "That they may be one **as we are one**." (v. 22.) There is the ideal. Strive to be united as perfectly as God and his Son Jesus are united. Jesus was united with the Father because he always was ready to do the Father's will. "I came down from heaven, not to do mine own will, but the will of him that sent me." (John 6:38.) So, he was dedicated and consecrated to doing the will of the Father, even when it cost him his own life and every drop of his precious blood to obey the Father's will. "He became obedient unto death, even the death of the cross." (Phil. 2:5-11.) When we are dedicated to God's will like that, we can come into one body, and have unity.

### One Spirit

Paul further said, "There is one Spirit." (Eph. 4:4.) The one Holy Spirit leads us into that one body. "By one Spirit" —the one Holy Spirit—"are we all baptized into one body." (1 Cor. 12:13.) That one Spirit, **by his instruction, by his teaching**, leads us to be "baptized into one body." Paul then said, "We drink into one Spirit." (1 Cor. 12:13.) There is the reception of the Holy Spirit after we have been baptized— as led by the Spirit, through his teaching, through the gospel, to be baptized in water into the one body—then we "drink into" and begin to "partake" of the Holy Spirit so that he dwells in us. The "one Spirit" in leading us gives us laws by which to be governed; hence, "The law of the Spirit of life in Christ Jesus hath made me free from the law of sin and death." (Rom. 8:2.) The Holy Spirit has a law—a law of pardon for aliens, and a second law of pardon for erring children of God. It is different from the first: no baptism is required in the second law of pardon. (Acts 8:22-24.) But the same inspired preacher (in Acts 2:38) put baptism in the first law of pardon.

### Law Of Spirit

We must follow the "law of the Spirit." He has a law of worship, and it is "the law of the Spirit of life," a rule of life. Law is a rule by which we must be governed. The

Holy Spirit has given us law, but he has also given us "liberty." (2 Cor. 3:17.) However, the Holy Spirit has given us no liberty to violate law. He has given us no choice when God has spoken. When God specifies a thing, we are not to do something else, nor substitute something else for it. We cannot be led by the Spirit and substitute like that.

When the Holy Spirit tells us to do a thing, the thing is authorized. But if he did not tell us **how** to do the thing, but left that up to our option and our judgment, then there is liberty. And "where the Spirit of the Lord is, there is liberty." (2 Cor. 3:17.) There is always liberty connected with the Christian life, under **generic** law. In **specific** law, there is no liberty—we must do the very thing specified. If God specified the "way" to do it, then the "how" becomes a part of the law—it must be done as specified. But if God does not give the way, then there is liberty.

So Paul says, "Endeavoring to keep the unity of the Spirit in the bond of peace." (Eph. 4:3.) That means then, that we must press it upon people to do what the "law of the Spirit" says. (Rom. 8:2.) We must enforce that. We are to discipline people who won't follow the Holy Spirit. We should never allow anybody to go to the judgment in our fellowship who is not on the way to heaven while going to the judgment. If we know a man is on the way to perdition, and we can't turn him, get him to live right we ought to withdraw fellowship from him. (2 Thess. 3:6.) (Of course, we sincerely seek to convert him from "the error of his way." Jas. 5:19-20.) Hence, there is liberty. "Stand fast therefore in the liberty wherewith Christ hath made us free." (Gal. 5:1.) There is "liberty" in Christianity. However, it is not **all** "liberty," nothing but "liberty." No; there is also "law." If a man wants to get into jail, just let him get out here and violate the law. He has a lot of liberty, although we may be losing some of it, for aught I know. (It seems to me we are losing many liberties, in allowing the federal government to take us over, so Communism can just grab the 'steering-wheel' so we will live under Communism. It seems to me there is a danger involved.)

## Matters Of Liberty

But, coming back to the main point: there is "liberty." In the great commission, when God said, "Go preach the gospel" (Matt. 28:18-19; Mark 16:15), he "bound" or specified the thing to be done—and we must "go"—we must do that very thing. **But he did not tell them "how" to go.** There is liberty there. Hence, we can have peace by each allowing the other to have that "liberty" which God gave. Brethren do not have to build all meeting houses alike. God did not prescribe the type building. (In fact, he did not even command that we build a house at all.) The building comes in under the generic authority that authorizes us to assemble. (Heb. 10:25.) He requires us to "come together into one place" (1 Cor. 14:23), but left that place to our judgment. That's a matter of "liberty." There ought to be no division about things like that. If it is a congregational matter, the elders decide it. If the elders decide that we are going to meet at 9:30 for Bible school on Sunday morning, instead of 10:00 o'clock, we ought to have unity in that. If it is the decision of the elders that we sing three songs before we have a prayer, we can all go along with that, just as when the leader says we are going to sing "No. 20," we all unite in it. **Nobody accuses the leader of making a law.** He has not made any law. If we are going to sing at all, we are going to have to sing one song at a time. Certainly, we would not be singing "decently and in order" (1 Cor. 14:40) if one started singing, "Jesus, Lover of my Soul," while another sings, "What A Friend We Have In Jesus." You would have confusion, and "God is not the author of confusion." (1 Cor. 14:33.)

If we are going to observe the Lord's supper at 12:00 o'clock, and somebody says, "No! I'm going to wait until 3:00 o'clock"—you would have division that way. You would have trouble in the church. You would build up a faction before you knew what happened. And so, in expedients, the Spirit has left us free, and left us "liberty," by authorizing the thing, but leaving the method, the "manner," to human judgment. To the extent that there is anything about it that is optional with us, to that extent God's law is **generic**.

Brethren, you may not have observed it—I was a long time learning it—but **a command may be both "generic" and "specific."** Take the command to baptize: it is **specific** as to the act. It is a burial, an immersion. Baptism is not sprinkling, nor pouring. But "baptize" is **generic** as to where it is performed—in a river, or lake, or baptistry; in warm water or cold, muddy water, or clear. All such matters are left to human judgment. When people start fussing over things like that, they are trying to make laws for God, or to obey a law some other fellow made. So, don't make a law that a man must be baptized in a baptistry, and don't make a law that he must **not** be. You will destroy liberty. If you change "generic" law into "specific" law, you pervert the word of God. Do not begin to change these things where God left us liberty. Where God tells us to do benevolent work, let us do it. If he tells us "how," authorizing all the details, then follow them. (I deny that God has done that, however.) He has not told us the "how," and we must not let anybody make a certain "how" into a law, or forbid any "generic" way of doing it. Use "liberty" there. The "unity of the Spirit" involves liberty.

### One Hope and One Faith

"There is . . . one hope of your calling." (Eph. 4:4.) That "hope" is heaven. And there is also the "one faith." (Eph. 4:5.) There is a difference between **faith**, and **opinion**. It is a matter of "faith" that we go preach the gospel; it is a matter of "opinion" as to how best to travel. It is a matter of "faith" that we are to be baptized, be immersed; it is a matter of "opinion" as to whether to immerse in a baptistry, or in a river. It is a matter of "faith" that we sing; it is a matter of "opinion" which song book to use, whether to sing soprano, alto, tenor, or bass—and how to get the pitch is a matter of opinion. In matters of "opinion" where the whole church is involved, let the elders decide; where the decision is going to affect all of us, let them make it. They are not making laws, but are just deciding that we will do it a certain way.

Our elders at Jasper, Alabama, decided back yonder more than thirty years ago that we would not use instrumental music in our auditorium, or on our premises, in connection with weddings. A few years ago a young couple wanted to use instrumental music in their wedding ceremony, and asked to bring in the instrument. The young man, a member of the church, asked, "Do you think it is a sin to use instrumental music in a wedding?" I said, "No." "Do you think it would be sinful to use it in this auditorium?" I said, "No, not per se, apart from the worship, as in a wedding." "Well, then, we are going to have it." I replied, "No you are not, either. The elders have decided that we will not have it, and I will not be a party to it. They would hold me responsible, and rightly so. We are not going to have it." He was becoming very stubborn about it: "You are making a law!" I said, "No, I'm not; I am just making a choice, and upholding the elders in their choice. I believe we could use, or not use, it (apart from the worship). But the elders have decided we will not. It would get up a lot of trouble, and we are not going to have it. We are going to help the elders 'keep the unity of the Spirit in the bond of peace' while we have peace." So then, you can see that there is a choice to be made under "generic" authority. But if we had made a law that it would be sinful for a couple to get married in connection with the use of instrumental music in the ceremony, we would be in the wrong. We are not going to get ourselves into such trouble. We will look upon it as a matter of indifference, and let elders decide such matters of expedience which involve the congregation. (This very couple obtained a denominational church house so they could have instrumental music, and wanted me to say the ceremony—which I did. But when they wanted me to pray to the instrumental accompaniment of "The Lord's Prayer," I refused, saying, "I can't do that. That would put me to praying with instrumental music. I'm not going to do that. You do your own playing and your own singing; then when you get through, I'll say the ceremony and lead us in prayer as best I can.") We need to have convictions about such things where the truth is at stake. Of course, there are times when some contend where there is no principle at stake—they just contend for contention's sake.

### One Lord

But there is also the "one Lord" (Eph. 4:5) who has all authority. (Matt 28:18-20.) He has authorized certain things **specifically**, and other things **generically**. And we must teach it like he did. When it is **specifically** taught, we teach it **specifically**, and **practice** it thus. If he has taught it **generically**, we teach it that way, and practice it thus, and allow or extend "liberty." He is our authority.

### One Baptism

And then there is the "one baptism." (Eph. 4:5.) That baptism is baptism in water which brings us into that one body.

### One God

There is "one God . . . who is above all, and through all, and in you all." (Eph. 4:6.) This God is back of the whole scheme of human redemption. All of it grows out of his marvelous, and amazing, and wonderful love, exhibited in the gift of his Son, that we might be saved. The gospel is the sweetest story that has ever been told or heard in this world! By it, and it alone, can we be saved, and know the "unity of the Spirit."

### Bible Basis Of Unity

All true disciples should be united upon faith in Christ and obedience to him. All who believe in Christ and implicitly obey him will certainly go to heaven at last, and if we go there we must eventually be with them forever. We might as well be with them now, and they with us, here in the congregations of the saints. To walk by faith and to do his commandments embraces the whole Christian life, and is enough to save all men. (Rev. 2:10; 22:14.) No one can possibly be a Christian without faith in Christ. Neither can one be a Christian who will not obey Christ. (Gal. 3:26-28; 1 John 2:3-4.)

### Individual Matter

Each of us must believe in Christ whether others will let

us be in their fellowship or not. (Acts 16:30-34; Rom. 1:17.) And we must obey Christ in all things and do his will in order to go to heaven, whether or not others will let us be in their fellowship. We must not compromise concerning our faith in Christ and obedience to him. (Heb. 5:8-9; Heb. 11:6-30; Luke 12:51-53.)

## A False Way Of Unity

Some preach, teach and follow a false way of unity. They actually cause divisions contrary to the doctrine of Christ by their false doctrines and practices. By their good words and fair speeches they deceive the hearts of the simple. (Rom. 16:17-18.)

Some want us to unite with them in their modernism and unbelief. They reject the truth of the virgin birth, the deity and Sonship of Christ, his miracles, his atoning blood, his death for our sins and his bodily resurrection, ascension, and the like. They want all to unite with them in rejecting the authority of Christ and his commandments. We can have no scriptural church, nor unity on anything less than wholehearted faith in Christ and obedience to him. Those who reject the authority of Christ and his commandments may be united, but they are united in sin and iniquity. Let us not overlook the fact that sinners may be united, as well as the saints of God.

## Strong Faith Will Always Obey

We should all be united in obeying the gospel of Christ. (Rom. 10:16; 1 Pet. 4:17; 2 Thes. 1:7-9.) We must not change the Lord's plan of salvation to be united with others. Neither must we change the divinely appointed worship in the interest of some sort of unity. And we must not change the organization of the church to please men. Where the Lord has spoken we cannot compromise. We must have unity in the faith of the gospel, and not in error and false teaching. We must abide in the doctrine of Christ, whether others like it, and unite with us in doing likewise or not. (2 John 9-11.) We must unite in teaching and preaching the truth, believing and obeying the truth. This is the unity of the Spirit which we are to endeavor to keep in the bond of peace. (Eph. 4:3.) The Spirit, by his word, leads us into this unity, if we will follow his teaching in the New Testament. (2 Cor. 3:6; Heb. 9:15-17.)

### What About Specific Authority?

Liberalism trifles with specific authority. It disobeys, adds to, takes from, or substitutes something else for those things which Christ has commanded and specified. This produces vain worship and vain religion. (Matt. 15:9; Mark 7:3-13.) When Christ and his apostles specify that a certain thing be done, we must unite in doing it, whether others join us in doing it or not. The very thing specified must be done, if we would love and obey Christ, and if we would go to heaven at last. (Matt. 7:21; Luke 6:46.) Faith and obedience to Christ unite men in these things.

### What About General Authority?

Just as liberalism trifles with specific authority and specific commandments, "anti-ism" trifles with general commands, or generic law of Christ. Under general commands there are matters of human opinion and judgment in which we have liberty of option or choice. There is to be unity, but not necessarily uniformity, in this field of church activity. God commands us to "go" and teach all nations. (Matt. 28:19-20.) This is a general command telling us WHAT to do, but it gives no details as to HOW to travel. The method of going is a matter of option, choice or human judgment. We must unite in going, but there is liberty in the methods of travel to be chosen. Here there may be no uniformity—all may not choose the same method. Some may choose to walk, others to ride, and others to go by automobile or plane. We can unite in having no confusion and division over these matters. (1 Cor. 1:10.) In individual Christian activity, let the individual choose and exercise his God-given liberty. If it be a congregational activity, under general back-ground law, let the church, or its elders, choose the method or way of doing the thing commanded, and choose in the best interest of the congregation, whether it be what hour to meet, what song book to use, what preacher to invite for a meeting, and a thousand other things not regulated by divine specific law. Teaching, baptizing, assembling, incidentals of the worship, such as individual communion cups, Bible classes, literature, women teachers, and all such matters as are left to human judgment, should be handled in such a manner as to promote peace and happiness in the church, and to expedite its work.

### Making Laws Causes Division

"Anti-ism" trifles with general commands, and makes laws to restrain God's people where He gave them liberty of choice as to some method, way or manner of doing something specified in divine law. It is as sinful to make laws for God as it is to break the laws which God himself has made.

### Some Examples Of Man-Made Laws

God said for us to "go" and "teach" all nations, etc. (Matt. 28:19-20.) The command to "teach" is generic—it does not tell us how to do the teaching. But here the "Anti-Sunday school" brethren try to divide the church by their man-made law against our conducting Bible classes on the Lord's day morning before our regular worship. They make a human law that we must give up our classes in the interest of unity with them in having only one class. We do not make a law that the churches must have classes, and try to force it upon the brotherhood. But they do make a law against our having classes, and that in the realm of liberty where God left us free to choose our own method of teaching.

### The Pioneers

The pioneers had as their motto the statement, "In matters of faith we should have unity, in matters of opinion or human judgment, liberty, and in all things charity." We are still pleading for this scriptural principle. A church does not have to have Sunday morning Bible classes, but it has no scriptural right to put on a campaign of false doctrine that it is unscriptural for other congregations to have them, if they so desire, and thus become a sect or faction to divide the church.

The same is true of the "anti-individual communion cups" brethren. Christ said for us to take the cup—the fruit of the vine—and divide it among ourselves. (Luke 22:17.) He did not tell us how to divide it, but left us the liberty of dividing it by the use of individual cups, if we so desire. We make no law for the Lord here, to enforce it upon the' brotherhood to the division of the churches. A church has the liberty to use one vessel or many, as it may choose, but it has no divine right to force its opinion on other churches to their disturbance. It is a sin to go out to force the churches to use individual cups, and also a sin to make a law to prohibit the use of them. But anti-ism proposes to take away this liberty by its man-made law against individual cups.

You can make the application of these principles to the various matters of expediency under general authority, such as the located preacher question, the baptistry, orphan homes, church owned meeting houses and preachers' homes, and the like. These are in the realm of liberty under generic authority.

### Who Caused The Division?
Some take the position that we must give up everything that is not specifically commanded in order to have unity. But this is not the scriptural solution to the problem. If we must give up everything to which some disgruntled brother objects, which is not commanded by **special mention,** then the church will become a fiftieth-rate sect. In that situation, some brother may move in and object to our Bible classes, literature, and women teachers for some children's classes. Another comes in and objects to our individual cups. Still, another comes in and objects to our having a local preacher. Another comes in and objects to the church's owning and having a meeting house, and a baptistry, class rooms, rest rooms and office rooms, drinking fountains, etc. Another objects to the church's contributing to an orphan home, and another to the church's helping another church to put on a radio program. Such anti-ism is just about anti-everything that is expedient in building up the church and preaching the gospel to the world.

### Paul Not Compromise
Paul refused to give over to the Judaizing hobby-riders

even for an hour, that the truth of the gospel might remain with us. (Gal. 2:1-5.) Paul stood for the liberty in Christ Jesus under divine authority. He circumcised Timothy, as a matter of liberty and expediency, but refused to circumcise Titus as was demanded to satisfy a man-made law of the Judaizers. (Acts 16:1-4; Gal. 2:1-5.) Orphan homes and cooperative radio programs are matters of liberty under general law which requires that the THING be done, but does not give the details for doing it. Let us, therefore, have brotherhood unity, and have it upon faith in Christ and obedience to his will. Let us unite in doing the very things required in specific divine law, and still have unity in matters of human judgment under general authority, by allowing that liberty for which Paul contended. (Gal. 2:1-5.) Let elders oversee the church, and let us be done with the idea of turning the church over to a disgruntled minority of factionists and church dividers.

On the other hand, let the churches stay within the authority of Christ in all religious matters. Let us do nothing religiously unless we have either specific, or general authority for it.

### A Word About Examples

If an apostolic example had back of it a specific command as to the details, then that example was binding on the early Christians and would, for the same reason, be binding upon us today, such as examples of baptism, a thing commanded and exemplified. (Matt. 28:19; Mark 16:15-16; Acts 8:35-39; Acts 18:8; 22:16.)

But if the background command for doing something did not give any details as to how to do the thing commanded, then such details were not bound on the early Christians, and for the same reason, their chosen method of doing the thing would not be binding upon us, though it would be authority for us to choose to do as they did if we should so desire.

### When Follow Examples?

We are bound to follow the examples of the early Christians only in so far as they were bound to leave us the detailed examples as they did, and beyond this their example would be optional with us, as it was a matter of choice with them when they left the example. Certain things were then bound, and certain things loosed. (Matt. 16:19.) Christ bound the going into all the world and preaching of the gospel to the whole world—but loosed the how to go, and the method of teaching. He bound baptism, and loosed the place to perform it, whether in running water, or in a pool, etc. He bound the meeting of the saints, but loosed the place. He bound the singing, but loosed the matter of having a song book, use of tuning fork, etc. He bound the prayers, but loosed the posture; bound the supper, but loosed the number of cups; bound the contribution, but loosed the matter of collection plates; bound the teaching, but loosed the classes, literature, etc. LET US NOT BIND WHERE GOD LOOSED, NOR LOOSE WHERE GOD BOUND. LIBERALISM LOOSES WHERE GOD BOUND, and ANTI-ISM BINDS WHERE GOD LOOSED. BEWARE OF SUCH "ISMS " IF YOU WOULD HAVE THE UNITY OF THE SPIRIT. May God bless you, every one.

# BLASPHEMY AGAINST THE SPIRIT
## OR
## THE UNPARDONABLE SIN

I have been requested to speak to you at this time on the subject of "THE UNPARDONABLE SIN." The subject is an interesting one to most people. First of all, many wonder if they may have committed at some time in life what they usually call "the sin against the Holy Ghost." Others simply want to know what the Bible teaches on the subject. But all are interested in any representative discussion of the subject. Like most Bible subjects, what God says concerning this matter is not always faithfully taught and respected. However, the fact that there are many conflicting and popular theories concerning this subject is no proof that what the Bible says on the subject cannot be understood. Of course, no exhaustive study of the subject would be possible in the time allotted.

Any proper study of the subject must begin with the context, for Jesus introduces the subject with the word "wherefore," meaning that what he is about to say on the subject is to be said because of what had just been said and done on that occasion. He said, "Wherefore I say unto you, All manner of sin and blasphemy shall be forgiven unto men: but the blasphemy against the Holy Ghost shall not be forgiven unto men. And whosoever speaketh a word against the Son of man, it shall be forgiven him: but whosoever speaketh against the Holy Ghost, it shall not be forgiven him, neither in this world, neither in the world to come." (Matt. 12:31-32.)

Before noting the context of this passage, let us observe that there is no difference between what is here called "the blasphemy against the Holy Ghost," and "speaking against the Holy Ghost." The word "blaspheme" is defined: "To speak impiously or irreverently of (God or sacred things)

2. To speak evil of; abuse. 3. To utter impious words." It follows, therefore, that this sin is committed with the tongue. Jesus says, "Whosoever speaketh against the Holy Ghost, it shall not be forgiven him." (Matt. 12:32.) It is not the sin of murder, as bad as that sin is. Moses murdered an Egyptian, and was forgiven. (Ex. 2:11-12.) The Jews on Pentecost were charged with the murder of the Son of God and those who would accept pardon were forgiven. (Acts 2:23, 36-41.) Saul of Tarsus was a murderer of Christians. (Acts 7:52; 8:1; 9:1; 26:9-11.) He was an accomplice in the crime, and yet he obtained pardon, as did Moses and others; so murder is not the unpardonable sin. Neither is it adultery, for Jesus offered pardon to a woman guilty of this very sin. (John 8.) Paul mentions a catalogue of sins, such as fornication, idolatry, adultery, theft, drunkenness, reviling, etc., and says some guilty of these sins had been forgiven. (1 Cor. 6:9-11.) Hence, none of these is the unpardonable sin.

And the unpardonable sin is not simply blasphemy; but it is blasphemy against the Holy Spirit—it is a certain kind of blasphemy. Paul says he was a "blasphemer" before his conversion. (1 Tim. 1:13.) But he did not blaspheme, or speak against, the Holy Spirit. He believed in and respected the Holy Spirit, and God, the Father; but he blasphemed the name of Jesus, for which sin there was forgiveness offered. Jesus said, "Whosoever speaketh a word against the Son of man, it shall be forgiven him: but whosoever speaketh against the Holy Ghost, it shall not be forgiven him." (Matt. 12:32.) So, in blaspheming Christ, Paul was not guilty of an unpardonable sin. "Whosoever shall speak a word against the Son of man, it shall be forgiven him: but unto him that blasphemeth against the Holy Ghost it shall not be forgiven." (Luke 12:10.)

But what was in the context which gave rise to these statements of the Master? Please remember that Jesus introduced this lesson because of something which had been said and done in the context. Because of those things, he said, "Wherefore I say unto you," and then gave us what he had to say about speaking against the Holy Spirit.

In the context, he had healed a man possessed with a devil, blind and dumb. (Matt. 12:22-23.) No one could deny or in any way gainsay the miracle of healing, which, like his other miracles, confirmed his claim to be the Christ, the Son of God. (John 20:30-31.) But the Pharisees were so prejudiced and determined to destroy his influence over the people that they made the foolish charge that he did the miracle "by Beelzebub the prince of the devils." (Matt. 12:24.) Jesus then demolished their explanation and showed its utter unreasonableness by pointing out the fact that if Satan were casting himself out of people in any such fashion then he was divided against himself and would eventually destroy his own kingdom. Then Jesus explained how he did the miracle. He said, "I cast out devils by the Spirit of God." (Matt. 12:28.) Therefore, their explanation was, in fact, just another way of saying that the "Spirit of God" was "Beelzebub the prince of the devils." Here they actually blasphemed against the Holy Spirit, or spoke against him impiously and irreverently by calling him a devil, and by giving Satan credit for healing the man, which credit was due the Holy Spirit. This was blaspheming the Holy Spirit, or speaking against the Spirit. This was therefore an actual case of committing this sin. This is the one kind of blasphemy that is not pardonable. One may be forgiven of all kinds of blasphemy other than this. "All sins shall be forgiven unto the sons of men, and blasphemies wherewith soever they shall blaspheme: but he that shall blaspheme against the Holy Ghost hath never forgiveness, but is in danger of eternal damnation: because they said, He hath an unclean spirit." (Mark 3:28-30.) Yes, "They said, He hath an unclean spirit;" but he actually had the Holy Spirit, and cast out devils by Him. (Matt. 12:28; John 3:34.) Hence, they called the Holy Spirit an unclean spirit. This is blasphemy against the Holy Ghost. This is so plain that I do not see how any one can misunderstand it without expert help to do so.

But many actually deny that this sin is **unpardonable**, and that there is any such sin. But this, too, is a false interpretation of the passages dealing with the subject. They think this sin is only an **unpardoned** sin, but that pardon is offered for it. But Jesus said those committing this sin are "in danger of eternal damnation." (Mark 3:29.) The American Standard Version reads: "Is guilty of an eternal sin." It is contrasted with sins that are pardonable. Jesus says, "All sins shall be forgiven unto the sons of men . . . but he that shall blaspheme against the Holy Ghost hath never forgiveness." (Mark 3:28-29.) This should be final on the point. No one guilty of this sin can ever get forgiveness for it, though there is forgiveness offered for other "sins . . . and blasphemies," other than this one. Yes, Jesus says, "All manner of sin and blasphemy shall be forgiven unto men: but the blasphemy against the Holy Ghost shall not be forgiven unto men." (Matt. 12:31.) This being true, there is an **unpardonable** sin, as well as sins **unpardoned**.

No sin will be forgiven unconditionally, and without obedience to the terms of forgiveness. There are terms of pardon for the sin of speaking against Christ, and sins other than speaking against the Holy Spirit. Jesus says, "Whosoever speaketh a word against the Son of man, it shall be forgiven him: but whosoever speaketh against the Holy Ghost, it shall not be forgiven him, neither in this world, neither in the world to come." (Matt. 12:32.) "This world" was the Jewish age under which Jesus then lived and said this. "The world to come" meant the Christian age which later began on Pentecost, Acts 2. The Greek word for "world" in the passage means world in the sense of an age. Christ died in the end of the world—in the end of the Jewish age or world. "But now once in the end of the world hath he appeared to put away sin by the sacrifice of himself." (Heb. 9:26.) So, this sin against the Holy Spirit would not be forgiven in "this world"—this age—the Jewish age, nor "in that (world) to come"—the Christian age that was then to come—was then future. It follows that this sin, therefore, could be committed during the personal ministry of Christ, and was then committed, as we have seen, and could also be committed under the gospel age or dispensation. They could have attributed the works of the Spirit to Satan after Pentecost, the same as before.

When some take the position that "the world to come" means in the life after death, they are accepting the Roman Catholic argument on purgatory. The Catholics argue that it means this life and the next, and that since there will be no forgiveness in the next life for one sin—the blasphemy of the Holy Spirit—there will be pardon extended in the future state for all sins except that one. But, as already pointed out, "this world" meant the Jewish age in which Jesus was then speaking, and "the world to come" had reference to the Christian age, or dispensation which was then future, but which came afterward on Pentecost. There can be no forgiveness after death. Jesus said if you "die in your sins: whither I go, ye cannot come." (John 8:21.) Man will be finally rewarded according to "the things done in his body, according to that he hath done, whether it be good or bad." (2 Cor. 5:10.) The Catholics are wrong about these passages. The Bible does not teach the doctrine of  purgatory;  but when the wicked go into punishment, it will be "everlasting punishment." (Matt. 25:41, 46.) Just so, any  brother  who argues that "this world" in the passage under study means merely this life, has already fallen into Catholic hands on the purgatory argument. Therefore, any theory that teaches this sin could not be committed before Pentecost is wrong.

There is a theory which holds that one could not blaspheme against the Holy Spirit before he came on Pentecost and began his work of revealing and confirming the gospel. But Jesus says it could be done "in this world"—"this age" —which was the Jewish age, at the end of which Christ died (Matt. 12:31-32; Heb. 9:26.) Christ had the Spirit without measure. (John 3:34.) He cast out devils by the power of the Holy Spirit. (Matt. 12:28.) And when the Pharisees said he did this by "Beelzebub the prince of the devils" and that he had "an unclean spirit," they were blaspheming the Holy Spirit, and there was to be no forgiveness for such an awful sin.

Think about it! If their false explanation of the miracles wrought by Jesus had become the commonly-accepted view and explanation, Christ would have failed to  prove  his Deity and Sonship, and his mission on earth  would  have been a colossal failure; for his miracles were to confirm his claim to be the Son of God. (John 20:30-31; John 3:1-2.) As long as his enemies could get by with their foolish explanation that he was in league and partnership with the devil and did these things by the power of an "unclean spirit" or a wicked spirit, the purpose and mission of his coming to earth was in danger of being thwarted. So, he nipped their theory in the bud, and pronounced such an awful condemnation on one guilty of such offense as would deter and restrain men from accepting this new doctrine of the Pharisees. And there is no record of any one else's ever committing this sin. Furthermore, I doubt that any other human beings have ever been guilty of this sin. It is true, great multitudes are going out into eternity in rebellion against God to be finally and eternally lost; but it is for rejecting and neglecting pardon graciously extended in the gospel while they live, not because they have committed the unpardonable sin.

But there is another theory which says the unpardonable sin is simply going through life and dying in sin without obeying the gospel. This is a very popular theory, and one of those theories which denies that this sin against the Holy Ghost could be committed before Pentecost. But according to this theory, one dying in disobedience to the gospel would get forgiveness of all his sins except the sin of rejecting the gospel. He would be almost saved, but not quite saved—just lack pardon of one sin! For did not Jesus say: "All manner of sin and blasphemy shall be forgiven unto men: but the blasphemy against the Holy Ghost shall not be forgiven unto men"? (Matt. 12:31.) So, if the unpardonable sin is simply failing to obey the gospel, one can get forgiveness of all his other sins without obeying the gospel, and if so, then obeying the gospel would not bring remission of sins, as Peter said it would. (Acts 2:38.) Why, a simple failure to obey the gospel would not be any more a blasphemy against the Holy Ghost than it would be of God, or of Christ. For the gospel is called the "gospel of God" and the "gospel of Christ." (Rom. 1:1-2, 16.) One is obeying Christ in obeying the gospel. (Heb. 5:9.) And he is disobeying

Christ and saying "No" to him when he refuses to obey the gospel. This is as much a sin against Christ as it is against the Holy Ghost. But in Matthew 12 and Mark 3 the sin was **directly** against the Holy Spirit: it was against the Spirit by which Jesus did his miracles. They called the Holy Spirit "an unclean spirit"—a wicked spirit. (Mark 3:28-30.) Let us here draw a circle on the blackboard to represent Christ, then this small circle in the center of the larger one and let it represent the Holy Spirit by which Jesus did his miracles. Now, did the Pharisees directly speak against Jesus? (Here the speaker draws an arrow so as to point to the larger circle representing Jesus.) No, they did not deny that Jesus wrought the miracle; they admitted it. If they had denied the miracle and claimed that Jesus was only a magician or trickster deceiving the people, they would have been speaking against Christ, and Jesus said there is forgiveness for that sort of sin. But, no, they spoke against the Spirit, saying Jesus did his miracle, but did it by a wicked spirit, the spirit of the devil; and this was speaking directly against the Holy Ghost. (Here speaker drew another arrow to point to letter "S" in the inner and smaller circle representing the Holy Spirit.) This was therefore, speaking "against the Holy Ghost," and was the unpardonable sin.

Furthermore, if merely rejecting the gospel is the unpardonable sin, then if a man ever rejects the gospel invitation one time he is guilty of an unpardonable sin, and could not be forgiven if he were to obey it the next day. This is true unless it be proved that rejecting the gospel one time is not sinful, but that one would have to reject it a whole life-time to be guilty of rejecting it. If it is not a sin to reject the gospel once, how could it be a sin to reject it twice, three times, or for the whole of one's life? If it were not sinful to tell one lie, could one ever tell enough lies for it to become sinful? No, my friends; this sin for which there is no forgiveness could be committed in the Jewish age, before Pentecost, and therefore before the gospel was preached in its fullness. (1 Cor. 15:1-4.) The failure to obey the gospel would be an **unpardoned** sin, until it is obeyed; but the same is true of all other sins. But Jesus makes a distinction between sins: some are to be forgiven when the terms of pardon are met, but one sin is not to be forgiven; but, is called "eternal sin."

There is one more theory which I can examine only very briefly at this time, and that is the theory that the Holy Spirit strives with man directly, and if you reject this direct striving and operation, the Spirit may finally go away never to return, leaving one without any impulse to be saved, and therefore lost forever. This theory is built on a false interpretation of Gen. 6:3 where God said, "My spirit shall not always strive with man, for that he also is flesh: yet his days shall be an hundred and twenty years." This was before the flood when men were living eight and nine hundred years. But God said his Spirit would not strive with them "always" or throughout the normal span of life in that era, but the flood would come in one hundred and twenty years destroying the wicked. They would be destroyed in early life! Hence the Spirit would not strive with them eight or nine hundred years, as he had been doing with their fathers. The Spirit was striving with them through Noah, "a preacher of righteousness." (2 Pet. 2:5.) The Spirit spoke and strove with men through inspired men. "Holy men of God spake as they were moved by the Holy Ghost." (2 Pet. 1:21.) The Holy Spirit continued to strive with those before the flood so long as they lived— one hundred and twenty years. (Gen. 6:3.) The Spirit does not strive with dead people, and they were all dead in one hundred and twenty years; but the Spirit did not forsake them and cease to strive with them until the flood came. So long as they lived, the Spirit spoke to them through Noah who preached unto them "righteousness." The Spirit now calls us by the gospel. (2 Thess. 2:14; 1 Pet. 1:12.) The Spirit says, "Come" and he will not cease to say this as long as we live. (Rev. 22:17; Heb. 9:27.) One who resisted the Spirit yesterday by rejecting his message in the gospel may accept and be saved today. He has not committed an **unpardonable** sin. Of course, he may harden his heart by continually resisting the Spirit, by rejecting his word; but this also is not the unpardonable sin; it is rather an **unpardoned** sin. (Heb. 3:7-8.)

It seems that all sins committed today are pardonable, and that all can be saved, if they will. I have never found a man in the twenty-seven states in which I have preached who was guilty of saying the Holy Spirit by which Jesus wrought his miracles was a wicked spirit, the spirit of Satan. But one might as well be guilty of the "eternal sin" and go to perdition because of it as to go to the same place of "everlasting punishment" guilty of sins which were pardonable and for which forgiveness was offered, but rejected or neglected.